Branding Black Womanhood

Branding Black Womanhood

Media Citizenship from Black Power to Black Girl Magic

TIMEKA N. TOUNSEL

Rutgers University Press

New Brunswick, Camden, and Newark, New Jersey, and London

Library of Congress Cataloging-in-Publication Data

Names: Tounsel, Timeka N., author.

Title: Branding Black womanhood: media citizenship from Black power to Black girl magic / Timeka N. Tounsel.

Description: New Brunswick: Rutgers University Press, 2022. | Includes bibliographical references and index.

Identifiers: LCCN 2021039303 | ISBN 9781978829909 (paperback) | ISBN 9781978829916 (hardback) | ISBN 9781978829923 (epub) | ISBN 9781978829930 (pdf)

Subjects: LCSH: Branding (Marketing) | Women, Black—Public opinion. | Women, Black, in popular culture. | Self-perception in women. | Communication in marketing.

Classification: LCC HF5415.1255 .T68 2022 | DDC 381.082—dc23

LC record available at https://lccn.loc.gov/2021039303

A British Cataloging-in-Publication record for this book is available from the British Library.

References to internet websites (URLs) were accurate at the time of writing. Neither the author nor Rutgers University Press is responsible for URLs that may have expired or changed since the manuscript was prepared.

♾ The paper used in this publication meets the requirements of the American National Standard for Information Sciences—Permanence of Paper for Printed Library Materials, ANSI Z39.48-1992.

www.rutgersuniversitypress.org

Manufactured in the United States of America

For my grandmothers, Bonnie Jean and Erthlene,
who refused to dim

Contents

Branding Black Womanhood

Prologue

Black girls who grew up visiting beauty salons where issues of *Essence*, *Ebony*, and *Jet* were plentiful had access to a masterclass in commercial empowerment. My interaction with these magazines began in a makeshift hair salon in the basement of a mid-century Tudor on Burnett street, on Detroit's west side. During biweekly trips to a beautician from first grade through twelfth, I spent hundreds of hours meditating on the women that lived on those pages. Eventually, somewhere between age eight and eleven, I began to think that the images circulating throughout the world of Black popular print culture were attached to my identity. For one thing, all the women in the magazine world were intentionally and exclusively Black. Those icons came to occupy the same parts of my mind where I grappled with the models of womanhood that lived and breathed around me at church, school, and my home. Certainly, I enjoyed ABC's Friday-night lineup of family programming, various Saturday morning cartoons, and Blockbuster rentals on weekends, but the magazines were a unique portal to a place that felt closer to reality than fantasy.

The owner-operator of the salon I grew up patronizing, a close family friend and fellow church member, stocked between five and six titles for her customers to browse. She was the sole beautician and never took more than one client at a time. This meant that I had free rein to scrutinize each publication every other Friday, when my mother and I went to her house for our regular appointments. Carefully absorbing the editorial and advertising content alike, I noticed the basic similarities between the models in the ad pages and the story subjects pictured in the others. Although the personalized address label on the magazine covers suggested that the salon owner must have had a subscription to each title, I do not recall her updating her miniature newsstand regularly.

New issues emerged slowly, and when they did, they shared space with the older copies. It could take months or longer for a single magazine issue to disappear from the large coffee table where they resided in the basement.

This collection became my first archive of the Black image economy. I returned to the same issues over and over again, never boring of them, and always managing to have what felt like a new reading experience each time. My favorite days in the salon were the Fridays when only my mom was serviced. Escaping the inconvenience of actually getting my hair styled, the coffee table and sturdy, rust-colored sofa positioned farthest away from the television and the hum of the blow dryer became my laboratory. Here, I began the practice of seeking to know Black womanhood through mediated images.

Around age nine I began reading the articles. Prior to that time, only the photographs, titles, and occasional captions had held my interest. The text, however, did not add much to my meditations; my nine-year-old intellect made most of the topical matter inaccessible and, by that time, the message of these lifestyle handbooks had already captivated me. The African American beauty salon, one that many of the women at my church also patronized, was the most conducive context in which to communicate a narrative about the project of Black womanhood. Collectively, the magazines and the environment in which I engaged with them proclaimed that the Black female self was forged and performed through images, gestures, and symbols; intimate and public, commercial and political, mundane and extraordinary.

What I did not fully understand as a child but came to comprehend in adulthood through stints at Black-targeted magazines and, finally, through the research for this book, is that consumption is a crucial act Black women perform to assert and elevate our identity. Commercial entities market their goods and services by stitching them into the imagined lifestyles of their target consumers. Consumers also deploy advertising texts and products as building blocks of identity, forging a coherent subjectivity that aligns with the imposed parameters communicated through popular culture. Within this image economy, visibility is a form of capital and brand patronage is a political practice; not political in the sense that it yields civic power, but political in that it allows for greater mobility. And for Black women in particular, shopping, watching, spending, and engaging are some of the mechanisms we use to be seen, to appear legible in contexts where we might otherwise go unregistered.

As a young, but faithful reader, I did not get the impression that smoking Kool cigarettes, using Revlon cosmetics or even subscribing to a particular magazine, once I was old enough to do those things, would make me more powerful. I did, however, feel an overwhelming sense of pride and recognition when I engaged the magazines that other go-to texts from my (pre)adolescent years— Beverly Clearly novels, episodes of *Boy Meets World*, issues of *CosmoGirl*, and the occasional episode of *All My Children* that I watched with my grandmother—could not match. *Essence* and the other cultural texts that it referenced had developed a commercial empowerment enterprise that hails Black women as consumer citizens so effectively that even before becoming a teenager, I had become a believer. I believed that the best version of what I could become rested somewhere in the glamour of those pages. Too young to understand that the allure of the editorial content and the promises of the advertising content were mutually constitutive, I concluded that if this was the world where Black women were legible, then I needed to access it at whatever cost. It was not power that I sought, but a kind of cultural enfranchisement; I just wanted to be acknowledged in the mediascape as easily and broadly as white women and girls.

The content platforms that center Black women consumers in their profit strategies, including legacy media like Essence Communications Inc. and product conglomerates like Procter & Gamble, have come to understand that longing for recognition, and how to monetize it. As a result, they offer their target audience media citizenship, a conditional form of agency bound to the image economy. It is this transactional arrangement between Black women and the corporations that hunger for our dollars that undergirds the commercial project explored in this book. *Branding Black Womanhood: Media Citizenship from Black Power to Black Girl Magic* theorizes public recognition's appeal and situates the struggle for cultural enfranchisement within the longer struggle for full Black citizenship. It is my effort to make sense of the gratification I sought in the pages of *Essence* as a girl, which is the same benefit that companies have promised to Black women for decades in exchange for our consumer loyalty. I offer this study not from an intellectual position that would minimize the pleasures of the marketplace. Rather, I have written *Branding Black Womanhood* from a place of hope, believing that the better we understand affirmative visibility and how it becomes commodified, the better our chance, as Black women, of reclaiming the authority to decide when and how we intend to be seen.

Introduction

Black Women and the
Twenty-First Century
Image Economy

In 2013, CaShawn Thompson tweeted a simple, yet compelling celebration of Black women's resilience and excellence; she aimed to facilitate a movement with "Black Girls Are Magic" as its rallying cry.[1] Her words resonated with social media users in such an astounding way that soon celebrities used the hashtag to caption their posts and other online authors integrated the phrase into their own content. Rather than guard the mantra as a personal asset, Thompson delighted in the fact that others felt inspired enough to make it their own. She followed her social media campaign with a collection of t-shirts that echoed the slogan.[2] Soon the four words that she issued as a community affirmation functioned as their own kind of magic, awakening corporate brands to a consumer market that has experienced multiple cycles of obscurity followed by focused attention. While Thompson's mantra is a twenty-first century emergence, its monetization is part of a longer history whereby Black women's empowerment has been commodified and tethered to media. For decades, commercial entities have marketed dignity to Black women, fashioning their pitches with the language of protest anthems and other edgy period parlance. Thompson's mantra—which social media users shortened to an even more spreadable hashtag, #BlackGirlMagic—would prove to be just as susceptible to corporate appropriation as predecessors like Black is Beautiful. By 2017, two companies were fighting over trademark rights to the phrase.

FIGURE I.1 Attendees at the *Black Girls Rock! Awards* show applaud First Lady Michelle Obama at the March 28, 2015 taping. Actress Cicely Tyson stands to her immediate right, followed by former Black Entertainment Television CEO Debra Lee, and Black Girls Rock! founder Beverly Bond. Credit: Official White House Photo by Amanda Lucidon. Public domain.

Essence Communications Inc. (ECI), the company that publishes *Essence* magazine and manages the Essence Festival of Culture, and Beverly Bond, founder of Black Girls Rock! were the opposing parties in the legal dispute over Black Girl Magic. Bond, who originally filed a trademark application in 2014, claimed to have neither prior knowledge of the term's origins, nor of Thompson, who is most often credited as its creator.[3] A former model and disc jockey, Bond is known for translating her vision of empowering Black girls and women into a youth enrichment organization and commercial enterprise, including an annual televised awards show. The *Black Girls Rock! Awards* show, which has aired on Black Entertainment Television (BET) since 2010, has featured appearances from the likes of First Lady Michelle Obama (see figure I.1) and superstar-turned entrepreneur Rihanna and boasts sponsors such as AT&T and Nissan. Having already monetized one Black girl affirmation, securing the trademark for another would seem a practical move for a savvy entrepreneur like Bond.

Decades before Black Girl Magic was considered valuable enough to be the subject of legal disputes, ECI had already probed the worth of a commercial project that fused empowerment and femininity. The company's first property was a glossy magazine for Black women, *Essence*, that launched in May 1970. While the magazine was not the first of its kind, those who worked under the

Essence banner in its nascent stage were largely responsible for constructing Black women as a legible consumer niche in the twentieth century and for developing the strategic approach to Black female publics which pervades marketing rhetoric in the new millennium. ECI asserted that they had just as much a right as any brand to capitalize on the idiom of the day and made plans for a content series that they intended to title "Essence Black Girl Magic," ultimately prompting them to block Bond from gaining control of the phrase.

Remarkably, CaShawn Thompson had been excluded from the legal proceedings concerning the terminology that she had created. Attempting to maximize their own profits, two well-known businesses had written Thompson out of a narrative that she launched to affirm Black women. She had never intended for Black Girl Magic to become an income generator for herself or anyone else. Yet, what most disturbed Thompson about the phrase's monetization was that the original sentiment of magic as an everyday superpower that any Black women could access had been lost. "It turned into a thing that actually alienated women like me," she said in an interview with *For Harriet* blog founder, Kimberly Foster. "After that commodification it was easy to turn [Black Girl Magic] from a state of being to a thing that you own, like all commodities. Once that happened, it was hard for me to get it back."[4]

Branding Black Womanhood: Media Citizenship from Black Power to Black Girl Magic examines the infrastructure that absorbed Thompson's mantra, a decades-long project to configure Black women's empowerment as a business enterprise. While the terminology may have changed over the years, mainstream brands and mass media companies have consistently sought to acknowledge Black women's possession of a distinct magic or power when it suits their profit agendas. Working both in conjunction and competition with Black media platforms and professionals, these corporations turn to otherwise overlooked niches in order to gain an edge in the marketplace. Thompson's particular phrase of affirmation emerged just as the culture industries were rediscovering Black women consumers. The first decade of the new millennium had seen a harsh decline in Black women's images and voices, but by 2010 the image economy began to shift. A Black First Lady had ascended the international stage, beaconing toward a new configuration of African American womanhood. Importantly, Michelle Obama's magnetism was not only compelling on a political level; as the sold-out fashion items that she was seen in proved, hers was a bankable enchantment. As if on cue, the culture industries made room for this dignified Black woman figure in the hopes of captivating an underserved market.

The BET Her cable network, the reformulated Oprah Winfrey Network, Procter & Gamble's *My Black Is Beautiful* campaign, Black Girls Rock! and dozens of other multimedia efforts that launched or expanded in the 2010s suggest Black women's ascent to a position of prominence. Compared to this population's relative absence from the media landscape in the early 2000s, the projects that emerged in the second decade of the new millennium indicate progress, even if only momentary. Black Girl Magic is therefore a route to a kind of cultural enfranchisement that I call media citizenship.

Popular culture is among the most important producers and disseminators of ideologies that refute Black civility. By offering a basis for excluding Black Americans from citizenship status, this institution has been an important battleground within racial advancement struggles. Furthermore, the neoliberal orientation of the twenty-first century image economy which treats individuals as brands has increased the value of visibility such that being magical is equal to being perceived or visualized as such. I refer to Black women as media citizens to emphasize how mass media representation and being valued for one's dollars and engagement are prerequisites for citizenship. Indeed, the branding of Black womanhood has only been successful when stakeholders have convinced consumers to accept publicity and affirmation as forms of power.

If we invest in the foundational credo of the Black Girl Magic enterprise—that the world has finally recognized "the sheer glory of being born a Black girl" as Beverly Bond proposed during her 2019 awards show speech—how do we make sense of the material constraints that Black women continue to confront?[5] Even if we limit this elevated status to commercial culture, the conditions under which Black women have returned to mainstream visibility—under the auspices of corporate profit agendas—prohibit simple or celebratory assessments. Furthermore, CaShawn Thompson's exclusion from the legal right to capitalize on terminology that she created indicates that whatever benefits there are to be gained from Black Girl Magic, they are not universal. It is therefore crucial to interrogate how this form of capital is unevenly distributed, expressed, and performed.

Branding Black Womanhood explores these dilemmas and provides insights on what we gain by approaching Black Girl Magic and other terms of empowerment not as movement generators, but rather byproducts of an enduring marketing logic and as media frames. In the twenty-first century image economy, Black Girl Magic functions as a mandate that marks the parameters of legibility. In other words, the primary means through which we recognize Black women in mass media is through proximity to the magical. Those who do not fit within this mold because they fail to embody beauty, excellence, resilience, and wokeness are deemed incapable of authentically imaging Black womanhood and unworthy of attention. Furthermore, this media frame rests on a marketing logic which requires that proponents accept visibility as a form of capital and consumption as a vital political act.

Marketers and media professionals who target Black women consumers would have us believe that "being a Black, female consumer is pure power," as one executive expressed in 2017.[6] These Black Girl Magic ambassadors read broader recognition from corporations as purely a cause for celebration. While tempting, this interpretation denies the more tangled history of empowerment as a commercial enterprise. Marketing dignity through product campaigns and tailored lifestyle media such as magazines is a well-worn pathway to Black women's purses through our hearts and minds. By considering the twenty-first century in relation to earlier periods, *Branding Black Womanhood* reveals the conditions under which periods of intense corporate attention recur and their commercial impact. Beginning with the late-1960s inception of the *Essence* brand, I trace the development of a modern image economy that operates as both a sacred space for Black women and an easy hunting ground for our dollars. At the turn of the 1970s, Jonathan Blount, Cecil Hollingsworth, Edward Lewis, and Clarence Smith—the founders of *Essence* magazine—sold Madison Avenue the notion that a "new" Black woman was emerging who demanded a lifestyle guide to facilitate her evolution. They not only understood the magazine to be a financially profitable, image-bound cultural project; they also believed it to be a mechanism for advancing Black entrepreneurship and, by extension, racial uplift.

The four men envisioned Black women's spending power—and the general ignorance of this fact—as an opportunity. By assuring disinclined corporate advertisers of their audience's value, *Essence* forged a gateway that benefits media outlets beyond their own brand and continues to complicate the terms of Black women's visibility within mass media. It is a singular force in the construction of Black women as an underserved consumer niche ripe for targeting. Through exploring the company's beginnings and evolution, I demonstrate how institutions and individuals monetized Black women's empowerment at the height of the Black Power and Women's Liberation movements, who benefited from this enterprise, and the legacy that it has left vis-à-vis Black Girl Magic. Drawing on memoirs, interviews with Black women media professionals, oral histories, and other archival data, *Branding Black Womanhood* considers the corporations, transactions, government policies, and marketing strategies that facilitate the political economy surrounding Black womanhood.

Defining Black Girl Magic

Although the expression did not become viral until 2013, Black Girl Magic's undergirding sentiment belongs to a centuries-old legacy of self-affirmation cultivated among subaltern Black female publics. The intention that drives this praxis is a demand for agency in naming and a desire to repudiate external misrepresentation. Self-definition has been central to Black women's theorizations of freedom and power (see figure I.2). And yet, because dominant vocabularies were not designed to address Black women's subjugation in the Americas, few terms capture the magnitude of our everyday triumphs. Magic, then, is

FIGURE I.2 Black Girl Magic has been integrated into political rhetoric as demonstrated on this sign, which appeared at a Black Lives Matter protest on July 2, 2020. Credit: Ivan Radic. Creative Commons License.

terminology that developed to fulfill a longing for dignity unmet by external arbiters.[7] In light of this history of resistance, some scholars have charted Black Girl Magic's proliferation as a political resource. For example, Julia S. Jordan-Zachery and Duchess Harris conceptualize the twenty-first century iteration of magic as the philosophical descendent of Alice Walker's theories on Black women's self-articulation. Harris and Jordan-Zachery read the "girl" in Black Girl Magic as indicative of affection and familiarity as well as a fluid term that "defies social categorization."[8] Many Black females, regardless of age, understand themselves as belonging to a collective with intersecting fates and use girl, as in sister-girl or girlfriend, to name that sociality.[9] Harris and Jordan-Zachery were most interested in this "community building" function of Black Girl Magic and therefore situated their study outside the sphere of celebrity and commerce.[10] In this way, their 2019 volume aligns with CaShawn Thompson's intentions for the terminology and avoids analyzing the ways in which it has been repurposed as a marketing device.

Branding Black Womanhood is concerned with the parallel genealogy of magic in the commercial sphere, which defines it as a quantifiable "sway" that "self-made and self-reliant" women wield over popular culture and their own destinies.[11] The marketing logic explored in this book aims to woo Black women as consumers and is less attentive to age distinctions; therefore, I use Black Girl Magic and magical Black womanhood interchangeably. In their 2017 report *African-American Women: Our Science, Her Magic*, Nielsen uses "magic" as code for influence and spending capacity. This magic is both intrinsic and a future projection of a better, latent self that will only emerge under appropriate disciplinary conditions. Thus, what marketing firms refer to as Black Girl Magic in the 2010s is derived from a neoliberal conception of the self and an altogether different device than what CaShawn Thompson used in her original tweet. The complexity of this empowerment mantra lies in the fact that it bears an alluring dignity often withheld from Black women, but it does so at the cost of injury and oppression. Magic has been used to obscure vulnerability and the unique frailties that threaten well-being. If Black women (or girls) are magic, then we are hyper-capable and have no need for the kinds of support afforded our counterparts. By fixating on Black women's capacity to achieve in spite of lack, dominant institutions offer admiration in lieu of adequate provision.

Accordingly, magic within the Black image economy is synonymous with beauty, power, and strength, as in the Strong Black Woman.[12] While these terms change over time to accommodate prevailing sensibilities, their co-option as marketing devices is recurring. For example, the rhetoric of strength has been replaced by the emergent frame of magic because the former could easily be contorted to function as a pejorative. Even within popular discourses that appear to celebrate women as accomplished figures, strength remains an excessive quality of the feminine. The privilege of being considered a respectable or desirable woman requires that one relent to a restrained capacity that always concedes to men's superior strength. Magic, on the other hand, circumvents an association with gender deviance by reformulating strength as an attribute of otherworldly-ness with spiritual connotations. As I discuss in chapter 2, media figures such as Susan L. Taylor and Iyanla Vanzant, who infused their public performances with religious symbolism, bridged neoliberal understandings of self-empowerment and the philosophy that Black women are divine beings.

At the height of her prominence, however, Taylor herself would not have been called magical. Rather, as editor-in-chief of *Essence* magazine during the 1980s and 1990s, she was the quintessential *Essence* woman. For ten years editors produced a monthly column spotlighting women who fit this moniker: self-empowered and enterprising agents who, no matter their personal circumstances, took responsibility for managing their fate. Like the companies that advertised in its pages during the 1970s, *Essence* was looking for ways to siphon energy from heightened political moments—Black Power and Women's Liberation—and channel it for their bottom line. So, they affirmed Black women's beauty and strength while also suggesting that those attributes could be enhanced with the right products. The sentiment endured after the "Essence Woman" column faded in the early 1980s: Black women were born powerful but needed the appropriate tools and direction to maximize their potential. This principle was the philosophical bedrock upon which *Essence*, and other lifestyle media targeting Black women, could normalize continuous self-regulation and position themselves as the caring guides that would shepherd their audience to fulfillment and happiness. Under this logic of empowered Black womanhood, sisterhood became a key resource for actualizing the best self. Sister–role models are reminders of the distance between one's present state and the empowered self yet to be realized. Thus, while the magical Black woman is primarily concerned with individual ambitions and endeavors, she is ever aware of opportunities to uplift the race. She must always perform "wokeness," bringing her thoughts, words, and deeds into alignment with dominant ideas of racial authenticity.[13]

Ultimately, to be magical is to be celebrated for satisfying contemporary dictates of the ideal, self-managed Black woman despite unsuitable conditions. Multiplatform advertising campaigns, awards shows, and women's lifestyle magazines perform much of this celebratory work. Affirmation manifests across these platforms as an image-based project. For example, in a speech at her 2019 awards show, Beverly Bond cited Black women's increased presence at executive boardroom tables, writing rooms, and behind cameras and podiums as a turning point. Moreover, she offered that organizations like hers, which counter "stereotypical social constructs of Black womanhood," stood to address inequity in society more broadly.[14] "History will see Black Girls Rock! as the demarcation point of when we rose," she said. "This movement induced a seismic paradigm shift that armed our spirits and recalibrated the measures of our humanity, womanhood, Blackness, and beauty so that we could reclaim our power."[15] Bond's remarks frame visibility as both a threat to accurate self-perception and a route to self-empowerment. A televised awards show like *Black Girls Rock!* can operate as a racial uplift tool because it remedies stereotypical representations with a buffet of affirming images. Since she centers degrading depictions—and the risk of internalizing them—as the obstacle Black women must conquer to "reclaim our power," Bond envisions the *Black Girls Rock!* stage as a political resource. All may be born with a "repository of Black girl juju" but that property becomes particularly potent when expressed through a media platform.[16]

Queen Latifah is another media mogul and empowerment symbol who has publicly linked magic with cultural recognition. When asked to define Black Girl Magic at a panel during the 2017 Essence Festival, Latifah explained it as an "indescribable elixir that comes with a Black woman," but one that popular culture was slow to celebrate.[17] Having first emerged on the male-dominated 1990s hip-hop scene, Latifah has experienced the sting of invisibility and the power of recognition. "For a long time it wasn't Black Girl Magic," she said. "It wasn't the uplifting that should've been."[18] The multihyphenate star emphasized this point by contrasting the media landscape of the 2010s with previous eras when, save for *Essence*, few outlets were interested in Black voices. "Thank God for *Essence* magazine showing that beauty, showing that strength, and telling our stories," she said, identifying the company as a pioneer in valuing Black women before others deemed it a priority.[19] Along with ECI, Latifah cited self-publishing platforms like Instagram that afford Black women the capacity to self-manage our images as crucial to elevating our status in the mediascape. The opportunity to curate and publicize the self to a primed audience is an advantage that a new generation of Black women have which our older sisters could not access. Celebrity endorsements like this one illuminate that while magic is acknowledged as an organic property that oozes from Black women in mundane moments, the ability to mediate and publicize that magic increases its value.

Why Visibility (Still) Matters

While it is true that magical Black women must assume full responsibility for recognizing and cultivating power from within, it is also true that this intrinsic labor yields visibility. Public attention and affirmation are both the rewards that await Black women who effectively comply with the mandates of magic and the metrics through which one assesses their power. In the twenty-first century we have been directed to think of identity as a commodity and visibility as the primary means for gaining and expressing agency. But the condition of exposure is not new for Black women, rendered sub-human figures valuable only for their (re)productive capacity in the slave economy. Generations under surveillance have necessitated strategies for navigating a marketplace where our very images are objects that bear social and commercial value. To this end, our labor of self-making has never been divorced from market demands and incentives. Still, visibility, or cultural recognition, has political limitations. Scholars such as Herman Gray and Kristen J. Warner have unsettled the correlation between representation and structural change, but mass media images are still used as a gauge for the Black condition.[20] Similarly, Beretta E. Smith-Shomade and Robert E. Weems Jr. have shown that commercial projects that tether consumption to empowerment, like the BET network, tend to fall short of their stated mission.[21] Nevertheless, in a capitalist society, commerce remains an important battleground where struggles over citizenship transpire. Minoritized groups whose liberation efforts are especially susceptible to capitalist co-option do not have the luxury to forgo participation in the marketplace. Black Girl Magic therefore exists within a larger system, or economy, of images and products where Black people cultivate, reject, and otherwise negotiate various gazes with the aim of achieving dignity and political agency.

While representation has sometimes been perceived as a means to an end, in other periods such as the 2010s, Black women's visibility or presence in mass media has been accepted as a victory unto itself. This slippage between visibility *as a means to* power or a channel through which one might access citizenship, and visibility *as a form of* power or the evidence of citizenship status, easily occurs for two reasons. First, as Herman Gray argues, self-communication technologies have made visibility more easily achievable and the corporations who have monetized such platforms work to make self-promotion more appealing. Second, the racist and patriarchal ethos that privileged a narrow form of white masculinity as the singular mode of citizen has reconfigured as color-blindness, rendering diversity a valued symbol of individuality and a self-branding device. Being a Black woman was once an intersectional locus of oppression that cast groups into the margins of the culture industries. It is now—in certain contexts—a unique selling proposition for individuals.

Gray argues that the enduring focus on representation within Black liberation struggles is outmoded since "the legal capacities, cultural assumptions, and social circumstances that produced the necessity for this recognition [of subordinate and marginalized communities] in the first place have changed."[22] Yet one can hardly come to this conclusion without a critical understanding of the institutions and processes that undergird popular culture. Furthermore, for many Black women, the twenty-first century media landscape does not feel altogether untethered from historic controlling images. The conditions under which Black women have become hypervisible do not necessarily offer this audience an affirming or empowering affect. Indeed, it was the feeling that Black women were under assault, especially across social media platforms, that prompted CaShawn Thompson to create a hashtag-ready resistance motto in the first place.

Rather than critique the ideology that undergirds a fixation on Black representation or consumption in general, I examine the particularities of the commercial sphere where empowered Black womanhood circulates as a product. As an empowerment enterprise, Black Girl Magic sits at the intersection of ideologies which naturalize the relationship between capitalism and Black Power on one hand, and spending power and femininity (or girl power), on the other. Such conflations have occurred under "the increasing marketization of all aspects of public and private domains," also understood as neoliberalism.[23] Under this paradigm, political frameworks associated with women's empowerment like feminism have succumbed to what Sarah Banet-Weiser describes as an economy of visibility, which have rendered them down to a set of marketable goods: "self-esteem, confidence, competence."[24] Banet-Weiser argues that white women's bodies have become the most visible representation of this branded feminism. We need only look to Black Girl Magic, however, to see that Black women have also been targeted by the "new" ethos of the culture industries—identity as commodity, self as brand, and exposure as capital. While the Black brand of women's empowerment is less likely to include the word, it makes many of the same promises and demands as Banet-Weiser's "popular feminism." One key distinction, however, is that the logic of Black Girl Magic takes seriously the benefits of self-curation for raced and gendered bodies. *Branding Black Womanhood* considers Black women's attempts to capitalize on our visibility within popular culture and the collective consequences of such endeavors.

The Fight for Cultural Enfranchisement

The value of Black women's visibility is a byproduct of the marketplace's entanglement with struggles for Black citizenship. For marginalized audiences with constrained political agency, brand loyalty operates "as a particular kind of citizenship practice."[25] What and how we consume matters only because we are legible as a niche market and therefore recognizable as a factor in a profit model. In *Breaking Up America: Advertisers and the New Media World*, Joseph Turrow explains how media companies began to engineer "primary media communities" in the 1980s that combined "income, generation, marital status, and gender into a soup of geographical and psychological profiles they call[ed] 'lifestyles'."[26] These profiles were inevitably racialized and intended to help companies generate broader consumer loyalty by creating content that made audiences feel like they were engaging that which aligned with their identity;

the content that best suited people like them. Media texts could then "[draw] the 'right' people and [signal] the 'wrong' people that they ought to go away."[27] That is not to say that consumers did not retain agency to participate in audience communities that did not align with their imposed lifestyle category, or that these marketing categories foreclosed renegade fandoms. Nevertheless, to predict and manipulate audience behavior, stakeholders have attempted to manufacture taste, directing an audience in what it *should* desire and what it ought to consider pleasurable. In this way, as Banet-Weiser argues, the marketplace configures identity as a function of "purchases made and a loyalty to brands."[28] We therefore demonstrate and maintain our power, our sense of belonging, by publicizing our brand loyalties and engagement activities so that they can be easily tracked and used to quantify our capacity to impact a company's financial strategy. The marketplace is significant, then, because it has offered a pathway to citizenship to persons historically disenfranchised.

The U.S. Constitution failed to adequately designate who had access to citizenship and what such a status entailed. It was those persons whose condition and concerns ranked lowest in the framers minds—white women, immigrants, indigenous people, and Blacks—that forced Congress to draw parameters around the body politic.[29] As their struggles for agency played out in court, the press, and the marketplace, these marginalized groups exposed the fragility of America's democratic experiment and lawmakers' willingness to continue redrawing the boundaries of citizenship such that even as more groups were allowed to become citizens their social status did not necessarily improve. The (post-) Reconstruction period offers a poignant illustration of citizenship's dynamism and dilution. Since the condition of enslavement excluded most Black Americans from becoming rights-bearing members of the nation-state, there was less need to formally prohibit access vis-à-vis racist legislation. Once bondage ceased to be a proper barrier, white supremacists petitioned to obstruct Black Americans' full participation in society on the basis of their race. These actions framed them as inferior subjects who could not handle the liberties and responsibilities of citizenship in a civilized society.[30] So, even though the passage of the 14th amendment in 1868 meant that Black people were legal citizens, they could not do as much with their new status as white men; theirs was a second-class citizenship.

Of course, Black Americans never accepted subjugation to a lower tier of power. In addition to resisting degradation, they also theorized citizenship according to their own frameworks within an alternative, Black public sphere. They did not limit their liberation project to struggles for inclusion, as Derrick Spires explains in *The Practice of Citizenship: Black Politics and Print Culture in the Early United States*; rather, they imagined a more perfect union constituted through an altogether different set of arrangements and practices.

[B]lack activists articulated an expansive, practice based theory of citizenship, not as a common identity as such but rather as a set of common practices: political participation, mutual aid, critique and revolution, and the myriad daily interactions between people living in the same spaces, both physical and virtual. They rejected definitions of "citizen" based on who a person is, a preordained or predefined subject or subjectivity, in favor of definitions grounded in the active engagement in the process of creating and maintaining collectivity, whether defined as state, community, or other affiliative structure.[31]

The recognition that nineteenth-century Black writers sought extended beyond formal government bodies to include other institutions, especially those with a social orientation. Rather than limiting their sense of belonging to the letter of the law, they asserted it through the cultural texts they produced and the enterprises they supported with their dollars. The newspapers and magazines where African Americans circulated their conceptions of citizenship served multiple purposes: they facilitated deliberation on civic matters and, as entrepreneurial endeavors, provided an opportunity for Black business ownership and professional growth. As Black Americans progressed beyond the terrors of post-Reconstruction and into the 1900s, an emergent class of specialists began to approach the Black press as a buttress for a burgeoning yet overlooked consumer market. Their actions helped to normalize the link between representation, consumption, and political progress.

Early twentieth-century advertising professionals who specialized in African American consumers understood the possibilities of consumer citizenship and directed Black audiences to privilege dignity as the primary qualifier for gratifying content. Dignity is a dynamic conception that has shifted over time, but it is fundamentally concerned with inclusion and affirmation. Marketing professionals understood cultural representation to be a potent tool that could either undermine or bolster the notion that Black people were capable of participating in civilized society. They discerned that advertising discourse was one of the ways that groups secure cultural enfranchisement in America. Businesses signaled which groups mattered through the audiences they selected to address in their promotional messages. Thus, advertising and marketing specialists guided Black audiences to (only) appreciate and patronize those companies that addressed them directly and portrayed them in a positive manner.

Civil rights organizations such as the National Association for the Advancement of Colored People (NAACP) also attended to oppression in mass media and the marketplace.[32] Since Black civility was always on trial and never taken for granted, they used commercial culture to circulate the notion that Black people could belong, that they *did* belong. In 1942, NAACP Executive Secretary Walter White collaborated with some seventy Hollywood executives to establish an ad hoc committee to elevate Black representation. White addressed the collective—which included the president of the Association of Motion Picture Producers and the heads of the directors, screen actors, and writers guilds—at a luncheon held at the 20th Century Fox Studio café. He argued that if the entertainment industry committed to broadening portrayals of Black Americans, they would ultimately be serving the more profound political objectives that the nation was fighting for in World War II (which the United States had just recently joined following Japan's December 7, 1941, attack on Pearl Harbor). Among those impacted by misrepresentation, White explained, were Black soldiers eager "to win this war for the preservation of the democratic way of life."[33] White further asserted that: "Restriction of Negroes to roles with rolling eyes, chattering teeth, always scared of ghosts, or to portrayals of none-too-bright servants perpetuates a stereotype which is doing the Negro infinite harm. And showing him always as a mentally inferior creature, lacking in ambition, is one of the reasons for the denial to the Negro of opportunity."[34] Activists like White found no value in disaggregating the various layers of racist disenfranchisement and proceeded to fuse commercial, social, and civic grievances in institutional rhetoric. They perceived that a group's integration into popular culture in favorable terms was a barometer for that group's status in the body politic. When a segment of the population was misrepresented or altogether dismissed from society's cultural discourses, that dismissal threatened their significance and worth. Being excluded from or denigrated within the dominant cultural record made it more difficult to argue that one's voice (or vote, or dollars) mattered.

Struggles for full Black citizenship during World War II paralleled an increased focus on economic practices—labor and consumption—as patriotic expectations. The state expected citizens to contribute to national prosperity by participating in the marketplace. In exchange, they instituted policies that made it easier for people to acquire goods and services they would not be able to afford in cash. Consumption became a civic act. For their part, shoppers expected the government to ensure that they be able to make informed purchasing decisions and to guard against swindlers who would misrepresent their products or otherwise cheat the consuming public. Established in 1914 as part of the Woodrow Wilson administration's efforts to eliminate monopolies, the Federal Trade Commission received expanded authority to police "unfair and deceptive acts or practices" in 1938.[35] Amendments to the original act signed into law months before the war erupted included specific provisions for false advertisements in the food, drug, and cosmetic industries. Such policies relied on the notion that legislators could not adequately protect consumers by lumping them together with businesses competing in the marketplace; they demanded specific laws and enforcement bodies. The protections came in time for a post-war acceleration in available goods, many of which would be aimed at female shoppers.

White women marshalled their dollars as civic power making what was otherwise considered a private and inferior practice (compared to men's public labor) into a generative political resource.[36] Blacks, however, struggled for equal recognition as consumers. Even advertisements positioned Black Americans as somehow being outside of the consuming public. To the extent that they were present in such material at all, Blacks were objectified and positioned as props to accentuate a product's authenticity or efficacy.[37] The ideological abyss between economic object and economic subject compelled these socially, culturally, and politically disenfranchised people to carve out a space for themselves in the body politic and thus redefine the contours of citizenship.

Having themselves been largely excluded from the most prestigious firms in their industry on the basis of prejudicial beliefs, the Black men and women who played an increasingly important role in branding and promotion in post–World War II America had good reason to connect representation, consumption and political progress. After all, they had been hindered from fully participating in their chosen professional sphere in large part because many corporate executives were not convinced that African American consumers were a significant enough segment of the population to demand a targeted promotional strategy.[38] In other words, these marketing specialists understood that if Black dollars could be dismissed, then members of their racial community could experience other kinds of discrimination, including industry exclusion and career stagnation. Thus, they fought to establish Black Americans as what Jason Chambers describes as "a valuable and recognized part of the consumer democracy in which everyone's dollar/vote was equal."[39]

The African Americans who worked in marketing and media were perceived as curating a visual record of Black citizenship through commercial culture.[40] These "[B]lack image professionals," as Brenna Wynn Greer refers to them, were crucial to the broader struggle for civil rights because they portrayed Black people in a dignified manner. By the 1960s, shifts in the U.S. economy and perceptions about niche markets, purchasing power, and culturally specific spending practices brought new voices to conversations around Black consumers. These emergent interlocuters included politicians and government appointees concerned with reformulating Black Power as a movement for Black capitalism, as well as advertising and marketing professionals responsible for managing new African American growth strategies for the country's household brands. In September 1966, U.S. Secretary of Commerce John T. Connor published "A Guide to Negro Marketing Information." Aimed at the nation's white-owned and managed companies, Connor framed the 55-page guide as a resource that would "[bring] both the Negro consumer and the Negro businessman into full participation in economic society" and yield "a better, happier, healthier America for all."[41] These kinds of appeals became increasingly frequent in the 1960s as the seemingly more radical Black Power movement began to gain traction over the conservative elements of the Civil Rights movement. The founders of *Essence* launched their business into this dynamic marketplace, willing their ambition to grow into an empire where politics, consumption, and the interior lives of Black women could coagulate as a glossy package.

Commercial media and citizenship are therefore intertwined in how Black Americans, and Black women more specifically, fit into the dominant national narrative. In *Branding Black Womanhood*, media citizenship speaks to the terms under which belonging is unevenly distributed, how one's positioning along the spectrum of belonging fluctuates, and how it is expressed and performed through commercial culture. Moreover, by focusing on mass media, I am invoking broader arenas of enfranchisement. Media citizenship is concerned with social, economic, and political realities. The "magic" in Black Girl Magic provides access to citizenship because it is the primary avenue through which Black women's agency has been branded—that is, commodified and tethered to images. While media citizenship is bound to the image economy, magic for Black women is an interactive property that connects the imaginary to material possibilities. It is a cultural manifestation of a type of power and dignity that Black women hope to be able to realize beyond the screen.

Studying Black Women as a Self-Informant

My impetus for pursuing this work on Black womanhood, commercial culture, and citizenship, was my indignation with the way that the culture industries scrutinized, shamed, and silenced Black women for much of the first decade of the twenty-first century only to claim a few years later that we were self-empowered, magical creatures. In 2006 the U.S. Census Bureau released its American Community Survey showing that 45 percent of Black women in the country had never been married.[42] Hannah Brueckner, a sociologist at Yale University, found the trend to be most prevalent among college-educated Black women, leading her to conclude that their professional achievements had "come . . . at the cost of marriage and family."[43] These statistics incited a media-fueled panic about the demise of the Black family, which fertilized the ground for a new genre in the Black self-help marketplace to blossom. Comedians, little known actors, and filmmakers emerged as self-appointed experts that would guide Black women out of the darkness of single-*doom* and into the light of traditional Black family units through their books, movies, and other texts. Importantly, the figures who profited most from this genre were Black men with their own obvious romantic deficiencies, such as the twice-divorced Steve Harvey, and Hill Harper, who had never been married when he published his first relationships guide.[44] While the men developed distinct approaches to their audience, their message was consistent: a) Black women's professional success had caused us to establish unattainable and inappropriate demands for potential Black male partners, and b) it was Black women's responsibility to mitigate the crisis of Black female single-*doom* by remaking ourselves into more suitable partners.[45]

What intrigued me most about the shift in Black women's representation during the 2010s was that the same traits that deemed Black women unmarriageable under one paradigm rendered us magical just a few years later. The culture industries had first reconfigured Black women consumers as inherently deficient to sell us lifestyle guides for becoming better women. They then peddled the idea that we were already beautiful, fierce, and capable and should only offer our dollars and attention to companies that recognized this truth. Both narratives proliferated in the name of Black women's empowerment. The study that I have undertaken in this book explores how commercial culture could fashion, or brand, Black womanhood in such disparate ways in a short period of time and why these narratives were appealing.

In order to fully understand the audiences and multimedia brands that animate this book and the commercial environment that has sustained them, I rely on a range of primary sources. These include interviews with Black women media and marketing professionals, field research at events such as the annual Essence Festival, oral histories, memoirs, and trade periodicals. I also utilize print and broadcast news coverage of key figures and entities, as well as editorial and advertising content from the institutions under examination. Combining data through various collection methods yields a study that is comprehensive and unbound by the limitations or biases of any one particular source. My professional affiliation as a former *Essence* intern enhanced my access to current and former media professionals. I began recruiting for this study by leveraging my connection to gatekeepers who have worked with the following media organizations as a freelancer or permanent employee: Aspire TV, Essence Communications Inc., GlobalHue,[46] Viacom, SpringHill Entertainment,[47] Johnson Publishing Company, and NBC Universal. Upon interviewing participants from among my personal contacts, I sought additional participants through snowball sampling. I also reached out to content creators with whom I had no prior relationship and ultimately conducted interviews with professionals from organizations of different sizes and geographic regions. Some companies were Black-owned while others were subsidiaries of large media conglomerates. In addition, I recruited women from various rankings; professional titles among the participants at the time of data collection included editor, editor-in-chief, producer, vice president, manager of branded entertainment, CEO, and social media strategist, among others. Informants agreed to participate in the study under the condition that I would maintain their confidentiality. Therefore, I refer to them using pseudonyms and obscure other identifying traits where appropriate.

In recognition of my identity as a Black woman, a former media professional, and a current consumer of most of the texts and products examined in this inquiry, I use first-person pronouns (we, our) throughout the book. I use third-person pronouns where it is clear that I am not included in the particular grouping being discussed, as in cases when reference is made to historical events that precede my birth.

Overview of Chapters

The story of Black women's empowerment as a commercial, image-driven enterprise begins with four Black men: the founders of the Hollingsworth Group (later ECI). As the first company of its magnitude targeting Black women, ECI helped to determine the contours of media citizenship for its audience. Chapter 1 examines the "new" Black woman that *Essence* executives fabricated at the dawn of the 1970s, probes how Black men became primary architects of Black womanhood in its commodified form, and explores what Black women editors contributed to this effort.

ECI thrived, at times, in spite of the men who managed it. For example, although they dismissed the first editor-in-chief Ruth Ross before the inaugural issue hit newsstands, it was Ross who offered them the *Essence* name. The founders had no idea that many in their target audience would be offended by a magazine called *Sapphire*, the title they planned to use until Ross gave them a better idea in 1969.[48] Of the nine women who succeeded Ross as chief editorial executive at ECI in its fifty-year history, none have been more iconic or instrumental to the company's profit-driven racial uplift project than Susan L. Taylor. Chapter 2 examines how Taylor appropriated empowerment as a self-branding tool, packaging her image through books, speaking tours, and an inescapable presence in all things *Essence*. In doing so, the budding self-help personality pioneered a more capacious form of media citizenship whereby she came to own her image.

Chapter 3 progresses to the dawn of the twenty-first century, when Black women are an established consumer market and the idea of Black Girl Magic, or empowered Black womanhood, has become tangible through figures like Susan L. Taylor. Corporate brands now perceive these consumers as a market primed for commercial messaging in part because Black media companies have nourished audiences on affirmative vocabularies that entangle consumption and empowerment. With a focus on Procter & Gamble's *My Black Is Beautiful* and Ford Motor Company's *Built Ford Proud*, I probe what these multiplatform product marketing initiatives signify about Black women and who they benefit.

Although it is true that these campaigns serve corporate interests far better than the grand political promises they make, some producers have found ways to appropriate Black Girl Magic to advance a more expansive and inclusive vision of media citizenship for Black women. The fourth and final chapter explores how those with access to magic may leverage this privileged status to engineer an alternative pathway to dignified Black womanhood. Mara Brock Akil (creator of *Being Mary Jane*), Issa Rae (creator and star of *Insecure*), and Lena Waithe (creator of *Twenties*) strategically deploy vulnerability in their television series to reframe Black women as simply human, countering the Hollywood convention of representing such figures in extremes. In doing so, each auteur leverages her agency as an empowered media citizen to emphasize and expound on a form of personhood beyond magic.

1

The Black Woman That
Essence Built

Movement chants and the rumble of marchers were a common refrain on America's streets in 1970. This was especially true for New York City's well-known avenues, where the metropolis's assemblage of governmental and commercial gatekeepers made it a strategic target for dissenters protesting everything from the Vietnam War to urban blight. Members of the New York Radical Feminists and the National Organization for Women were among those raising their voices in the firestorm of critique from marginalized groups that characterized this period. In March of 1970, they set their sights on what they perceived to be a pillar of popular culture's most degrading images of women and descended on the headquarters of *Ladies' Home Journal*. A dominant women's lifestyle magazine of the era, the *Journal* boasted a monthly circulation of 6.9 million readers. Despite its tagline—"never underestimate the power of a woman"—the company reserved top positions on its masthead for men.[1] In addition to petitioning for all-female editorial and advertising staffs, the 100-plus demonstrators who marched to 641 Lexington Avenue on March 18 demanded greater influence over their representation. They presented a prototype for what they hoped would become a special issue of the magazine, featuring articles on topics that reflected their concerns. Ultimately, they sought to liberate their image from the control of men who did not understand their struggles.

Further downtown, at 102 East 30th Street, a much smaller party of dissenters had invaded a different women's lifestyle magazine. Unlike the crowd at

Ladies' Home Journal, these were Black men insisting on their authority to police images of Black women. *Essence*, still in its first year of operation, had been riddled with competing expectations from its stakeholders since its launch. The few initial investors and advertisers that had taken a chance on the magazine were most concerned about numbers: subscriptions, single-issue sales, and readers' spending power. Other outsiders wanted the publication to meet their personal metric for Black consciousness. Whereas seven major magazines tailored their content to women in general, only one had identified itself as speaking to and about Black women. *Essence* may have been stepping into a void in the mostly white magazine world, but it was entering a fervid debate in Black (print) culture.

According to then-editor Ida Lewis, the magazine's loudest critics were Black men in the community who felt they had a right to "[tell] us what we couldn't do and what we'd better do."[2] Sonny Carson, an activist known for his work with the Congress of Racial Equality, led the charge on the *Essence* headquarters that night in 1970.[3] "They came in—invaded the offices—and confronted us," recalled Lewis. "Like, 'What are you about and what are you going to do? What kind of publication are you going to present to the Black community?'"[4] Given its target market, *Essence* would also have to contend with angst about what empowered Black womanhood looked like in the post–Civil Rights period. Four interrelated questions drove this anxiety: Did Black women have a place in the Women's Liberation movement? What role should Black women play in race-based political struggles? To what extent should one's lifestyle reflect their political leanings? And how could a Black woman be independent without crossing over into the territory of an emasculating matriarch? The recently published Moynihan Report, which blamed women-led and otherwise dysfunctional family units for the ails facing impoverished Blacks in America's cities, incited panic.[5] Many Black women felt pressure to defend themselves from this fiction while simultaneously resisting men whose ideas of Black liberation hinged on female subservience. *Essence*'s pages were bound to be tinged with the rhetoric that fueled this drama.

The founders soon learned that simply creating a platform, however significant, was not enough. An irresponsibly managed commercial magazine aimed at Black women could be just as negligible as if none existed at all. Disparate ideas of what the magazine should be doing for Black women and the broader racial community buzzed about *Essence*'s founders and inaugural editors. If it did not effectively manage audience expectations, it would struggle to find its way into the right readers' hands: upwardly mobile African American women ages 18 to 34 who were "inquisitive and acquisitive."[6] If it could not secure a large enough audience that sponsors deemed it attractive, the company would fail. As several men—investors, advertisers, founders, and community activists—

claimed ownership over some piece of it, the magazine that was supposed to center Black women initially struggled to serve that mission.

The tension between the promises *Essence* made to its audience and its obligations to investors and advertisers complicated matters. Edward (Ed) Lewis, founder and inaugural publisher, envisioned the periodical as a vehicle that would "portray the Black woman as she's never been portrayed before . . . [and] show her in the light that other publications such as *McCall's*, *Ladies' Home Journal* or *Cosmopolitan* had not."[7] By defining the magazine in relationship to an existing commercial framework, Lewis set the tone for how *Essence* would navigate its early days. Since they were targeting a niche not yet fully legible in the marketplace, Lewis and the other executives became default guardians managing how the commercial sphere interacted with Black women. In this paradigm, the reader was a consumer first and foremost. Her Blackness was a unique selling proposition—the factor that set *Essence* apart from the period's leading glossy women's magazines known as the seven sisters. Simply put, Lewis and the other founders had stepped up to fill a void because the market demanded it, not because of some political urge brought on by the Women's Liberation and Black Power movements. Still, *Essence* would have to be more than a consumption vehicle if it wanted to hold Black women's attention in a changing social climate.

This chapter examines the complicated figure at the foundation of Black Girl Magic whom Essence Communications Inc. (ECI) constructed to manage its disparate constituencies. The *Essence* woman that the company hailed through its editorial vision established a pattern for how Black women would be represented in the image economy. Like the magical Black woman of the twenty-first century, she was susceptible to co-option. Nevertheless, female editors framed the *Essence* woman as a figure who cared about realizing her own power and drawing on it to support her Black brothers and sisters. She not only functioned as someone that readers could aspire and relate to; importantly, advertisers could figure her into their profit models.

Two editorial features illustrate how ECI managed the tensions and overlap between commerce, empowerment, capitalism, and citizenship during its first decade: the "Essence Woman" column published during Marcia Gillespie's tenure as editor-in-chief; and Susan L. Taylor's fashion and beauty pages. The "Essence Woman" column ran from 1971 until the early 1980s, when Taylor was transitioning into the dominant editorial role. The critical maneuvers that company leaders executed during this period reveal how they responded to the political attitudes of the day and produced a philosophy of feminine power that accommodated Black nationalist and neoliberal principles. Much like the two versions of the *Essence* woman, these seemingly contradictory impulses coexisted in the company and produced a fertile ground where the commercial

Black Girl Magic ethos would later thrive. The formation of Black woman-hood that *Essence* constructed came into being through complicated maneu-vers that women staffers and male leaders advanced. The resilience of this image of empowered womanhood is a testament to its allure and polysemous nature. ECI did not simply bombard its audience with promotional content cloaked in hollow political symbols; editors developed a method of address-ing, framing, and goading Black women that felt authentic. They conceptu-alized the *Essence* woman as a cultural product that could serve political and entrepreneurial agendas, a means to collective and individual power.

Cashing In on Black Capitalism

Essence was never intended to be a pink microphone for the Black Power move-ment. Jonathan Blount, Cecil Hollingsworth, Edward Lewis, and Clarence Smith had assembled with the intent of creating a profitable business; a maga-zine they hoped would become the eighth member of the elite class of women's service magazines that were known as the seven sisters. They desired to build an empire around Black womanhood that would profit them in the same way that *Redbook*, *McCall's*, and *Ladies' Home Journal* enriched their white male founders. Furthermore, the men presented themselves as intercessors who would redirect a spirit of resistance by offering Black women dignity through consumption. *Essence* emerged at a time when underrepresented groups were troubling the status quo. Some of these groups, furthermore, were doing so in more militant ways than had been popular in previous years. Emergent Black companies were expected to tame Black Power by spreading the gospel of enter-prise as a pathway to freedom. Edward Lewis asserted in his memoir that he and his partners were able to secure funding for their idea because "as bold [B]lack men who were also educated professionals [they] were . . . less threat-ening than the ghetto boys who were burning down their own neighbor-hoods."[8] *Essence* was poised to become a testament to the pragmatism of Black progress vis-à-vis commercial ventures.

In the late 1960s, economic development moved to the center of Black lib-eration discourses and spurred a range of political and commercial responses. New alliances and businesses emerged as Blacks strategized ways to eliminate the poverty obliterating America's so-called "Negro" ghettos and, in some cases, to access the highest echelons of financial power. Meanwhile, white elites in government and private enterprise were devising plans to make the focus on racism and wealth work for them. Recruiting, training, and hiring Black pro-fessionals was one tactic intended to satisfy a cacophony of demands for eco-nomic inclusion without upsetting a prosperous national climate. This white and elite project was framed as mutually beneficial because it put more money into Black people's hands, which meant greater spending power and higher profits for businesses. Another initiative developed during this time centered Black entrepreneurship; the guiding philosophy held that Black people with access to venture capital, reasonable loans, and a chance to compete for large contracts could become their own employers and build self-sustaining communities.

Even Richard Nixon—whose more popular anti-Black rhetoric appealed to segregationist whites—discussed Black empowerment and uplift in speeches during his presidential run in the spring of 1968. Nixon asserted that what Blacks were really asking for in their marches and riots was the opportunity to compete in the private enterprise system rather than dismantle it. He argued that America should not dismiss their request; on the contrary, it should respond with more jobs and support for Black businesses. According to Robert E. Weems, then-candidate Nixon's talking points were more indicative of astute political strategy than a sincere desire to see Black citizens woven into the nation's financial markets. In a turn away from the "law and order" stance that he had taken to curry favor with white Southerners, Nixon's "Bridges to Human Dignity" speeches offered a sanitized reading of Black Power aimed at Black militants. At its core his version of Black capitalism was "a monetary incentive to move away from notions of 'Burn, Baby, Burn,'" an invitation to participate in the free market rather than challenge it.[9] Some notable Black activists like Floyd McKissick accepted the summons and endorsed the Republican candidate.[10] McKissick's stamp of approval was no small victory, as he had participated in organized civil rights work since the 1940s and served as President of the Congress for Racial Equality. In an apparent exchange for his endorsement, McKissick later received federal grant money to establish Soul City, a planned community for Black people in North Carolina.[11]

Conversely, many minoritized citizens who planned to vote for Nixon's opponent—Hubert H. Humphrey—rejected his Black capitalism program as being insufficient to address the systemic ills that impoverished many Black Americans and relinquished them to make do in resource-poor neighborhoods. Bayard Rustin, organizer of the famed 1963 March on Washington, charged that Nixon's scheme would amount to a mere "crumb to the [B]lack community."[12] Other activists, including women who belonged to the Congress of African People, had already been calling for a revolt from "monopoly capitalism" and saw no potential for Black liberation in Nixon's plan.[13] Some critics advanced their own economic development projects as alternatives. By disavowing mainstream consumer brands that disregarded Black communities these social justice innovators also helped to make the late 1960s and early 1970s a more opportune period for Black entrepreneurs like the *Essence* founders.

Jesse L. Jackson was one such leader who urged commercial retailers to employ more Blacks and use Black-owned firms for the work that they contracted out to independent vendors. Jackson led Operation Breadbasket—a

Chicago-based offshoot of the Southern Christian Leadership Council designed to address Black economic oppression—which boycotted companies that refused to comply. While Jackson rejected Nixon's Black capitalism as a "gimmick" and a "false goal" that would intensify intra-racial class divisions, he believed that his alternative strategy was more comprehensive.[14] He described the rationale behind Operation Breadbasket's approach in a 1969 article in the *National Catholic Reporter*: "In our approach of just getting jobs all we were doing with our power leverage was to make the companies hire more Negroes, and all that was being accomplished was to make more consumers. What was needed was a way to create Negro capital. The ultimate tragedy of [B]lack separatism from the mainstream society is in the dependence of [B]lacks upon whites for everything vital in their lives. Black people have been reduced to being dependent consumers without being allowed to become an independent production force."[15]

Under Jackson's leadership, Operation Breadbasket built an infrastructure that allowed Black entrepreneurs to compete alongside their white counterparts. In this vein, he was realizing the self-empowerment thrust of Black capitalism that Nixon espoused. Once elected, President Nixon made good on his campaign promises (in theory) by signing an executive order establishing the Office of Minority Business Enterprise in 1969.[16] This action inspired various institutions and individuals to join in the effort to expand Black economic opportunity in whatever way they found most reasonable. For example, an assistant dean and director of adult and continuing education at a Chicago city college added a course to his school's catalogue specifically aimed at aspiring Black entrepreneurs. The administrator credited Nixon's program with spurring him to introduce "Soul Food as a Small Business," a course that was free for Chicago residents.[17] Other ventures, including culturally specific publications and television shows, emerged to take advantage of the nation's growing interest in Black dollars. Recognizing that the proliferation of Black commercial media provided an opening for marketing firms, several African American advertising professionals established their own agencies in the sixties and seventies. Much of their business relied on the ability to confirm the Black consumer market's vitality and facilitate ad placements in Black media. Thus, they too had a vested interest in the endurance of a commercial vehicle like *Essence*.

In addition to proving that Black consumers had value, media and communications outfits also had to argue that brands needed to design distinct campaigns to reach this niche. The cultural resistance movement that was unfolding in the late 1960s facilitated this paradigm shift. Tom Burrell, who founded his own firm during this period, credits icons Stokely Carmichael and Malcolm X with contributing to a Black pride sensibility in American advertising. Inspired by Black Power rhetoric and its potential to transform their industry, professionals like Burrell began to unapologetically focus on Black consumers. Decades later, he described the dawn of the seventies as a turning point:

> That was the time of the daishikis and the Black handshake and all the things that kind of accompanied the idea that we're okay. The afro came into vogue. So that was the beginning of the whole process. And so Black business development, Black advertising agencies kind of came out of that whole idea, that we could be different and be okay. Because had we not done that, then we would not have had Black advertising agencies because it was all based on the premise that Black people are not dark-skinned white people. . . . Meaning that . . . based on our history there are psychological, sociological, anthropological differences that manifest themselves in different marketplace behavior.[18]

The *Essence* founders had therefore ventured into the marketplace at just the right time, a moment when Black people were finally being recognized as consumer citizens.

Creating the Eighth Sister

Many of *Essence*'s early advertisers were newly interested in Black commercial periodicals. While some were emergent brands specifically designed to monetize the aesthetic shifts facilitated by the Black Power movement, others were established corporations who had been lured by the notion that Black citizens could serve their financial interests. This Black consumer boom was especially evident in the cosmetics industry, where the marketplace for women of color was expanding at a rate of 15 to 20 percent each year.[19] Flori Roberts Inc.— named after its white founder—was one of the first national brands to target Black women with tailored product lines in 1965. The company began advertising its "melanin make-up" in the very first issue of *Essence*.[20]

ECI founders Blount, Hollingsworth, Lewis, and Smith also benefited from the Black capitalism push through their connection to someone who had been an early advocate: Russell L. Goings. The men first met at an entrepreneurship workshop sponsored by Shearson, Hammill & Co. in response to Nixon's call to support Black economic empowerment. Goings, a vice president at the New York firm, thought Nixon's framing of Black Power as "[B]lack pride, [B]lack jobs, [B]lack opportunity" had potential and had called the meeting in November 1968 to give African American businessmen an opportunity to network.[21] A former professional football player, Goings entered the world of investment banking at a time "when the only [B]lacks there . . . were shining shoes and delivering coffee."[22] Identifying corporate newcomers like Edward Lewis who would take to the gospel of Black enterprise was part of his mission to upset that pattern.

Lewis was the ideal recruit for Goings' efforts. A former University of New Mexico student council member, Lewis had envisioned a more civic-focused career for himself when he departed Albuquerque with undergraduate and graduate degrees in political science. Accepted into law school at Georgetown University, he dropped out after second semester exams revealed that he was not a good match for the institution. Following this experience, a mentor from college helped him secure a spot in an executive training program at First National City Bank in New York. Like other corporate institutions who had answered a national call to support Black business enterprise, the bank had developed a recruitment pipeline for promising African Americans and members of other disadvantaged groups. As a law school dropout-turned-banker, Lewis's job at First National City Bank was a chance at personal redemption.

Like Lewis, each of the other *Essence* founders had made enough of an impression in the corporate world to be invited to a Black entrepreneurship seminar at a brokerage that would soon merge with Hayden Stone, Inc. to become one of Wall Street's largest firms.[23] With the exception of Clarence Smith, who was in his mid-thirties when the men first met, the founders were twentysomething professionals working for companies like Prudential Life Insurance and New Jersey Bell Telephone Company's Yellow Pages. Cecil Hollingsworth, whose name would be incorporated into the official title of the business partnership, was an entrepreneur consulting on graphic design projects for companies like Merrill Lynch. Jonathan Blount, despite being the youngest and least experienced of the group, had spent the most time pondering the idea of a glossy magazine for Black women. He recalled multiple times in his youth when his mother openly wondered why such a periodical did not exist. So Blount's ears perked up when A. Michael Victory (one of the Shearson, Hammill executives present at the seminar) suggested that the firm would be likely to invest in something specifically geared toward Black consumers. While Victory's mention of "a Negro women's magazine" may have simply been a cursory example to him, it was the exact concept that Blount had been hoping to explore at the workshop.[24] At the onset, none of the men who went on to establish The Hollingsworth Group (the original name for the company that launched *Essence*) had an answer to the question that Blount's mother had asked. Nevertheless, they soon discovered that however promising the idea seemed, bringing it to fruition would demand a multipronged strategy involving a crucial resource that they all lacked: the lived experience of being a Black woman.

While the economic and political atmosphere of the late 1960s was fertile ground for their intended crop, *Essence*'s founders still needed to labor consistently and methodically to reap a harvest. Because newsstands at the time mostly aimed their feminine lifestyle offerings at white women, creating a Black women's magazine was a risky proposition. The leading publications in this category, known as the seven sisters, included *Good Housekeeping, Family Circle, Women's Day, Redbook, McCall's,* and *Ladies' Home Journal.*[25] Like *Essence,* they too were founded and managed by men, but they were proven investments. Luckily for The Hollingsworth Group, by 1970 the marketplace was shifting from "mass" to "class" publications.[26] According to Ellen McCracken, magazines began pitching their smaller, niche audiences as a more efficient choice for sponsors to compete with television. "Advertisers could avoid spending money to reach people unable to purchase their products, as frequently occurred when ads addressed mass segments of the population."[27] A magazine that provided access to a desirable niche "could raise advertising rates because it now targeted an affluent audience."[28] Jonathan Blount, Cecil Hollingsworth, Edward Lewis, and Clarence Smith planned to sell the *Essence* reader as the newest market segment that advertisers were overlooking. Rather than deconstruct the established system in which women's service magazines thrived, they sought to expand it to include those who had been excluded.

When they approached potential advertisers, Lewis and Smith talked about a "new" Black woman that was emerging in the midst of America's resistance movements. They argued that she would need a lifestyle guide to facilitate her evolution and that *Essence* was well-positioned to fill that void. General interest magazines like *Ebony* and white magazines like *McCall's* were not focused enough to meet her unique needs; neither could these periodicals effectively serve advertisers interested in this consumer niche. *Essence*'s pitch relied on advertisers being able to imagine this "new" Black woman as someone whom they wanted to reach in the first place. Thus, these sales presentations became the drawing board for the emergent *Essence* woman. In his memoir, Edward Lewis offers a glimpse into how this figure began to take shape and what she represented: "Clarence [Smith] would craft a sales story so compelling, original, and authentic that it became real, and created a new niche in the American marketplace. The story he told introduced the Essence Woman, a striver, who in 1970 was now educated, worked in new careers, had discretionary income, had the ability to influence, and wanted information geared specifically to her and her needs in media that reflected her."[29]

Even as women of all races interrogated their status as citizens and their representation within popular culture, four Black men envisioned themselves as being suited for the task of defining and publicizing the "new" Black woman as a consumer niche. By assuming a dominant role in the financial, logistical, and editorial operations, the four founders and Gordon Parks (the founding editorial director) positioned themselves to circumscribe Black women's movement within the media landscape. The advertiser-friendly *Essence* woman compelled corporations to confront their biases and recognize that Black women's dollars mattered. The men who managed the company's bottom line appreciated the significance of this victory given the rejections they encountered during sales pitches to potential sponsors, particularly in the magazine's early years. As Lewis recounts: "Judging by the attitudes of advertisers in 1970, you would think that [B]lack women and their families did not eat cereal, use toothpaste, drive cars, have bank accounts, use makeup, sleep on sheets, take vacations, or consume any of the other myriad goods and services that typified American life."[30] An *Essence* woman who was not only visible but appealing to advertisers represented progress in the commercial sphere.

Complicating the *Essence* Woman

While *Essence* executives believed that they were manufacturing a certain kind of ideal Black woman consumer, they struggled to prioritize Black women's voices in shaping the magazine. Inaugural editorial director Gordon Parks, then an acclaimed photographer and filmmaker, dominated Black women editors. His name was listed first on the masthead, and he steered the magazine's initial issues toward his own vision of creating a Black version of *Vogue*. Parks displayed women's nearly nude bodies in ways that he thought would emphasize beauty and glamour but that carried hints of the blaxploitation aesthetic he sometimes deployed in films.[31] *Essence* was not *Vogue* and Parks's editorial formula did not compel enough readers to make the magazine profitable. He left the magazine in 1972.[32]

Just over a year into the magazine's existence, *Essence* executives were already searching for a third chief editor who would shore up the young publication's identity. The new leader would need to project a coherent image of Black womanhood that calmed doubts incited by a scandalous development. When news broke that Playboy Enterprises, Inc. had invested $250,000 in the magazine and acquired one seat on the board, skepticism arose about who controlled this Black media platform. Jonathan Blount and Ida Lewis, who had been dismissed as president and editor-in-chief, respectively, charged that the company had deviated from its original mission under Playboy's influence. Blount's claims seemed plausible to readers who thought it explained *Essence*'s visual identity. It was logical to them that the infamous Hugh Heffner, who had built an enterprise on bare breasts and butts, would be covertly directing magazine staff to exploit Black women's bodies. Thus, the next editor-in-chief needed to restore faith in the magazine and breathe life into the image of Black female empowerment that the founders had sold to Madison Avenue.

Marcia Gillespie announced that she wanted to be considered for the role and unilaterally moved into the editor-in-chief's office before the publisher had an opportunity to appoint a successor. "I just assumed that once they saw me behind the desk and I looked like I belonged there they would have said: how could we have avoided her for so long," Gillespie stated in retrospect.[33] The

26-year-old had served as managing editor during Ida Lewis's tenure and cap-tivated executives with a confidence and fierceness that surpassed her youth. It was clear that Gillespie knew how to reach the targeted reader because she was one of them. She articulated a vision of the *Essence* woman—a self-empowered, race-conscious striver—that advertising executive Clarence Smith could sell in his appeals to potential sponsors. The reader was "interested in the quality of her life and interested in loving her man and finding ways to bridge the gap that this kind of nightmare society builds up between the two."³⁴ Because Gil-lespie's vision was effective—the magazine became profitable for the first time during her tenure—it became a prototype for the empowered Black woman image that *Essence* and other media platforms exploited for decades to come.

Gillespie's *Essence* woman was a precursor for the magical Black woman of the twenty-first century, but the images she advanced were less tidy than the manufactured reader profiles Clarence Smith would have referenced during advertising pitches. Gillespie understood that concern for the race—not just skin color—separated the *Essence* reader from women that titles like *McCall's* pursued. Thus, she steered the magazine with an eye to the target audience's status in the body politic. In her inaugural editor's column, published during the anniversary month of Nat Turner's 1831 slave rebellion, she touted *Essence*'s commitment to advancing Turner's objective of Black liberation and affirmed Black women's role in the ongoing struggle.³⁵ "Nat Turner's battle still rages," she wrote. "Although the shackles and whips are gone, our bondage continues—poverty, denial, dreams deferred."³⁶ For Gillespie, the *Essence* woman was a righteous warrior battling alongside men to realize a "[B]lack nation"—by which she meant cultural, social, and economic self-determination.³⁷ The pur-suit of these goals, however, did not require Black women to relinquish their independence. They could approach their identity and community in the ways that best suited them, regardless of whether they offended camps that thought them to be overly autonomous or assimilationist.

Under Gillespie's leadership, *Essence* presented an alternative definition of Blackness untethered to "an afro," "African dress," or "Swahili."³⁸ The new editor-in-chief understood that part of the magazine's mission was affirming the spectrum of complexions, sensibilities, and circumstances that framed read-ers' lived experiences of Black womanhood. "*Essence* comes as a statement that hey, you are beautiful," she said. "And you're beautiful 'cause you're chocolate brown, or you're light tan, or you're cafe au lait and you got red hair and it's nappy, or you got black hair and it's straight, or whatever you are."³⁹ The maga-zine expressed that affirmation through a column that put faces, names, and biographies to the kind of woman they were targeting. Beginning in Octo-ber 1971 the "Essence Woman" profiled individuals, often aged 25–40, who reflected a heterogeneous population of Black American women. While they tended to reside in urban areas with high Black populations like Chicago and were mostly professionals with some form of post-secondary education, they varied in their adornment choices, ambitions, and ideas about how to approach Black womanhood. As writer Marjorie Moore wrote in the conclusion of the very first profile, the content was intended to bolster "spiritual unity and communication" among Black women regardless of their worldview.[40]

With its spectrum of Black femininities, the "Essence Woman" feature reflects an arena where the woman-led editorial strategy strained the glossy construction of womanhood that the magazine's founders wanted to monetize. Most of the individuals profiled were self-disciplined role models who symbolized what one could attain by taking responsibility for one's own destiny. However, in grouping Black women according to their shared concern for racial progress rather than common commercial desires, the editorial staff used the "Essence Woman" column to (re)humanize their audience. They addressed readers not simply as high-achieving Black women who were only as valuable as their most recent accomplishment, nor as mere style mavens useful for fashion and beauty tips; rather, they were approached as full beings with anxieties, hurts, flaws, and struggles. Editors also made room in the column for contradiction and controversy, unsettling the notion that Black women should approach the volatile seventies with the same mindset. Thus, the "Essence Woman" was an editorial space where different viewpoints abounded about marriage, Women's Liberation, gender roles, Black Power, class divides, sexuality, motherhood, and the ways in which these issues complicated how Black men and women related to one another. While there were lines that the profiles did not cross—such as violating the magazine's pro-Black, anti-separatist (read feminist) agenda—the diverse opinions and lifestyles captured in the "Essence Woman" fractured any notion that the magazine's audience was a monolithic class of affluent Black women and an easy target for advertisers.[41]

The premiere "Essence Woman" profiles in 1971 capture editors' struggle to appeal to a broad readership. While the first three women all fell into the 28–32 age range, they came from distinct regional backgrounds and exhibited a spectrum of approaches to femininity from conservative to less traditional. By offering a point of entry for women of various sensibilities, *Essence* constructed a Black woman in its pages that was more difficult to pin down than the figure it sold to advertisers. Hulan Watson, a Texas-based community organizer and chairwoman of the Western Region Branch of the Tenants' Rights Association, was featured in the December 1971 column. She discussed her evolution from fulltime homemaker to a fulltime activist who did not always make it home for dinner. On days when work kept her away from home, she always arranged for her three sons' care and forged ahead with the confidence that the example she offered them through her activism was more valuable than her physical presence at every meal or activity. Watson also talked about how male colleagues challenged her in meetings, not simply because they disagreed with her ideas but because they did not appreciate her demeanor. They often complained that her self-presentation was unbecoming of a lady. Watson resisted such attempts at dismissal and made it clear that she had no interest in whatever social capital might have come along with conceding to her male peers' ideas of femininity: "I've never been a lady, whatever that means. I'm a woman and I'm important to this movement. I have a mind. I can contribute just as much as any man, when I know what I'm talking about. If I make an intelligent statement based on fact, all I ask is that they respect it."[42]

Conversely, Janice Terry, a 32-year-old wife and mother of three, clung to traditional beliefs. She described herself as "very weak" in the November 1971 issue and indicated that she was happy to let her husband provide for her.[43] "I need a nice, strong, hard, intelligent, secure man to take care of me; to hold me when I cry," she said.[44] Whereas Watson reported feeling so troubled by the government's mistreatment of Black citizens that she could no longer be content as a homemaker, Terry prioritized her family responsibilities over other endeavors. She had stopped modeling and teaching to support her husband's work, which took the family to Vietnam during the war. She was content to focus on her husband's ambitions and felt no impulse to carve out space for personal projects. When she was featured nine years later in the May 1980 issue, Terry revised her position and claimed that it was something she had said because she assumed it was necessary to support the male ego. "That was one *BS* statement," she said. "I was *never* weak, I'm *not* weak."[45]

Lydia Rose Cade, the first person to be featured as an "Essence Woman" in October 1971, fell somewhere in the middle of the other two. Cade was working for the UniWorld Group, a Black communications firm based in New York City, when her profile appeared in the magazine. Her winding career path had taken her from the publishing world to the music industry and required multiple interstate moves. Described as "a mover, a doer, creative," single and college-educated 28-year-old, Cade appeared to be the quintessential modern Black woman, untethered from the lifestyle requirements that encumbered previous generations.[46] It may have been this aura of independence that prompted Cade and the writer to emphasize the conventions she held onto. The first sentence of the feature reads like a dating profile: "She's fine, she's bright, loves men, wants children, and stands five feet, ten inches tall with pride and dignity."[47] This description communicates that despite being unmarried and nearing the age when women were expected to have settled into motherhood, Cade was still interested in these conventional roles. She had not veered so far off into modernity that she had no use for a man.

It was customary for "Essence Woman" profiles to participate in such apologetics for the independent, professional 1970s Black woman. Some women were anxious to distance themselves from the tropes of sapphire and matriarch and wanted to express that they had not "eschewed revolutionary procreation for corporate life," as one *Essence* writer stated.[48] Many profiles featuring unmarried women articulated their familial ambitions along with their career goals. In this way, the *Essence* woman presented as an every-woman who would bring home the bacon and fry it up in the pan. Advertisers could rest assured that even if she did not yet have a family to tend to, she would one day be in the market for bacon, pans, and other domestic products aimed at married mothers. Her career achievements also meant that unlike the fulltime homemaker, the modern Black woman would also need all the trappings that made life as a professional more manageable.

To this end, it was common for individuals featured in "Essence Woman" to have a public service record just as impressive as their professional resumes. For example, Ada Evans, who was profiled in the July 1975 issue, was a fulltime teacher and mayor of Fairplay, Colorado, an unpaid position at the time. Evans managed these roles along with her domestic responsibilities as a wife and mother of two. In the April 1975 issue, readers met Maria Broom: a classically trained dancer and head of WJZ-TV's Public Defender Unit in Baltimore. In addition to her telejournalism work, Broom taught a Saturday dance class for local youth. La Deva Davis, who was featured in the November 1975 issue, hosted a PBS show called *What's Cooking* and managed Philadelphia's Frekoba Africans Afro-American Drum and Dance Ensemble with her fiancé. Through these profiles, *Essence* communicated the importance of a woman maintaining her commitment to racial uplift while she worked to realize her career ambitions. One was not to eclipse the other.

Community work signaled that Black women could be career-driven without becoming competitive and self-centered—traits that would have classified them as masculine. Furthermore, their service was almost always targeted to Black communities and indicated that no matter how far Black women climbed up the corporate ladder, they would not abandon their racial heritage nor reject Black men. Anxiety around Black women outpacing their male counterparts professionally and joining with white women in what was perceived as a man-hating crusade lurked in numerous profiles. For example, Lydia Cade, the single New York City–based communications professional featured in the inaugural "Essence Woman," denounced Women's Liberation as a white women's campaign. "Any time a movement tries to separate the goals of Black women and men or hinder their efforts for a total result, I say to that movement—forget it!"[49] The afro-donning Cade presented herself as fully committed to a collective liberation agenda. The author of the profile contextualized her stance with a brief discussion of how mainstream feminism was ignorant of Black women's lived reality. "The media," she wrote, "is talking about women's lib . . . letting women get out there and compete with men. White women have had all the protection that a society can muster, while Black women have always been out there for socio-economic reasons."[50]

Such an interpretation of the movement would have been expected given editor-in-chief Marcia Gillespie's stance that the women's movement amounted to a "family dispute" among white people.[51] "I have never had a chance to be locked into a suburb with a dishwasher and a maid to find out if I need to escape," she once stated.[52] In alignment with the editor's point of view, "Essence Woman" columns tended to present gender and race as distinct identity vectors and suggested that Black women were expected to choose the latter over the former in their political alliances. Cade's profile thus emphasized her employment at an all-Black company, her desire for marriage and children, and her community work with Black children to present the modern Black woman as independent, yet self-sacrificing; empowered, but not emasculating.

Other women profiled throughout the seventies espoused conservative gender roles despite career paths that seemed to contradict their beliefs. For example, Vy Higginsen, a radio disc jockey and former advertising executive, described herself as a woman with old-fashioned values in her December 1972 profile. "Yes, I am the 18th century female's female," she said. "I refuse to compete with a man on a man's level. I like the idea of being a woman and a lady."[53] Higginsen was unmarried at the time of the interview and was working toward her pilot's license. Her remarks distanced her from the "aggressive Black woman" trope that *Essence* accused mass media of fueling during this period.[54] Still, Higginsen's comments suggested that a war between the career-driven, modern Black woman and the Black man was real and that women needed to make their allegiances clear.

A similar issue came to the fore when *Essence* profiled Janet Singleton in May 1975; two years after California State University in Hayward had appointed her director of the Intercultural Education and Resources Center. Singleton discussed "her fear of competing for the job and subsequent reluctance to accept it after learning that she won out over several minority men."[55] On the one hand, the profile celebrates Singleton's achievement as the first woman to ascend to such a role in California. However, it also frames Black men's relative stagnation as the downside to Black women's advancement. In response to this tension Singleton declared that "the women's lib thing" was not responsible for her accomplishment.[56] She insisted that she earned the job because of her qualifications, which is to say that she had not been the beneficiary of some reverse sexism agenda.

None of this is to suggest that the *Essence* woman had to be opposed to any philosophy that acknowledged the importance of gender as an axis of oppression. The magazine published an essay entitled "Black Women's Lib?" in 1972 urging readers to consider how many of the questions that the movement raised were relevant to Black women. Even though the struggle tended to privilege white middle-class concerns, the writer reminded Black women that "any sister who feels that she has more than babies to contribute to the [Black] liberation struggle" needed to be concerned with intra-racial conflict fueled by sexism.[57] Delores James, a 26-year-old psychiatric counselor featured in the April 1972 issue, echoed the sentiment that Black women could relate to some of the arguments that white women were raising. She spoke about going to a local meeting organized by activists in Atlanta. Although she reported being the only African American woman present and admitted that she was still uncertain about where she stood on several major agenda items, she expressed unease about how Black men related to their female counterparts. "Black men should stop blaming Black women for their misery," she said. "We seem to get caught up in bickering with one another, rather than with the society that causes us both to suffer."[58]

Many of the columns profiled women who were less occupied with what men needed and more concerned with how Black women could lead fulfilling lives. For example, Priscilla Howard left her husband behind when he refused to leave Mississippi. In the January 1975 issue, Howard explained that she wanted to move to Chicago to realize a better life. The opportunities that she believed awaited her and her three sons in the midwestern metropolis outweighed the mandate to comply with contemporary gender norms by conceding to her husband's desire to stay put in the town of Richton, Mississippi. The fact that her son, George, went on to found Johnson Products Company and grow it into the largest Black-owned haircare manufacturer in the world read as proof that Black women could find victory when they took charge of their lives and bet on their own ambitions. Rosemary Brown, who appeared in the October 1975 issue, echoed the opinion that Black women should not abandon their dreams at the altar. She remained committed to her personal professional endeavors despite being a mother of three and wife to the lieutenant governor of Colorado. "I feel that I have to remain as much an individual and total person as possible," she said.[59] Brown believed that if women held onto their sense of self in marriage, the resulting satisfaction they enjoyed would benefit everyone else in their family as well.

The "Essence Woman" profiles normalized Black women's pursuit of happiness whether they were married or single, childless or mothering. If some tradition or dominant gender role got in the way of a woman's peace and joy, it was acceptable for her to deviate from external expectations. This sense of autonomy and choice is a characteristic of empowerment still embedded in the twenty-first century configuration of the magical Black woman. Making self-determination a fundamental trait for the *Essence* woman and her modern descendant was crucial for appropriating the image as a marketing device. Consumption could only be fashioned as a political act if it entailed some measure of resistance. However, the "Essence Woman" profiles did not resign empowered Black womanhood to the commercial sphere; rather, they documented how women expressed a newfound sense of agency in their domestic arrangements, romantic relationships, and careers.

Fern Stanford was a 28-year-old artist and single mother profiled in July 1972. Stanford realized her autonomy by protecting her creative time even from her own daughter's disruptions. She explained that she expected her preteen to be more independent to allow for times when an all-night painting session kept her locked away and necessitated her sleeping in the next morning. She considered herself "an artist before . . . anything else" and determined that anyone who was part of her life would have to accommodate her creative practice.[60] Whereas Stanford bucked the image of the self-sacrificing mother to honor her vocational ambitions, other *Essence* women like Eddie Bernice Johnson found freedom in singlehood. In her profile, Johnson expressed that getting divorced afforded her the agency she needed to run for public office. "If I were married, I wouldn't be in the legislature. I'd still think of it as a man's place," she said.[61] Johnson worked as a nurse during her fourteen-year marriage and ascended to supervisory roles that brought her to the front lines of injustices she would later address as a lawmaker. An unexpected victor, Johnson defeated her opponent to become the first Black woman from Dallas to be elected to the Texas State House of Representatives in 1972. Upon being reelected in 1975, she became the first woman of any race to chair the House Committee on Labor.

The liberty to forge one's identity also transcended career choice. For *Essence* women like 25-year-old Michele Freeman, happiness meant reclaiming her individuality and upsetting dominant notions about racial authenticity. Having once agonized about whether she was perceived as sufficiently aligned with Black culture, Freeman asserted in her June 1972 profile that she would no longer capitulate to external arbiters: "It almost seemed that, liking flowers, soft music and good food, quiet evenings and good books, was not being Black. I think that while we are struggling to attain freedom and justice, we must not lose the freedom as individuals, to enjoy what our tastes dictate to us is beautiful. I know that I'm a Black woman, period."[62] Freeman's profile confirmed a core tenet of the *Essence* woman that continues to be relevant in the Black Girl Magic era: that no matter a Black woman's personal or professional roles and obligations, empowerment means that she is free to be an individual.

The *Essence* woman was both distinct from previous generations of Black women and free to orient herself toward traditional or progressive gender norms. In the *Essence* universe, Blackness and femininity became accessories that she could refashion and stylize as she saw fit. By making Black womanhood customizable like a brand, *Essence* could appeal to a broader audience and present Black women with a buffet of commodities designed to help them express their individuality. The "Essence Woman" profiles therefore doubled as clarifying statements about the lifestyles that Black women led and the kinds of marketplaces and consumption behaviors that accompanied those lifestyles. If the modern Black woman wanted to sport an afro, she needed the right products to keep it well-coiffed for the office or church, or both. If she was intent on living single and climbing the corporate ladder, she needed the right vehicle to keep her mobile without forcing her to rely on a man to maintain it. No matter where her life took her, she could trust *Essence* to guide her toward becoming her best, most empowered self.

Taken together, the *Essence* woman that editor-in-chief Marcia Gillespie constructed was a community-minded citizen who used her agency for personal and racial uplift. Her decisions and expressions were authentically Black because she was Black, not because they fit some imposed script. In broadening the parameters of Black womanhood, Gillespie validated a range of styles and corresponding purchases needed to achieve them. Yet, even the purchases held political significance for the editor. She aimed to equip readers with the information they needed to patronize Black-owned businesses. For example, after readers complained about what they perceived to be inadequate attention for Black beauty and fashion companies, Gillespie and her team introduced a "Designer of the Month" feature spotlighting Black artisans. And when a white designer complained that the feature was an act of reverse racism, Gillespie held her ground: "I hope he sues me 'cause I think it's funny. I think it's funny that after all these years of never, never having Black people who were talented have any place to tell the world about it, that when we start doing it, somebody's gone call us racist, in a racist society."[63]

Many editors in Gillespie's position—that is, leading a new women's magazine—would have considered it an easy compromise, if not an obligation to indulge fashion gatekeepers. Filling the magazine's pages each month demanded negotiations with talent and executives, publicists and advertisers. One miscalculation could have easily jeopardized *Essence* in its nascent stage. Nevertheless, Gillespie persisted in her mission to make it more than a chocolate-dipped *Ladies' Home Journal*. She centered Black subjects at the risk of offending others and cast an editorial vision that maintained a standard even in its commercialism.

With a bottom line to meet and a readership with wide-ranging interests, *Essence* could not abandon its fashion and beauty coverage altogether. The editors needed to speak to the part of the *Essence* woman that was a consumer without upsetting her political values. Susan L. Taylor, whom Gillespie promoted from freelance beauty writer to beauty and fashion editor, found a way to marry these interests. This position situated Taylor at the crux of the magazine's most difficult competing factions: reluctant advertisers still demanding that the periodical prove its worth and readers who did not see themselves nor a vision of what they aspired to be when they looked at *Essence*. Taylor's success hinged on her ability to repackage the magazine as something that Black women could relate to and read with pride. In a climate where masculinist views circulated throughout mainstream discourse scrutinizing women, she found a way to frame adornment as a personal liberation practice that elevated rather than diluted African aesthetics. Managing this dilemma equipped her to eventually take the reins of the magazine and cement it as the quintessential brand of empowered Black womanhood.

The Dilemma of Natural Beauty

Susan L. Taylor's role as beauty and fashion editor was especially important because she was responsible for the magazine cover and the beauty-and-style editorial content that advertisers relied on as the primer for their sales pitches. The cover, as Ellen McCracken has written, operates as a promotional tool for the magazine itself and hails the audience as readers and consumers: "The cover helps establish the brand identity of the magazine-commodity; it is the label or packaging that will convince us to choose one magazine over the competitors. We are to buy the magazine, however, not simply to increase the publisher's sales, but so that we will also purchase the goods and services advertised inside. . . . In effect, the front cover is the most important advertisement in any magazine."[64] Any editor directing the cover of a commercial periodical must be as adept at pitching as the sales team. Since editorial content must maintain at least the veneer of distinction from advertising, editors must also be inconspicuously persuasive. Taylor accomplished this by establishing a connection with the audience through strategic vulnerability, embedding product appeals in culturally specific spiritual guidance, and rooting Black American style in an African genealogy of elegance and flair.

Cultural nationalists who saw women's bodies as political sites that could be used in the fight for Black power complicated the work of a Black beauty editor emerging in the early seventies. Some male leaders within the Black Arts Movement argued that "natural" beauty—an embodied aesthetic free from artificial aides and props—signified psychological liberation.[65] Although several intellectuals challenged this patriarchal theorization of Black women's beauty choices, the notion that personal style was linked to racial consciousness persisted. Taylor understood the need to create a counternarrative to reach the *Essence* readers who were uneasy about cosmetic rituals that imperiled their performance of Black pride. "I would take it back to the motherland and tell them don't be ashamed for wearing cosmetics," she later remarked. "Don't let men tell you that you're not a traditional sister or a real sister or that you're negating your culture if you wear makeup."[66] She combatted the notion that cosmetic enhancement negated Black heritage by constructing a narrative that positioned African women as style originators whom the Western world imitated. "We took the earth and we pounded it and put it on our faces and used berries to stain our cheeks and our lips," she insisted.[67]

Taylor also persuaded the publisher to fund fashion shoots at sites across the African diaspora to exhibit the diversity of Black beauty. Her twelve-page fashion spread on Haiti published in the March 1973 issue included multiple brand tie-ins from American Airlines to the Charles of the Ritz "Total Skin Care System" designed especially for easy travel use.[68] While the article functioned as a promotional vehicle, it also afforded Taylor an opportunity to discuss the culture of Black resistance crucial to Haiti's history. She wrote about the country's people and customs, and, however subtly, brought attention to the legitimacy of Pan-Africanism.[69] Although the methods she used sometimes meant partnering with brands and corporate gatekeepers who did not share her goals, Taylor's writings reveal a desire for racial uplift. In addition to presenting readers with an alternative understanding of makeup, she reinforced their capacity to make meaning on their own terms and reject dictates from men who did not fully comprehend their experiences as Black women. Beauty was an accessible channel through which women could assert their Black consciousness and challenge men who presumed the right to establish rules for how racial pride should be embodied and expressed.

To be sure, Taylor's avowal that Black style was an arena of empowerment for Black women was neither novel nor exceptional. The use of beauty rituals and fashion for subversive and pleasure-boosting purposes is a tradition that spans centuries. During heightened political activity in the 1960s and 1970s, Black women fashioned their own sense of personhood through everyday acts including adornment. The work that they did in front of their mirrors, Tanisha C. Ford has argued, was just as important as the public protests unfolding on the streets.[70] Advertising rhetoric sometimes echoed these sentiments, especially when Black people were shaping the content. Caroline Jones was one of the few African American women who entered professional advertising in the sixties, when companies created diversity recruitment programs in response to increased scrutiny about their predominantly white, male ranks. Jones proposed that Aziza, a cosmetics company, design a new Bronze Beauty collection that capitalized on Black women's desire to replace white image standards with self-defined ideals.[71]

Advertisers alone did not develop Black women's consumer consciousness; companies also relied on Black media outlets like *Essence* to reinforce their efforts. The editorial and sponsored content needed to flow in a circuit of meaning that ultimately led readers back to the same ideas about consumption for the magazine to appease advertisers and audiences. Taylor approached this circuit of meaning with the deft touch of a philosopher; she knew how to manage practical concerns without losing sight of the spiritual. In one of her first pieces as a permanent editor, Taylor veered away from the superficial and discussed beauty in therapeutic terms. "To look special, you must think special thoughts," she wrote, "and begin a special program of total beauty care."[72] From the cosmetics resources she promoted to the toning exercises she prescribed her words pointed to the possibility that readers could achieve transformation through consumption and hard work. Taylor championed the connection between physical maintenance and soul maintenance years before penning her first "In the Spirit" editor's column in July 1981. In doing so, she normalized the connection between consumption and enlightenment.

Not all of Taylor's early work evoked personal empowerment. She also crafted stories that bent to the generic lifestyle magazine formula of directing women on how to accommodate the male gaze. For example, in a March 1972 article focused on exercise, Taylor used health and sex appeal as incentives for maintaining an ideal weight through a regular fitness routine. "We aren't advocating string beans, 'cause we know that our men do appreciate 'healthy' mamas," she wrote. "What we are saying is let's keep those curves in the right places. Our men want us round, *firm*, and fully packed."[73] A chart listing appropriate weight ranges for Black women based on height and body frame accompanied the article. Along with the chart, the tall and thin models pictured in various aerobic demonstrations worked visually to stifle readers' personal interpretations of a suitable physique. Hence, while it is true that some of her writings on beauty and fashion emphasized Black women's agency and affirmed their ability to make meaning on their own terms, other pieces foreclosed an active audience imagination.

Although it tapped into anxieties about romance and attraction, the March 1972 magazine spread on how to achieve the precise physique for male enjoyment also encouraged women's pleasure. Some exercises outlined in the article were designed to enhance sexual intercourse. Acknowledging that some readers may have considered a lesson in physical intimacy too "risqué," Taylor assured readers that sex was "the essence of life" and that the techniques would lead to a more enjoyable experience for all involved.[74] "By knowing how to maneuver your pelvis, a woman is assured not only of giving greater pleasure to her partner, but of having stronger and more frequent climaxes herself."[75] This article illustrates the tension constantly bubbling beneath the surface of Taylor's fashion and beauty coverage. While the pressure to concede to a narrow tone that reduced women's work on the self to a romantic scheme was ever present, Taylor generally managed to avoid that classic women's magazine technique. She emphasized self-pleasure and happiness as valid motives for the inner and outer work she directed readers to perform. These were benefits too often set outside the parameters of what Black women could and should desire. Taylor therefore penned a world where Black women would not be guilted out of buying and doing what made them feel good and feel beautiful.

Although this commercial world doubled as a hunting ground for corporations hungering for readers' dollars, it was also a space where meaningful consumption and self-indulgence were aids, rather than threats, to Black progress.

Expanding the Empowerment Empire

In the pages of *Essence*, advertisers found a pathway to increased profits and Black women found counsel for empowered living. The men and women who labored there were the settlers who laid the infrastructure upon which later initiatives like *My Black Is Beautiful* and Black Girls Rock! would be built. On one hand, the Black women whom marketing firms identify as "African American consumers" may resemble an organic assemblage emerging out of common consumption behaviors shared by a preexisting group. However, these marketing segments are also commercial configurations. It was during the 1960s that the contours of what the twenty-first century marketplace recognizes as the Black or African American female consumer took on a clearer shape. At this point the decades-long petition to recognize the value of Black dollars to the U.S. economy found more permanent footing. Black advertising professionals that rose in prominence in this period were instrumental by advancing new approaches for marketing to Black consumers and insisting that advertisers weave culturally specific media vehicles like *Essence* into their strategies. They helped to concretize Black women as a discrete consumer group that responded best to certain kinds of promotional triggers. Although this emergent infrastructure hinged on Black women, they had limited influence over it. Black and white men from the creative and business spheres negotiated an arrangement whereby they would brand Black womanhood and capitalize on that brand. In the process, they defined a critical moment in the history of Black American commerce.

The women of *Essence* were responsible for writing about the good life that awaited disciplined Black women, visualizing it photographically, and embodying it. The communications strategy that the magazine perfected in its first decade vis-à-vis editors like Taylor and Gillespie wooed Black women with affirmative vocabularies and normalized empowerment, beauty, and consumption as core to modern Black womanhood. In addition to championing an ethos of women's empowerment that elevated Black style, Taylor reinforced the logic of liberation through spending that *Essence* needed readers to embrace. By the late 1970s, Taylor refined her voice and developed a clear philosophy about Black womanhood and power. Through *Essence* she invited the audience into a world where beauty was not an appendage but rather the heart of the project to uplift Black women. Teaching readers that their lives, like their beauty, were best built from the inside out, she struck a balance between spiritual enlightenment and consumption that defined her tenure at the magazine and eventually her personal brand as a guru.

2

Self-Branding
Black Womanhood

The Magic of Susan L. Taylor

The meager staircase that Susan L. Taylor climbed to address congregants of the Apostolic Church of God in Chicago on a November Sunday in 1995 represented a monumental professional ascent. The editor-in-chief of the premier Black women's lifestyle magazine had gone from selling custom make-up blends in New York City to marketing self-empowerment to women across the Black world. The mega church in the Woodlawn neighborhood on Chicago's South Side was one stop on Taylor's sixteen-city book tour for *Lessons in Living*, her second monograph.[1] The opportunity to speak at Apostolic Church to promote a personal project was a testament to the congruous progression that the editor and her employer experienced together. Valerie Norman-Gammon, a parishioner who helped to coordinate the visit, began working with Taylor during Essence Communications Inc. (ECI)'s expansion in the 1980s. Norman-Gammon described her relationship with Taylor as a blessing because of her spiritual prowess. "I have been in shopping malls where people just want to talk to her and she is always, always ready to lend an ear," Norman-Gammon said. "Sometimes when we're working on some of the shows we have challenges. . . . And Susan will call me up and she'll say: *Val, it's all in divine order.*"[2]

As *Essence* grew—from a magazine to a multimedia platform for Black commercial culture—Taylor had also transformed into a guru for women of her race. Public speaking events where she performed culturally specific

FIGURE 2.1 After resigning from ECI, Susan L. Taylor became an advocate for vulnerable youth and established the National CARES Mentoring Movement. That work took her to Washington, DC, on February 28, 2012, where she met with representatives of the United States Department of Agriculture and the Department of Energy to discuss opportunities for youth in rural communities. Credit: USDA photo by Lance Cheung. Public domain.

monologues about personal uplift had become a staple in her empowerment enterprise (see figure 2.1). During the talk at Apostolic Church Taylor covered her usual points about the importance of ministry to the inner self, but she also appealed to her audience as Black consumers. Despite the personal objective of her visit—she stayed after service to sell and sign books—Taylor did not leave the pulpit without making a pitch for Black-owned media. "Black media needs you to be conscious consumers," she said. "We've given all of our power away supporting the very entities that don't support us. So, for your little twenty dollars you can get a subscription to . . . the Black-owned publications . . . that are really doing the work of moving our people forward."[3] Under Taylor's logic each purchase amounted to a greater civic duty. *Essence's* 5.2 million readers, she declared, were more than consumers, they were "brothers and sisters voting for us every month."[4] By presenting Black commercial media interests as aligned with the interests of all Black people, the speech elevated consumption to a matter of racial consciousness. This talent for cohering the spiritual with the cultural and the commercial made Taylor an indispensable force at *Essence* and a pillar in the Black image economy.

Using her platform at ECI, Taylor fine-tuned a manner of consumption that has helped to sustain the broader commercial infrastructure that promises to empower Black women through products and services. The first sprouts of her potential to be something more than a magazine writer emerged in the seventies as she elevated beauty and adornment in her monthly articles. By the time she ascended to editor-in-chief in 1981 Taylor had evolved into the quintessential *Essence* woman; she had learned how to rise above her circumstances and empower herself. She built an enterprise that taught other Black women how to tap into their own magic, which she often referred to as "inner beauty." With each editor's column, book, and motivational speech, Taylor was creating a space for *Essence* and herself in the lucrative personal improvement media marketplace. Furthermore, she set a precedent for self-branding in the "live your best life" arena that two other Black women—Iyanla Vanzant and Oprah Winfrey—have come to dominate. Vanzant and Winfrey have distinct commercial enterprises that exceed their predecessor's in terms of visibility, but this chapter will show traces of Taylor's style in their early work. Collectively these media figures exemplify how becoming magical is, among other things, a business strategy that affords Black women the latitude to monetize their labor and build self-managed multimedia empires. They therefore demonstrate how the commercial enterprise of Black women's empowerment benefits certain Black women not just financially, but also as media citizens.

Given the influence she has had on institutions and individuals that have shaped Black women's public images, Taylor's absence from public and scholarly discourse after her departure from *Essence* in 2007 has baffled me. By the time I met her she had already begun to fade into the margins of the mediascape, but she still managed to captivate a crowded room of mostly Black women college students. Some of us had followed her career and dreamed of one day working in the *Essence* universe that, as far as we were concerned, Taylor had created. The tingling mix of inspiration and fierceness that she unleashed in the room that evening in 2007 was all that I imagined it would be since the days when I would study her smiling face, beaming down from the cover of one of her books that my mother displayed in our small home library. What intrigued me as a young girl is the same thing that I believe astonished the crowd many years later at her talk for the Black Communications Society at Syracuse University, and the same force that allowed her to sustain a dialogue with Black women for some forty years. Taylor exuded a genuine desire to see other Black women accomplish for themselves the empowerment that she had been able to realize; this passion is what makes her brand compelling and messy.

Taylor's legacy as an empowerment guru hinges on competing ideas of magical Black womanhood. On the one hand, she has embodied the resilience, grit, and Black excellence that CaShawn Thompson aimed to celebrate when she coined the phrase "Black Girls Are Magic." Once a 24-year-old single mother making do in New York City without a college degree, Taylor has confronted many challenges. The steps she took to refashion her life, however, fit within a neoliberal discourse that glorifies self-regulation in an unbridled marketplace as the ideal form of modern citizenship. Under this ideological regime, empowerment is a depoliticized personal endeavor, personal responsibility is a scapegoat for structural inequity, and soul labor is tethered to consumption. With her emphasis on self-empowerment as a key to racial uplift, Taylor's message could easily be monetized and leveraged to sell products, the most important of which was dignified Black womanhood. By examining Taylor's particular brand of magic, I not only address a gap in the literature, but also lay bare the complicated role that iconic Black women play in selling empowerment.

The Rise of a (Beauty) Guru

Essence executives did not initially register Susan L. Taylor's fit for the top editor position when Marcia Gillespie departed the magazine in 1980. Since Gillespie had identified Daryl Roster Alexander, then the second-in-command, as her ideal successor, Edward Lewis trusted her decision. Subscription cancellations increased during Alexander's tenure, however, prompting the publisher to look for someone who could better connect with readers. At that point, Taylor was the obvious choice. After all, the magazine had allotted two pages to an interview with her in the January 1978 issue, reintroducing the beauty and fashion editor as a lifestyle expert and the quintessential *Essence* woman. Joyce White, who authored the piece, described Taylor as a "former actress, licensed cosmetologist and mother of an eight-year-old daughter . . . [who] sparkle[s] from head to toe with beauty, vitality and confidence."[5] Here the editor became more than a competent professional; the article framed her as a master at life who managed her responsibilities without neglecting self-care. She made time for a demanding career, parenting, and a romantic relationship while maintaining a fitness routine and time for meditation. The sparkle that the article says Taylor possessed—which would be considered magic in the twenty-first century context—is the intrinsic trait that enabled her to achieve the happy life promised to all *Essence* women. Going beyond typical musings on the editor's beauty and health regimens, the interview afforded Taylor the opportunity to address readers as a style coach. Using personal experience as a pedagogical tool, she focused her counsel on the connection between inner (mind and soul) and outer (body) beauty.

The interview also read as a response to the various critiques that *Essence* had encountered for its beauty and style coverage during its first seven years in circulation. Taylor had attempted to glorify the full range of Black women's allure in her work, but the state of the beauty marketplace in the seventies complicated this task. Advertising rhetoric that either implied that Blackness was an obstacle to beauty or disregarded Black women entirely made it difficult for some women to reconcile the tensions between their politics and the cosmetics industry. How could one consistently buy Black in a space that large white corporations increasingly controlled? Of the more than forty-five brands mentioned in one 1973 article that a reader lambasted, one was Black-owned: Johnson Product Company's Ultra Sheen.[6] The twisted irony of a Black women's magazine compelling readers to realize the fullness of their beauty by consuming products from white manufacturers was not easily overcome.

Taylor was therefore tasked with situating makeup more effectively within the context of Black beauty. She was expected to address the sentiment that Black women did not need to be "painted, streaked or straightened" to be stylish, all while directing readers to products that promised such effects.[7] Taylor reinforced the idea that "Black folks developed the art of making-up" to diffuse the tension between cosmetics and "natural" Black beauty.[8] In addition, she spent much of the interview espousing positive thinking and spiritual self-care as often underestimated, yet significant, building blocks to empowered Black womanhood. "Faith can make you and keep you beautiful," she asserted.[9] The foundation to the *Essence* woman, a woman who had unlocked her magic and fully realized her potential, was a sound mind and well-nourished spirit. Only when readers prioritized inner growth would they be able to exude true beauty, which the article framed as the result of hard work on the soul and the body: "We're only as beautiful as the sum total of our thoughts, our actions, and our deeds. What you put into you and your life is what you get back. If a woman goes to bed with makeup and grime on her face, she's going to have skin problems. She has to commit herself to a skin-care routine faithfully and do it because she loves herself and cares about her skin. We show how we feel about ourselves."[10] Taylor's words frame personal upkeep as an obligation and cosmetics as the tools best suited to perform this pleasurable work on the body. Along these lines, makeup rituals and products were conduits to a dignified Black womanhood available to any woman willing to commit to the proper disciplines. This vacillation between consumption as optional self-care and consumption as mandate is a persistent complication within Taylor's rhetoric and the broader grammar of empowerment that advertisers use to woo Black women. On the one hand, Black women are empowered because we enjoy a vast marketplace. And yet, the choice to not consume at all or to deviate from the brands that advertise in outlets like *Essence* is unavailable; that is if one desires to be recognized as a magical Black woman.

Taylor describes the spiritual and physical practices that constitute her self-care habits throughout the January 1978 interview. Although she insists that what works for her may not be suitable for all readers, the implication that self-maintenance routines are not optional is clear. In this context beauty is both an intrinsic property and something that can never be fully realized without proper management. This conception of beauty is synonymous with magic in that both render the Black female self an enterprising agent fully responsible for her happiness and life outcomes. Also, both beauty and magic function as disciplinary technologies that grant access to authentic Black womanhood only to those women who capitulate to a specific behavioral code. Importantly, the article suggested that self-management was not a burden, but a happy labor for Black women who really loved themselves. The daily and weekly rituals that Taylor testified to performing, from reciting Psalm 23 to a deep cleansing facial, reflected her positive self-concept. Within this logic, the greatest threat to Black women's empowerment was not how society viewed them, but Black women's lack of self-appreciation.

Nonetheless Taylor understood beauty to be deeper than the products one used to achieve a particular style; it was a spiritual property that Black women needed to access to recognize their value and reject the false images surrounding them. She recalled that the scarcity of affirming cultural messages she encountered during childhood caused long-term damage: "I remember . . . not feeling pretty and feeling like I was too dark, and my hair was too short, and my legs were too skinny; feeling like most Black girls, especially dark-skinned Black girls, felt at that time because we didn't have the images. We didn't have positive images of Black women on screen and in magazines. It was difficult to understand your beauty and your uniqueness, and it was before our appreciation of our African-ness."[11] Taylor held that her mission as a fashion and beauty editor was to use popular culture to deconstruct the distorted ideology that had once compelled her to rub up against a lighter-skinned childhood friend in the hopes that she might dilute her own darker hue. She sought to dismantle these strongholds so that they would no longer corrupt Black girls' (and women's) minds. Taylor's early work therefore exceeded profit motives. Amid her writings on Remington Mist hair curlers and Hanes hosiery she strategically placed nuggets of affirmation that she believed her readers needed: "You are beautiful because of what you are inside."[12] For Taylor, beauty was Black women's magic.

Lessons in Becoming Magical

Part of the reason why Susan L. Taylor's inner beauty philosophy moved Black women is because her ideas fit easily into the broader self-help and self-determination crusades that had been building in the seventies, eighties and nineties. She taught that a person could thrive once they committed to soul labor, or the work of developing productive thoughts and character traits and eliminating counterproductive ones. Certainly, she had developed a unique style for directing her audience to cultivate the inner being—mind and spirit—to achieve the outward trappings that accompany wellness and success. Nevertheless, the message and the specific pathway to empowerment she preached resembled emergent neoliberal discourses about self-governance. Thus, Taylor's work as a self-empowerment guru resonated with her audience in part because they were already enmeshed in the "literature, television, multimedia, and other products of self-help culture" that had become ubiquitous in "advanced capitalist societies."[13]

In the final decades of the twentieth century, self-help books, workshops, talk shows, magazines, and therapeutic devices such as recovery groups, became key tools that regulated private life. Under a prevailing, commercialized gospel of self, the personal eclipsed the structural as a societal focal point. Rather than look to institutions as the cause or solution to their problems, citizens were encouraged to look within. The self-help texts that fueled an appetite for knowledge about the inner life also offered strategies for self-improvement. Anyone who was dissatisfied with their life had the option and responsibility to change it. Politicians and self-help capitalists promised that this arrangement would bring increased personal liberty, but the major flaw in this argument is that it dismissed the inequities that prohibited certain individuals from accessing the better life that they envisioned. If a personality assessment revealed that one's ideal career was in art or medicine, for example, individual life circumstances—wealth, domestic obligations, etc.—would make a career change more feasible for some and nearly impossible for others. The gospel of personal responsibility that politicians like President Ronald Reagan espoused ignored these systemic differences.[14] Meanwhile this governing philosophy protected corporate practices—regardless of how greedy—with a sacred wall between government and private enterprise. In a move to minimize government, or more accurately to drastically reduce a government's responsibility to its citizens, state actors championed unbridled markets and directed citizens to eschew so-called handouts like welfare. They were expected to take care of themselves.

In the United States this brand of small government held particular consequences for Black women, who became the face of Reagan's crusade against welfare crooks and dependents—individuals who had either manipulated the system to gain more than they were legally due or had become so attached to public assistance that they lost the will to work.[15] Alongside this top-down campaign, an audience consisting mainly of young people sought therapeutic relief from the diminishing quality of life associated with unfettered enterprise. While critics interpreted this turn to therapy as "a narcissistic withdrawal . . . wrapped in the jargon of personal fulfilment, awareness, and authenticity," it ultimately functioned as a tool of political authority that facilitated absentee governance by way of self-control.[16] The appeal of self-help for Black people was its connection to self-determination, which had been a pillar in Black thought for several decades.[17] Self-help was attractive to the extent that it offered an opportunity to forge lifestyles according to their own values without white interference. Figures like Susan L. Taylor leveraged this version of self-help, extending their audience a route to empowerment that was both modern and culturally relevant. Furthermore, Taylor encouraged them to attend to their inner lives in a way that might have otherwise seemed overly indulgent. It was radical for Black women to see one of their own sanction personal quiet time, travel, and other happiness triggers as wise practices that would restore the soul and eventually impact the larger racial community.

Commercial women's magazines made for a convenient mass distribution center for ideas about self-care and self-discipline, but these periodicals and the self-help literature they promoted mostly targeted white audiences. If any media vehicle had a chance at transmitting similar messages—cloaked in the appropriate cultural tint—to large groups of professional and aspiring Black women, it was *Essence*. As the brand's chief steward, Susan L. Taylor and the staff she led bore the responsibility of ushering Black women into this national period of fixation with the self. Rather than mimic white sister media in form or function, she responded to her audience's particular sensibilities with tender guidance that reflected their realities as Black women and that privileged a triumphant racial history. Taylor's affiliation with ECI meant that her philosophies on living could not circulate beyond the corporate shadow where empowerment was first and foremost a marketing scheme. While she understood and respected her obligations to the company, she desired to spread her enlightenment gospel to as many Black women as possible for the sake of collective healing and uplift. What *Essence* and its sponsors meant for profit, Taylor meant for spiritual and physical wellness. In numerous speeches and writings she reiterated her belief that if those in the audience could transform their lives, they could join in a unified Black struggle for advancement. Nevertheless, her lessons could easily be emptied of their substance and reconfigured as superficial consumer directives.

Taylor's message that Black women should "set high goals and work toward them consistently" reflected her belief in personal accountability and testified to her audience's capacity to thrive despite what society suggested was impossible for them.[18] Her instruction to "declare ownership"[19] of your life and to "write your own script"[20] implied a level of autonomy inaccessible to many Black women, without enunciating the structures that constrained them. That is not to suggest that Taylor was ignorant of those external constraints, nor that she avoided them altogether. While she acknowledged the public and intimate opposition facing Black women, she emphasized self-honor and self-affirmation as corrective methods. "The recognition and affirmation of our intrinsic beauty, richness and grace are a particular necessity for women," she wrote in her 1993 release *In the Spirit: The Inspirational Writings of Susan L. Taylor*.[21] "That is the truth of who we are, the truth within us, the truth that the world teaches us to forget."[22] One could interpret Taylor's words as evasive, assigning Black women to correct an image of their community that they did not create and to heal the psychic damage from a toxic environment they did not design. At the same time, it is possible to read Taylor's message as a lesson in spiritual brico-lage, imploring Black women to use the resources available, however meager, to elevate themselves out of the degraded conditions to which they had been relegated.

Undeniably, these precepts fit within modern discourses that privilege self-work as crucial to productive citizenship. Laurie Ouellette and Julie Wilson describe self-work as "an entrepreneurial investment with payoffs for the individual" that renders the self "a site of labor as well as governmentality."[23] Under this self-disciplining regime, women manage dual sets of expectations in that their labor benefits the self, but more importantly, their spouses and children. While Taylor burdened her audience with other-directed care, her philosophy of empowered Black womanhood hinged on a broader racial uplift agenda instead of a strictly capitalist objective. Importantly, she framed racial uplift— addressing all that ailed the community and creating institutions that would allow everyone to thrive—as a shared project. Her philosophy prioritized self-care to correct a hierarchy where Black women situated themselves at the bottom of their care list. The lifestyle guru addressed this concern in her books and spoke about it during a keynote speech at the African American Women on Tour Empowerment Conference in 1994: "When you're not giving you what you need, you know what people say, *you sisters are evil*. Black women aren't evil, we're tired. We're tired! Because we give all of our stuff away. We have a history of tired in our bones. We don't know how to say no, don't know how to say I can't help you with that, don't know how to say you know you have to do that project without me."[24] By addressing stereotypes specific to Black women in her work, the magazine executive tailored her message precisely, making it clear that she had her audience's best interests at heart. She was not simply a master saleswoman hawking an unattainable idea; she was a true believer testifying to her transformation journey and teaching others how to claim their power.

For Taylor, a girlfriend's getaway, a magazine subscription, and beauty treatments were more than just trivial purchases or self-disciplining tools. They were passports to enlightenment and self-actualization that offered an opportunity to engage affirming images and to honor the divine power that each woman possessed within. Rather than adopt the managerial ethos common to self-improvement discourses, Taylor modeled her teachings off of an ideology that is both spiritual and focused on Black women's material concerns.[25] Womanism—a theoretical framework that Black women theologians began using in the 1980s to define their understanding of God and to challenge the masculinist bent of Black liberation theology—undergirded the author's philosophy and distinguished her writings from other woman-centered self-help literature that emerged in the late eighties.[26]

The term womanism, as articulated by Alice Walker, derives from the Black colloquialism "womanish" which describes a Black girl or young woman who has begun to test respectable boundaries through her demeanor and behavior.[27] Black girls observed as acting womanish were understood to be exploring and experimenting with their bodily and psychological agency. Womanist ethics, much like Taylor's behavioral code, demands that Black women exercise their agency to facilitate self-care and care for our community. It is equally a doctrine for personal wellness and a framework for advocacy and activism. Furthermore, Black women theologians have adapted womanism to name their distinct liberation struggle in accessing a divine heritage often denied them within Christian institutions that center white women or Black men.[28] In order to resist institutional subordination, Black women theologians insisted on a more democratic hermeneutic, one that included everyday Black women as valid knowers of the sacred. They emphasized the intergenerational, woman-to-woman networks through which Black women cultivated a practical theology across kitchen tables and knee-deep in Southern gardens.

Although Taylor's body of work aligns with womanist ethics, the tension between her spiritual and commercial urgings persists. In addition to tapping into womanism's spiritual ethos, Taylor also benefitted from and helped to facilitate what Monica Coleman calls a process of "commodification and commercialization" whereby Black women's intellectual products have been packaged and sold to benefit institutions that they often do not lead.[29] In other words, the "In the Spirit" column and the books that it birthed paved the way for ECI's entrance into a nascent market in Black women's religious thought and spiritual empowerment. For a mainstream consumer magazine to integrate spirituality into its standard editorial formula was rare, but with a predominantly Black women audience, faith-based content became a unique selling proposition for *Essence*. The magazine, especially Taylor's column, left room for readers to insert their own religious preferences into the spiritual framework of empowered Black womanhood. Although she leaned more toward Christian texts and figures than any other belief system, her words were strategically vague. The speech she made at Apostolic Church in Chicago in November 1995 exemplifies this point.

Having been baptized in an Episcopalian parish and raised in Catholic schools, Taylor has never concealed her belief in God and spoke often of faith in her monthly editor's column. Nevertheless, she made it clear that Sunday morning that her God was more a conceptual container for divinity than a specific deity with commandments. Even the name, as she communicated to the congregation during her talk, was insignificant; God, Allah, Mother/Father Spirit, Beauty were simply titles for a power that each human being held within. Teaching people how to recognize and access that power was the author's aim.

Since Taylor's professional journey is the kind of spiritually charged bottom-up narrative that fills self-help book catalogues, it was not difficult to translate into a product for the emerging marketplace. One of the stories she retold in books and speeches is of an epiphany she had on a long walk home from the hospital one cold November day. Overcome with anxiety, she had rushed herself to the emergency room with the fear that the physical pangs she had been feeling all week were heart attack symptoms. Hours later, she learned that her affliction was not physical, but mental; her body was responding to the stressors that had saturated her life in the form of a panic attack. She walked home in shock, unsure how to stabilize life for her young family that had recently decreased from three to two. Just a few months prior, in 1969, she was still married and adjusting to life as a new mother. William Bowes, then a beautician at a salon on Harlem's famed 125th Street, was her husband and business partner. At his encouragement, Taylor resigned her position as a performer with the Negro Ensemble Company and turned her attention to nurturing her new daughter and a new cosmetics company for Black women. Nequai Cosmetics had been lucrative, Taylor recalled, because she offered custom-blended makeup made with natural ingredients that matched Black women's unique skin tones. "I made so much money. It was incredible," she stated. "The investment that I made, I made back in three weeks. Women were thrilled with it. And that's how I came to the attention of the *Essence* editors."[30]

The company's success was short-lived, however; Nequai Cosmetics ended with Taylor's first marriage. Even though she had secured a freelance position at an up-and-coming magazine (*Essence*), at the age of twenty-four she found herself a divorced, single mother confronting monthly expenses that threatened to outweigh her $500-a-month salary. So, as she began the journey home from the hospital that Sunday in November 1970, she was convinced that financial insecurity was the culprit that had stolen her peace and sent her to the ER. Later that day, though, she heard a sermon that presented her with an alternative perspective. Desperate for a modicum of hope, Taylor randomly stopped at a church service she encountered along her route home, and for the first time, began to entertain the idea that she was far more powerful than she had ever realized. She used that experience to begin her first inspirational book, *In the Spirit*: "That night I heard a sermon that would change my life. The preacher said that our minds could change our world. That no matter what our troubles, if we could put them aside for a moment, focus on possible solutions and imagine a joyous future, we would find a peace within, and positive experiences would begin to unfold. . . . It was the beginning of my realization that our thoughts create our reality."[31] In order to commercialize womanist philosophy and praxis, Taylor first needed to ground it in Black women's everyday realities. Thus, exposing a lifetime of her own triumphs, failures, anxieties, and heartbreaks positioned the editor as equally relatable and aspirational. Taylor constructed a public image based on vulnerability that compelled her audience to peer beyond her glamourous title to ascertain the woman inside who was just like them. Since she embodied the *Essence* woman, her unearthed flaws were proof that beauty and power—the core traits of magical Black women—were both intrinsic and latent, accessible and costly.

The brand strategist consistently framed herself as a righteous racial authority, which concealed the possibility that the executive might be guided by profit motives or anything other than divine intuition. She considered herself to be "like a sister" to the *Essence* readers, presenting them with material that would be both affirming and aspirational.[32] What Taylor presented as beneficial for her "sisters," therefore, was thought to be good for the broader racial community. This power dynamic created tension between ECI and other notable Black figures on more than one occasion. For example, a 1985 *Wall Street Journal* article reported that Alice Walker had been shocked and troubled when *Essence* declined to publish an excerpt of *The Color Purple*, citing issues with the novel's depiction of Blackness. "They said [B]lack people don't talk like that," Walker is quoted as saying.[33] In response, Taylor wrote a letter to the editor insisting that *Essence* passed on Walker's pitch because they felt an abbreviated sample from her manuscript would be too easily misinterpreted outside of its fuller context. The letter also emphasized the company's consistent support of Walker throughout the years, hinting that the *Essence* spotlight had helped the author gain the broad visibility she began to enjoy in the mid-1980s. This incident demonstrates just how meaningful the empire that Taylor led was for some Black cultural producers. Even after *The Color Purple* received critical acclaim and was being developed into a film, Walker still bemoaned the fact that a powerful Black platform had shunned her work. A blessing from Taylor's *Essence* went a long way toward validating an idea, or text, or person, as positive Black representation. We should consider Taylor a crucial media figure then, because by becoming the quintessential *Essence* woman she came to occupy an elevated status as a media citizen whereby she could manage other cultural producers' access to her audience.

A Lineage of Black Women Gurus

The most prominent testament to Taylor's influence is making self-help rhetoric a core part of the ECI brand. Beyond editorial content, the company capitalized on faith-based personal development discourses through Essence Books.[34] Figures that readers encountered in the magazine re-emerged at enrichment workshops and in branded manuals like *21st Century Sister: The Essence Five Keys to Success*. The most prolific such self-help personality and author to find a lucrative home at ECI is Iyanla Vanzant. *Essence* readers first encountered Vanzant through a 1989 feature story, when she had not yet become a bestselling author or the star of an unscripted series, *Iyanla: Fix My Life*. Following Taylor's model of teaching through personal exposure, Vanzant testified to her transformation from teenage mother to single welfare recipient, to a dual-degree-holding professional and spiritual counselor. She encouraged readers to embrace Yoruba, an African cultural philosophy, for guidelines in how to attract the things that would enhance their lives. "The Yoruba message to Black women is actually basic and universal: What goes around, comes around; whatever we give to life in thought, words, and deeds is what we get back."[35] The Yoruba priestess would continue to espouse this philosophy each time the magazine called on her expertise, in spiritual, health, romance, and even finance-themed articles. She consistently referenced her past and present lived experiences as the body of evidence that validated her enlightenment ethos. If she could overcome childhood sexual assault, intimate-partner violence, and poverty, then so could the women who flocked to her public lectures and read her books.

In her most intimate exhibition, Vanzant allowed *Essence* readers into her Maryland residence for the July 1996 article, "At Home with Iyanla Vanzant." Instead of presenting the emerging self-help powerhouse's typical lifestyle rhetoric, this article used Vanzant's day-to-day routine to articulate her advice. The author described three altars within the home, each in a different room and each intended to facilitate a different meditative affect. There were also sticky notes fastened to various surfaces which carried messages like, "what you see you become."[36] Just as Susan L. Taylor's 1978 interview had framed the editor as a prototype for empowered Black womanhood, Vanzant's 1996 feature story communicated that she too was a magical Black woman with the personal disciplines to support her self-actualization claims. The two women displayed their lives as living proof that every woman was just a few positive thoughts and productive habits away from her own spiritual, physical, social, professional and financial liberation.

Essence featured Vanzant dozens of times during Taylor's tenure. Beyond the page, Taylor also shared her motivational speaking stage with her mentee whom she referred to as "an empowered being."[37] Just before offering the keynote address at a 1994 African American women's conference, Taylor directed the audience's attention to applaud "a sister that I love and admire so much."[38] In small moments like these and in more visible instances, like granting Vanzant her own monthly column, Taylor's support of the budding self-help personality was palpable. By 1999, Vanzant would be headlining her own national speaking tours, sponsored by the likes of automobile manufacturer Oldsmobile. Like Taylor, Vanzant emphasized personal accountability and Black women's capacity to create better lives by thinking positive thoughts in her workshops and books. While her subsequent televisual presence on *The Oprah Winfrey Show* catapulted Vanzant to a broader audience than the *Essence* readership, she identifies Susan L. Taylor as a mentor and an essential part of her public launch. In a 2019 interview, Vanzant stated that Taylor's decision to put her on the cover of *Essence* "taught people how to say [her] name" and brought her to the attention of one of the most magical Black women of the last hundred years: Oprah Winfrey.[39]

Before the mid-1990s, *The Oprah Winfrey Show* was known for some of the same content that Ricki Lake, Jenny Jones, and Sally Jesse Raphael used to drive ratings. The daily program's salacious stories were a far cry from the "become your best self" topics Winfrey would later use to rebrand herself. Still, she was a Black woman rising to the top of an industry considered hostile to Black people—and that was a worthy accomplishment to *Essence* editors. Winfrey's visibility had drawn the magazine's attention when she had just begun her television career at WLAC-TV in Nashville. In July 1974, they named her an "Essence Woman" alongside five other honorees from various industries. This early mentioning marked the beginning of Winfrey's relationship with the periodical.

In October 1986, a few years after becoming editor-in-chief, Taylor gave Winfrey the first of many cover stories. Winfrey, who would later start her own magazine with Hearst Communications, says that the 1986 article launched her face in the magazine world.[40] The issue hit newsstands just as Winfrey's show was entering national syndication and afforded her space to address common critiques, such as the accusation that she was more affectionate toward white audience members who visited her show. Winfrey appeared on the magazine cover again in 1989, this time accompanied by her romantic partner, Stedman Graham. The article, written in Winfrey's own words, focused on her seventy-pound weight loss journey and the steps she had taken to break her addiction to food and regain control of her life. An August 1987 interview where an already visibly leaner Winfrey sat down with Taylor is the moment when the connection between the kindred brands became more palpable.

In addition to low self-esteem, doubts about their appearance, and a longing for the kind of mother-daughter affection they viewed on shows like *Leave It to Beaver*, the interview also revealed Winfrey and Taylor's shared belief in the power of positive thinking. "I am where I am because I believed in my possibilities," Winfrey told Taylor. "Everything in your world is created by what you think."[41] Taylor had been writing about inner power and everyone's capacity to transform their lives in her monthly editor's column for several years at that point. As a longtime *Essence* reader (she has expressed her appreciation for the magazine on multiple occasions) Winfrey would have had the opportunity to see Taylor's brand bloom, just as she was setting out to establish her own public image. She was one of millions of African American women gleaning from Taylor's practical wisdom, but unlike most of them, Winfrey had the opportunity to capitalize on Taylor's (inner) beauty lessons in unmatched ways.

Scholars have pointed to slipping ratings, a desire to distance herself from other popular talk shows of the early nineties, and a connection with self-help author, Marianne Williamson, as catalysts for Winfrey's brand makeover.[42] However, Winfrey's ongoing relationship to *Essence* reveals that Susan L. Taylor's lessons in empowered Black womanhood were likely a strong influence in the talk show host's life. Years before a public announcement to change her show's format, she had described herself to the editor-in-chief as a woman simply "striving to magnify the Lord," and expressed a desire for her viewers to receive "a spiritual message" of personal responsibility and power through her show.[43] In light of the rising star's dialogue with Taylor, it is plausible that *The Oprah Winfrey Show*'s metamorphosis was just as much a move toward spiritual balance as it was a strategy to protect her competitive edge in the market. By aligning her outer work with her inner beliefs, Winfrey would have been following the exact formula for success that Taylor prescribed to all her pupils. Thus, scholars who point to Winfrey as the media personality most responsible for popularizing a twentieth century, gendered enlightenment discourse tethered to self-management without making mention of Taylor, have failed to fully comprehend the figures who facilitated this phenomenon. Taylor is a crucial part of the faith-tinged self-help industry not just because of her personal connection to Winfrey, but also because she leveraged womanist rhetoric to include Black women in the therapeutic marketplace.

The Mecca of Enlightened Consumption

If we approach her work as an editor and entrepreneur within the context of her intentions, then we must take seriously the extent to which Taylor performed a polyvocality as saleswoman, self-help expert, and philosopher. Each of these roles was vital to the development of enlightened consumption—a philosophy that allowed Taylor to reach an audience of Black women who would not easily be manipulated into purchases. Enlightened consumption best describes Taylor's practice of intentional spending and media patronage. She defined spending as a necessary tool in the broader life of an empowered woman.

Nowhere is the philosophy of enlightened consumption more perceptible than at the Essence Festival. The event started as a music festival in 1995, Taylor's fourteenth year as editor-in-chief. It was designed to be a one-time celebration of the magazine's twenty-fifth anniversary, but by 2020 it had evolved into the Essence Festival of Culture, an indispensable marketplace for corporate and indie brands who target Black women consumers.[44] The festival takes place annually over the course of three to five days around the fourth of July weekend in New Orleans, Louisiana.[45] This form of branded experience stretches the limits of traditional advertising texts to immerse the audience in a context where the lines between promotion and entertainment are blurred. In a typical commercial media environment, audiences are expected to navigate around the advertisements. Conversely, Essence Fest attendees make a personal financial investment to access this days-long promotional event where corporate and independent sellers hawk everything from movies to automobiles to banking services.[46]

None of the things that the event has become known for—a global stage for Black beauty, a warehouse for women's empowerment, a catalyst for Black-targeted marketing campaigns, a testing ground for emerging entrepreneurs—were a part of the initial vision. Edward Lewis, then publisher and CEO at ECI knew that he wanted to mark the 25th anniversary of the magazine in a unique way but could not quite imagine how to do so in a financially beneficial manner. The company was profitable, but as was the custom with most media brands, Lewis was ever cognizant of the need to diversify revenue streams. When a business acquaintance proposed that ECI host a music festival to honor *Essence*'s silver anniversary, Lewis saw an opportunity to combine dual efforts. George Wein, who pitched the idea to Lewis, was the ideal partner to guide the company through this foray into the live entertainment industry. While ECI had experience in hosting events, including the annual, televised Essence Awards ceremony, a music festival demanded a particular skill set that Wein had mastered: persuading corporate brands to underwrite most of the production costs.

Once Taylor and the rest of the executive team gave their approval, Wein and ECI agreed to split the profits from the event. In order to maximize this project, *Essence* would need to establish the festival in the discursive tradition that their audience had become accustomed to, while also speaking the language that most appealed to sponsors. Susan L. Taylor's brand of enlightened consumption was ideal for managing this dialectic between service and exploitation. It allowed ECI to present itself as a safe space in the media landscape where Black women could expect to be acknowledged, celebrated, esteemed, and protected from the evils of misrepresentation and degradation that lurked elsewhere. Nevertheless, this haven of affirming images depended on the same predatory sponsors whose advertising dollars also supported repressive images.

In the case of the largest sponsors, including Coca-Cola, Chase, Ford, State Farm, and Walmart, the festival was an opportunity to eliminate the competition altogether; they were each the only companies in their product category involved in the event. Such an exclusive promotional opportunity exemplifies the other commercial relationship that structures the festival. From the big business vantage point, ECI is the seller and their loyal audience of magical Black women is the product for sale. Despite ECI's emphasis on their devotion to Black women and framing of the festival as "home" and a place where Black women can "live [their] truth," the overlapping business dynamics make it virtually impossible for the company to satisfy audience and advertisers without compromise.[47] How can the company effectively protect the magical Black woman if it must sell her to the highest bidder in order to survive? More than any other property of the *Essence* brand, this event troubles the boundaries between ownership and sponsorship, visibility and commodification.

Given the way print publications have struggled to accommodate audiences with an increased appetite for free or low-cost digital content, the Essence Fest has become the most significant property in the ECI portfolio.[48] Nevertheless, it has also functioned as a site where Taylor and other company icons leap off the *Essence* pages. The festival is where Taylor became more than an image or ideal; she was a tangible figure who beckoned her audience toward an equally accessible form of enlightened living. Just as sure as they could touch her, they could also grab ahold of the better life that they had been dreaming of but had not realized. They could become magical Black women.

Within the visual and ideological framework of the festival, Coca-Cola, Ford, AT&T and the like function as the adhesive that sustains the magical or empowered Black woman. Through the intense brand presence, whereby one cannot attend a single event without being bombarded with logos, Essence Fest frames Black Girl Magic as a resource that must be cultivated and developed through various products and services. Each corporation dominates its own physical region within the festival's landscape, but they also deploy their logos and representatives to intervene in ticketed events for live commercials. The corporate brands host panels, workshops, and performances that promote consumption as the solution to every kind of struggle.

Taylor's philosophy of enlightened consumption is central to this interaction between brands and Black women consumers because it acts as a legitimating force, calming the tensions that would otherwise disrupt these strategic encounters. ECI compels festival sponsors to emulate the empowerment grammar that Taylor elevated because it is proven to be effective in raising the stakes of commercial transactions. Put simply, all of the products and services advertised at Essence Fest are multifunctional, with the primary operation being the ability to dignify and empower the consumer. The brands therefore deploy a visual and discursive rhetoric that is unique to the festival in terms of its focus on Black womanhood. Even those brands who already have an exist-ing marketing program targeting Black women will develop a separate collec-tion of focused promotional content for Essence Fest. This effort often requires companies to search outside of their typical advertising vendors to find mar-keting professionals, usually Black women, who have mastered the Black Girl Magic register.

The festival's function as a service to Black women would collapse without the self-empowerment logic of Black Girl Magic woven into brand activations and empowerment sessions. Originally, Lewis and Wein were content to host the festival as a party, but Karen Thomas, a sales and promotion consultant, suggested that they supplement the evening concerts with informative daytime programming.[49] These open admission events have given corporate brands the opportunity to communicate with consumers for hours each day without inter-ruption, under the auspices of helping attendees enhance their lives. Morn-ings and afternoons at Essence Fest have become bustling workshops of interior and physical transformation fueled by consumption where Black celebrities across generations and artistic genres host seminars in self-improvement.[50] Attendees can curate their experience from a buffet of sessions that accommo-date a range of ambitions, from the professional ("Elevating Your E-commerce Presence," sponsored by Walmart), to the emotional ("transform your look and drive your self-confidence through positive wardrobe choices").

Celebrities who are not offering a talk on the Power Stage, the official space for daytime personal development programming, are typically participating in an interview at a big brand exposition. For example, solo recording artist and former Destiny's Child member Michelle Williams, who has struggled pub-licly with mental health, participated in an interview about depression at the Walmart platform in 2019. Interestingly, there was nothing to buy at these branded exhibits (they actually gave away merchandise showcasing their logo), but that does not mean that they were not engaging participants as consum-ers. They were offering dignity in exchange for customer loyalty. What makes this transaction problematic is not its commercial dynamic, but the nature of the exchange. Rather than winning Black women's dollars because their prod-ucts and services outperformed the competition, these companies were pitch-ing their brands on the basis of their very presence at the festival, which signaled an appreciation for Black womanhood.

Nightly concerts at the festival pivot to a leisurely tone, but the aura of personal uplift lingers. During my first Essence Fest experience in 2015, for example, Iyanla Vanzant spoke between R&B performances by Kem and India. Arie. Her animated pitch about productive thought patterns was indistinct from the artists' musings about how they willed themselves up from homeless-ness and heartbreak. Furthermore, in an unprecedented move, the festival featured Michelle Obama as a headliner on the 2019 mainstage roster. Her discussion of marriage, motherhood, and owning your narrative immediately preceded a Mary J. Blige concert. Even under the thump of a hip-hop drumbeat, however, the festival motto was clear. The weekend was intended to be more than just a good time; it was also an invitation to tap into your inner strength, your magic, and strategize about how to become your best self. It is an "In the Spirit" column come to life, refashioned as a social experience.

ECI executives have therefore heralded Essence Fest as uniquely beneficial in that it provides small business owners and marketing consultants, many of whom are Black women, with a larger platform to expand their consumer reach. It also, in theory, allows the entrepreneurs to network with executives from large companies. Former ECI President Michelle Ebanks described these opportunities as two of the factors that make the festival a distinct service to the Black community: "This is a unique convergence, because we have our cultural class and also have many of the top corporations in the world, along with their executive leadership in attendance—from Walmart and AT&T to Chase—they're standing shoulder to shoulder with our entrepreneurs and understanding how they can engage."[51] To say that the independent entrepreneurs were close enough to big business to rub shoulders or even have a conversation at the 2019 festival would be an exaggeration. In the spatial hierarchy of the event, the largest brands occupied distinct colonies while the smallest businesses shared a large open space filled with booths. Moving from one part of the convention center to another felt like transitioning between two different commercial arenas. The sprawling Essence Marketplace, with its stalls and nameless salespeople beaconing women to try their wares by shouting promises about the quality of their products or shoving samples and promotional cards into their hands, felt like a bazaar. On the other hand, the extravagant exhibits that companies like Ford, Coca-Cola, and Disney constructed drew festival attendees through their sheer opulence. I remember being captivated by the towering virtual displays at the Walmart platform, which featured a single model in four different scenes that would rotate every few minutes (see figures 2.2 and 2.3). In each scene the model was seated on a different throne and styled in a different fashion.

While the Essence Festival's entanglement of empowerment and commerce, much like Taylor's philosophy of enlightened consumption, fits neatly within a neoliberal framework, it cannot be read as a purely profit-driven enterprise. Since its inaugural year, the event has created an environment that acknowledges attendees as full human citizens. Indeed, part of what makes the festival such a vivid demonstration of the logic of Black Girl Magic is an insistence on entangling spending power with other kinds of agency, particularly those basic rights and endowments that Black women have struggled to maintain. At the 2019 festival five democratic presidential hopefuls, all top-ten party candidates according to polling metrics, participated in interviews focused on topics that

FIGURES 2.2 AND 2.3 ECI divides the New Orleans Convention Center into several sections for the Essence Fest. Major sponsors like Walmart occupy large sections of the convention floor where they build elaborate interactive exhibits like the one pictured here and on page 65 from the 2019 Festival. Credit: Photo by Timeka N. Tounsel.

FIGURE 2.3 Photo by Timeka N. Tounsel.

FIGURE 2.4 Elizabeth Warren was one of five democratic presidential hopefuls who attended the July 2019 Festival. The senator is pictured here on the "Power" stage with Rev. Al Sharpton, who frequently participates in the festival as a commentator and host. Credit: Elizabeth Warren. Creative Commons License.

Essence readers reported as most crucial for the 2020 election (see figure 2.4). In addition, various panels included discussions around the role of anti-Black racism as a common denominator in a range of struggles—health disparities, economic inequity, mass incarceration. Essence Fest Sundays punctuate the multiday experience with worship services animated by contemporary leading gospel acts and preachers who are also bestselling authors. This concluding experience honors a religious tradition familiar to many attendees but tends to be pluralistic enough to accommodate guests with divergent beliefs. Therefore, the festival does not completely eschew the structural in favor of the personal. It holds space—albeit more limited—for attendees to express their political citizenship and spiritual urgings alongside their consumer citizenship.

Essence Fest bears the most enduring elements of Taylor's legacy as a chief editorial executive and lifestyle guru: how she used spiritual empowerment as the connective tissue to fuse beauty, style, and racial uplift into a model of Black womanhood that was both relatable and aspirational. Taylor recognized that Black women would not be satisfied with superficial pitches that offered quick product fixes. She also reasoned that her audience did not just want to see glossy pictures of themselves; they wanted a platform that made them feel heard and dignified and respected. They did not just want a role model; they wanted an advocate and representative. They did not just want an advisor; they wanted a sister-friend. As she evolved, Taylor went about creating a multipurpose brand that would fulfill these desires. Through sharing and theorizing her personal struggles and triumphs she built two mutually sustaining brands. To be clear,

Taylor's success at constructing herself as a brand that served ECI's commercial aims does not reflect a lack of depth in her work, but rather, an innovative capacity to use marketable vernacular to capture and theorize Black women's everyday realities.

By the time Taylor left ECI in 2006 to lead a personal enrichment program for youth, a new era in Black representation was dawning. The United States would soon elect its first Black president and welcome an African American First Lady into the White House. This momentous shift reminded corporate brands of Black women's significance as voters, consumers, and influencers, a significance they had mostly ignored for the past decade. Although Taylor herself would fade from public view during this period, her formula for hailing Black women was far too effective to disregard. Making her work accessible meant that it was versatile enough for other brands to later adapt for profit. Nevertheless, as the following chapter will demonstrate, the companies that have attempted to replicate her empowerment grammar in form have fallen short of delivering its substance.

3

Marketing Dignity

The Commercial Grammar of
Black Female Empowerment

More than 540,000 people attended the 2013 Essence Festival, setting a record for the event. While most of the attendees were vacationing, Kelly, a publicist, was there on assignment.[1] That year, Kelly's multicultural marketing firm was tasked with promoting Walmart as a viable beauty retailer for Black women consumers. She found the task difficult. "The biggest thing that we were trying to strategize about was how do we make Walmart seem like a go-to destination for an African American woman." The research that Kelly's firm collected indicated that the target demographic trusted the reliability and variety of luxury retail offerings over the narrower portions of drugstore beauty aisles labeled "ethnic" and "multicultural." As a twentysomething Black woman with her own cosmetic bag filled with Mac and Chanel products, Kelly did not need focus group data to tell her what her instincts had already confirmed. "If I'm a Black woman and I'm trying to look my best, I am not going to say *oh, let me go to Walmart and get my look.*" Faced with the dilemma of marketing something to Black women that—according to her firm's research—they did not want, Kelly and her colleagues opted not to focus their campaign on product quality. Instead, they centered the emotional aspects of beauty politics, priming their audience to recall hegemonic standards of pretty and the feelings of inadequacy that they often trigger.

Essence Fest—with its distinct composition of Black pride and women's empowerment rhetoric—was the ideal environment to launch the marketing program that Kelly's firm had developed. Since its launch in 1995, the festival had ballooned into a consumption-driven extravaganza of pleasure and self-improvement drawing small independent vendors and corporate titans alike. Kelly's all-Black female team strategized that the best way to distinguish Walmart would be to partner with Procter & Gamble (P&G), a manufacturer of the kinds of beauty brands sold at the budget retailer.[2] P&G had launched their own campaign focused on Black beauty, empowerment, and self-affirmation called *My Black Is Beautiful* in 2006.[3] As an extension of that project, P&G produced a documentary on African American media images and self-concept entitled *Imagine a Future* that they planned to debut at the 2013 festival.[4] Kelly and her colleagues rationalized that if they could leverage *My Black Is Beautiful*'s established charm, festival attendees would connect with Walmart on a deeper, cultural level. Framing the Walmart campaign as a project about Black history, pride, and budget-friendly makeovers would compensate for the fact that some consumers did not naturally envision Walmart as an ideal cosmetics destination.

The strategy that Kelly's firm used—leveraging symbols of racial adversity and empowerment to align with the target audience—has become the primary mode of addressing Black women in the twenty-first century marketplace. Such advertising campaigns invite shoppers to *become* something by *buying* something. Because the branded products in these campaigns are merely a mechanism for achieving and maintaining empowered Black womanhood, they are useful for marking the parameters of the magical Black woman. All consumers are subject to this manipulative promotional method that deviates from products to direct attention toward an appealing identity. However, white-managed corporations did not always approach Black consumers in this manner. Essence Communications Inc. (ECI) modeled this form of sales pitch, creating an environment where it could circulate unbridled and where recognition requires mediated visibility. Power, in this milieu, is realized through consumption.

Susan L. Taylor, who embodied the empowered Black woman that *Essence* idealized, was also instrumental in developing this commercial grammar. I use the term commercial grammar to describe Black Girl Magic's instrumentalization as a visual and discursive system aimed at wooing Black women. Given her aptitude for making spiritual lessons accessible and attractive, Taylor gave depth to the *Essence* woman, a precursor for the twenty-first century magical Black woman. Her womanist rhetoric elevated ECI's grand sales pitch so that it could be interpreted as a discourse on personal agency and community uplift, rather than simply cosmetics, hair treatments, and glamourous automobiles.

The advertising scripts examined in this chapter tend to conform to Taylor's discursive style: they articulate a proud African heritage and present Black women as self-empowered persons with a divine capacity to create our own destinies.

Within the political economy of empowered Black womanhood, purchasing power is the primary resource that Black women must wield to achieve, assert, and maintain their citizenship. Whether they are saving lives, piloting planes, or leading in male-dominated fields—all of which the figures in this study sample achieve—the Black women who occupy these story worlds are active agents because they are conscious consumers. The singular qualification for conscious consumption is to patronize companies that celebrate Black womanhood through affirmative vocabulary. For this reason, marketers who exploit the commercial grammar of empowered Black womanhood craft texts that read more like tribute psalms than sales pitches. Signifiers such as "fierce," "unstoppable," "strong," and "queen" enunciate a core claim about the target audience. The argument that Black women are innately magical cloaks the central tenet upon which all advertising logic hinges to drive consumption: that even magical women are constantly in need of conditioning and management.

The premise that attention from global corporations is a political victory is another anchoring assumption embedded in these marketing campaigns. Given the many years that mass-market brands spent ignoring and demeaning Black consumers, these companies must somehow address this tension if they wish to now capitalize on Black Girl Magic. One way of managing this rupture is to make Black women dominant figures in their marketing programs. The companies exhaust the image of the strong, glamorous, high-achieving Black woman in the hopes that this trope will replace its predecessor. The commercial grammar of empowerment sanitizes the truth behind why Black women—or any demographic, for that matter—find themselves a marketing target. It is not simply that corporations have become enamored with them or finally realized their power; rather, corporate attention signals a financial opportunity. While flattery, or in this case deep cultural pride, is a common pathway to consumer heart and purse strings, these affirming messages can only ever go so far. Even when advertisements proclaim to their audience that they are enough, this rhetoric will almost always be undercut by the tenet that most drives superfluous consumption: that one can never be, nor ever have, enough.[5] While Black women occupied an elevated space in the image economy of the 2010s, this elevation meant that we were caught in the crosshairs of a hunting machine known to seize its target by any means necessary.

Although product campaigns in nearly every industry have deployed empowerment rhetoric to target Black women, beauty and automobile advertisements—the nexus of this strategic communication practice—are the focus of this chapter. No random sites, each industry has a history tarnished with hostile points that strain their capacity to effectively woo Black women consumers. The racist and sexist biases that have privileged white men and women in car, beauty, and personal care sales strategies make these respective marketplaces important battlegrounds where marginalized communities can assert their dignity through retaliatory consumption. In other words, these are industries where Black women can disprove degrading myths by expressing the right to purchase the very products deemed to be outside of our social status.

Early car adverts hailed men as their natural audience because women were thought to be incapable of handling the powerful machine or maximizing its capabilities. In the same vein, hair and skin product manufacturers tended to frame Blackness as a physical impairment that excluded Black women from being able to achieve the effect their treatments otherwise yielded. It was thought that the most these women could hope to do was mute their undesirable racial attributes and move closer to a Eurocentric aesthetic. Product advertisements promised Black women a more bearable and respectable image—not beauty. Contemporary brands target this consumer niche by reshaping what they once defined as unassailable deficiencies into magical properties. The kinks, coils, and curves once in need of taming now occupy center stage as symbols of unique, natural beauty. The feminine traits once viewed as weaknesses now shine as indicators of Black women's strength, necessitating improved twenty-first century automobiles powerful enough to match the capacity of new millennium women. Within this marketing logic, the degrading rhetoric of the past and the ideological frameworks in which those promotional messages proliferated become triumph narratives. Black women fought a centuries-long war against toxic myths and misrepresentations and survived, slowly making strides to correct the image economy in the process, so the logic goes. Thus, we are far more than consumers; we are magical consumer citizens tackling injustice one purchase at a time.

I continue this chapter with an historical overview of corporate America's dealings with Black citizens. Some of that history emerges in contemporary advertising as subtext or central narrative themes. For example, Procter & Gamble's 2019 campaign "The Talk" sequences different parent-child conversations about racism in chronological order. This campaign is a product of P&G's broader *My Black Is Beautiful* (*MBIB*) initiative, a multi-brand strategy designed to target African American women consumers. P&G launched the *MBIB* project to bolster promotion for brands such as Pantene (hair care), Cover Girl Queen Collection (cosmetics), Crest (dental care), and Always (feminine hygiene). This chapter explores *MBIB* alongside of Ford's more recent *Born to Roll* and *Built Ford Proud*. After analyzing the various promotional vehicles connected to each campaign, I address what these marketing programs accomplish for corporations and consumers and where they fall short of their promises.

From Invisible to Powerful: The Rhetoric of Ethnic Marketing

The commercial grammar of Black women's empowerment did not emerge in a vacuum; rather, it fits within a broader genealogy of marketing rhetoric that has more often rendered Black consumers invisible than magical. Historically, brands have either ignored Black women altogether or worse, incorporated our bodies in the form of caricatured images to accommodate white customers. In addition to proliferating repressive tropes, companies also integrated terms like Mammy into product names. These marketing choices were not mere missteps but intentional acts that "graphically reflected the callous disrespect that many businesses had for [B]lack consumers."[6] Until the post-World War II commercial boom, most household brands saw no benefit in marketing to African American consumers. Consequently, there was no need to place their promotional content in Black media outlets.[7] This willful ignorance created a void that Black professionals who came to be known as ethnic marketing specialists worked to fill.

Gradually, Black consumer specialists leveraged government support and convinced corporate America that targeting previously marginalized consumers would be a worthwhile business endeavor. Still, many advertisers attempted to reach Black women through the same marketing campaigns they used to reach whites. Initially, companies did not think that it was critical to address Black women through voices and faces that reflected their own. In an effort to correct this misunderstanding, one African American marketing representative published a trade press article in 1966 alerting advertisers to the rules they would need to follow if they wanted their campaigns to be effective. Elsie Archer wrote:

One out of every four Negro families is headed by a woman, compared with one out of eleven of the white families, thus making her a prime target for decision-making on how Negro dollars are to be spent.

How do you reach her?

1 She wants to be *recognized,* and her particular problems understood.

2 She wants *identification* in terms which she can understand.

3 She wants a direct *invitation* to buy.

She wants advertising and marketing people to understand that her needs and desires are often different. For example, she does not want a blue-eyed blonde suburban housewife telling her to use a particular product, when she is faced with urban living. Particularly in the area of personal care products, advertisers should use extreme caution to avoid pricking the high sensitivity of the Negro woman. [...]

She does want to see pictures of Negro women in advertisements, using the kinds of products she uses, and under similar conditions. And, advertisers should keep in mind that Negro women used in print ads and commercials should be identifiable as Negroes.

She does want a personal, direct invitation to buy, through media oriented to her interests. The problems of women in suburbia are hardly the problems faced by Negro women in urban centers.

Another word of caution for advertisers is to remember to avoid stereotypes of Negro women, and keep in mind that today's Negro women in major cities can spell the difference often between a product's success or failure.

The Negro woman has a high degree of sensitivity that must be understood, and programming to her must meet the new image she holds of herself.[8]

Archer's guidance, as obvious as it may appear in the twenty-first century context, reflected a novel way of thinking about Black women in 1966 and required white-managed brands to reject established beliefs. The first new premise that corporations needed to embrace was that Black women were influential consumers who could direct household purchasing decisions and comprised a significant enough bloc to impact a company's profit margins.[9] It was not enough for mass-market brands to recognize Black women consumers in theory; rather, they needed to prove their understanding by adjusting their promotional strategies. Such modifications demanded change across the mass media landscape. For advertisers to provide "a direct invitation" that resonated with their new target audience, they would need to employ Black advertising professionals, actors, and models, and secure space in Black media outlets. The notion that advertisers would reimagine their marketing approach by employing Black brand ambassadors, sales representatives, and consultants was significant because it suggested that mere solicitation was not enough. These long overlooked, disrespected, and underestimated consumers would not leap at whatever whistle blew in their direction. They demanded a revised protocol that reflected their self-image.

Since they stood to benefit from this cultural shift, Black stakeholders across the public communications industries participated in the campaign to convert white corporations into believers and Black publics into dignity-seeking consumers. Of course, Black women were already shopping according to their own spending preferences and political sensibilities by the 1960s. Elsie Archer, an African American woman, and her comrades in commerce did not invent Black consumer niches. By emphasizing the connection between "Negro dollars," advertising, and "the new image" Black women held of themselves, however, they did construct a racially specific consumer market that would be legible and attractive to national brands. The commercial grammar espoused by market experts held a dual purpose. First, it went beyond the lower bar of avoiding offense and centered on Black pride. Second, this syntax sought to impress upon Blacks that commodities and their promotional texts were conduits to dignity and "key tools" in the struggle for broader access to citizenship.[10]

African American consumer experts continued their crusade into the 1970s by developing a specific rhetoric to reach Black women. The Black Power era and the years that followed each carried their own empowerment mantras aimed at this emergent consumer niche.[11] For example, the L&M Super King tobacco brand used "the bold earth colors of Africa" to remind women that they had "roots to be proud of,"[12] while Johnson Products integrated Swahili poetry into their Afro Sheen marketing campaign.[13] Other products invited Black women to "discover the [B]lack and beautiful you,"[14] fashioning the self on their own terms and rejecting imposed ideas and expectations. Blackness was presented as a core part of the self that could be stylized to fit a woman's needs and desires. As one *Essence* magazine promotional explained, it was something to be worn, cultivated, and even subscribed to.[15]

Seventies ad men and women constructed a world where women smoked their Virginia Slims cigarettes in dashikis and brightly hued head scarves that rested at the base of their perfectly coifed afros. While some brands eased into the affirmative vocabulary of the day, others who were just stumbling into African American marketing feigned authenticity, mimicking a style of speech that had also been integrated into big and small screen productions.[16] Blackness was beautiful, unique, and not to be subdued or diluted to blend into a white ideal; it was to be celebrated. Corporate brands joined the celebration by developing new product lines, like Honey & Spice Cosmetics, "created expressly to beautify Black women."[17]

Advertisements in the 1990s followed suit, echoing the emergent representations of proud, upwardly mobile Black Americans that starred in television series like *Living Single* and novels-turned-films such as *Waiting to Exhale*. From the variety of Black women's hair styles and fashion selections to their agency in romantic relationships and careers, their scripted lives suggested that power was about choice. Since corporate America had seemingly awakened to the reality of Black spending practices and adapted their offerings accordingly, Black women could shop confidently. Finally, as one cosmetic brand announced in 1996, "it's all about us,"[18] assuring Black women that their desires had been understood and that they would be presented with options tailored to "who we are, and what we need."[19] In this diverse marketplace consumers could access a plethora of products claiming "true to you"[20] effects that did not compromise Black style but enhanced it. Denying your indulgences was the only wrong choice in this paradigm. Consumption was no longer about aligning with some external ideal of civility but was instead about pursuing your pleasures without guilt and—especially for Black women—"empower[ing] yourself" to "successfully balance" the demands of a modern woman's lifestyle without losing "peace of mind."[21]

By the end of the twentieth century, ethnic marketing specialists had convinced many corporations that brand messaging geared toward Black consumers was a critical investment. Even as African American–targeted campaigns increased, however, these professionals' work did not necessarily become easier. The same biases that prevented corporations from taking Black capital seriously in the first half of the twentieth century continued to hover over sales pitches well into the new millennium. One multimedia professional who has worked at print and digital outlets shared with me that even in the 1990s, some brands continued to label Black women with inaccurate, pejorative traits like uncleanliness. Despite data showing that Black women spent more on personal care products than any other consumer group, for example, some shampoo brands were reluctant to advertise in Black media. They insisted that Black women's hair hygiene practices were too irregular to warrant a targeted campaign. Confronting antiquated stereotypes during sales meetings became so common that members of the advertising team sometimes returned to the office in tears.

In addition to disputing consumer data, corporations have also been known to resist Black specialists' expertise. Kelly, a former New York City–based publicist, recalled multiple meetings where corporate clients resisted her firm's recommendations in favor of their own assumptions.

> The biggest thing that has rubbed me the wrong way with meetings are people thinking that Black women are not educated and that we don't do our research or our due diligence. I think a lot of it is, *just tell them that [the product's] great and they'll believe it.* That's not how it works. We go into these meetings—and my department is all African American women—and they're kind of looking at us almost like we're Martians. We're sitting there saying to them, we're your target . . . you're speaking to me! So, don't give some dumb-it-down campaign and not think that this requires the same level of strategy that your general-market program would.

Kelly's account reveals that even firms that have developed culturally specific campaigns in the age of Black Girl Magic may harbor doubt that their new target niche warrants the promotional efforts they devote to their main clientele. Thus, while the turn toward Black female consumers in the 2010s represents a shift, it is neither comprehensive nor unprecedented. These periods of intense corporate focus are fleeting and recursive. They tend to occur when mass-market entities are experiencing a financial lull or otherwise need to bolster their profits. Though it is tempting to read pivots to marginalized consumer niches as corporate epiphanies that could lead to long-awaited industrial changes, the retraction to traditional market programs that privilege white customers proves that such an interpretation is typically inaccurate.

Empowered Beauty: Procter & Gamble's
My Black Is Beautiful Campaign

P&G was among the first corporations to pull their sponsorship from an NBC-Universal program when, in April 2007, the show's host galloped across the line between edgy and vile in commentary about a predominantly Black women's basketball team. The casual manner in which "nappy-headed hoes" rolled from Don Imus's mouth—between chuckles—as he contrasted the Rutgers University women's basketball team with their ultimately victorious opponents from the University of Tennessee suggested no concern that his words would cost him his platform in national radio and cable news. Within a week of those comments a cascade of revoked sponsorships and rebukes from national social justice organizations had damaged Imus's public profile beyond what his apologies could repair. What had amounted to a raunchy and misguided wisecrack for some, Black women recognized as a haunting illustration of an antagonistic white gaze. So long as dominant beauty standards privileged a genteel white aesthetic, Black women's bodies could always be dissected and offered up as evidence of unfemininity, excessive sexuality, and undesirability.

While Imus's racist and sexist commentary did not shock Najoh Tita-Reid, the outrage it triggered made her realize that the moment revealed a unique opportunity. Having recently been promoted from global brand manager for Pampers to P&G's multicultural marketing director, she occupied a singular leadership position at what was then the world's largest advertiser. Tita-Reid had already been quietly spearheading the development of a new initiative aimed at strengthening the company's position in the African American beauty and personal care market when the infamous comment began circulating throughout the nation. The widespread controversy had provided the perfect rhetorical storm that a project centered around Black beauty affirmation could intercept. P&G, which was already set to host its inaugural global summit for executives of African descent in the month immediately following the Imus blunder, decided to announce the *My Black Is Beautiful* initiative at the event. In an effort to fully seize the moment, Tita-Reid also interrupted her maternity leave to launch the initiative more publicly at the National Association of Black Journalists annual convention later that summer. Audiences at both events applauded the project and welcomed it as a much-needed counter to the persistent assault on Black women in the media landscape.

My Black Is Beautiful celebrated its decennial at the 2016 Essence Festival in New Orleans, Louisiana. Videos gathered at the live marketing experience carried the hashtag #BEAUTYEMPOWERED and featured praise from celebrities and unknown festival attendees attesting to the campaign's power. "I remember the first time I heard *My Black is Beautiful*, I was like YES!" actress Sheryl Lee Ralph shared.[22] "I think it's necessary to have bold statements like this," echoed singer, actress, and *MBIB* ambassador Letoya Luckett. "To make a bold statement and remind yourself constantly that you are enough."[23] Their messages confirmed P&G's self-description of the initiative as a movement to "uplift Black community and culture through the lens of Black beauty."[24] *MBIB* has outlived Tita-Reid's tenure at P&G and infused advertising for brands such as Pantene and Olay with a core message of Black beauty as a form of power. Over the years, the *MBIB* campaign has used promotional vehicles including live events, empowerment seminars, product demonstrations, a podcast series, a documentary project, and even a doll named Zoe.[25] In 2017, a corporate relaunch under the leadership of P&G executive Marc Pritchard spawned new content for the campaign's social media channels, including the award-winning commercial "The Talk." And, in 2019, the company partnered with Sally Beauty Holdings to launch the *My Black Is Beautiful* haircare product line.

As the first marketing project of its kind in the twenty-first century, *MBIB* set the parameters for how empowered Black womanhood could be operationalized as an idea brand. Swaminathan et al. theorize idea brands as "ideologies, initiatives, or other abstract, noncommercial notions that are identified by their stakeholders and the public at large using the same specific name."[26] In the case of *My Black Is Beautiful*, campaign creators proudly pointed to the slogan as a derivative of the "Black is beautiful" phrase popularized during the late 1960s and 1970s. That Black women's beauty was a galvanizing premise was not a revelation, nor was the notion that this idea could be translated into marketing rhetoric. Numerous beauty and personal care companies had already capitalized on the phrase by integrating it into their advertisements or otherwise infusing the idea into their promotional grammar, even if the exact phrase did not appear. Imus's epithet towards a predominantly Black women's basketball team led by a Black female coach was proof that for many Americans, these women and others like them would never amount to much more than nappy-headed hoes. Thus, 2007 was an optimal time to revive the "idea brand" of Black beauty. The media landscape and beauty marketplace had changed in the nearly forty years since the slogan's first run, however, and Procter & Gamble's campaign reflected those differences.

According to Swaminathan et al., one key characteristic of idea brands is that they "can evolve across time" and are "susceptible to hijacking."[27] Neoliberalism, with its focus on self-empowerment, self-governance, and self-realization, has changed the meanings of identity and difference. As such, the political sentiments that attended "Black is beautiful"—rejecting white culture in favor of reclaiming Black aesthetics—are less apparent in the idea brand's commercial derivative form. The possessive pronoun *my* in *My Black Is Beautiful* signals a conceptual shift in understanding Blackness. Rather than indicating membership in a broad collective of systematically marginalized peoples, race operates as a flexible marker of difference that can be easily exchanged for another marker such as gender identity or sexual orientation. In other words, if "I am what I make up" (as cosmetics company Cover Girl tells consumers), then Blackness is not a predetermined identity but a malleable property to be owned, interpreted, and expressed at will.[28] In the new millennium, culture industries frame Blackness as a symbol of individuality rather than a political subjectivity. Thus, the commercial grammar that has emerged in this period, with few exceptions, has prioritized interior consciousness over structural realities. According to this logic, what the world says about Black women can only have as much impact as we afford it.

The *MBIB* campaign and the products marketed under its banner present personal solutions to the disparaging comments and other assaults that Black women confront. The pronouncement of Black beauty is less a rallying cry in this frame and more of an encouragement open to individual interpretation. Rather than frame new millennium Black women as being engaged in a collective struggle, *MBIB* has emphasized each woman's individual power to choose how she will manage her beauty. The campaign narrative restricts power to a Black woman's self-generated capacity to style herself according to her own preferences and purchase the products that facilitate that look. This narrow form of agency is a given that exists independent of outside structures and can only be usurped if Black women deny our inherent power, or magic. In this way the campaign fits neatly within the ideological parameters of Black Girl Magic in its commercial form. Ancillary slogans that have emerged in connection to *MBIB*, including "My Black is Powerful" and "My Black is Magical," amplify this point. In this section I analyze how P&G has marshaled their affirmative mantra to promote hair care products under the banner of its Pantene brand.

When P&G revived *My Black Is Beautiful* in 2017, the corporation also launched a new product line under the existing Pantene brand. The Pantene Gold Series included a range of items with labels like "detangling milk" and "hydrating butter-crème"—buzzwords that had become popularized in the boom market for products designed to style Black hair without the intervention of straightening chemicals. Black entrepreneurs like Lisa Price of Carol's Daughter, Richelieu Dennis of Shea Moisture, and Mahisha Dellinger of CURLS, began laying the foundation for this emergent market in the 1990s and early 2000s. Taking notice of their profits, large corporate brands began adjusting their own product lines to better compete with the independent start-ups. In fact, two of those corporations, L'Oréal and Unilever, would eventually acquire Carol's Daughter and Shea Moisture, respectively. While the industry titans were already aware of the billions that Black consumers spent on beauty products, the pioneers of what would later be called the natural hair movement compelled these mass brands to update their sales pitches to fit the more affirming sensibilities of the new millennium.

Launching the Pantene Gold Series in 2017 made P&G late to the natural hair care party, which may have been why they attempted to be especially transparent in their marketing plan. One press release self-critiqued the brand's failure to adequately center and celebrate kinkier hair textures:

> There is still a level of inequality in how African-American hair is represented in popular culture and in mainstream hair care advertising. Mass brands, like Pantene, have inadvertently been a part of this pervasive hair bias with a history of advertising showcasing a limited representation of African-American hairstyles and textures and promoting long, shiny, smooth hair as the pinnacle of hair health and beauty. Pantene has set out to change this perception and empower all women to embrace their strong and unique hair because all strong hair is beautiful hair.[29]

P&G acknowledges past failures and proclaims a new mission for themselves in this statement: Empowerment through broader images. They suggest that changing their promotional rhetoric will give Black women the permission to "embrace" our hair.

In its press release P&G also admits that despite attempts to celebrate Black beauty, it conformed to a more Eurocentric standard in the earliest years of the *MBIB* initiative. While it centered Black models, it did not present a variety of hair textures. The Relaxed and Natural Collection, which directly preceded Pantene's Gold Series, hinted at diversity in its name; yet the promotion's visual rhetoric privileged styles achievable through chemical relaxers or hair straighteners. P&G aimed to correct its bias in a 2017 television spot featuring girls and women with a broad spectrum of hair textures and skin complexions. The commercial's poetic script and dramatic camera angles work to collapse the gap between Pantene and Black women consumers altogether. There is no trace of past flaws in the advertisement, as the corporation uses storytelling techniques that make it appear as part of the viewer's community.

> We are *proudly* born
> With hair that grows strong as a storm
> And doesn't conform to a beauty norm
> That isn't our own.
> So many wrong things are said
> About how it grows from our head.
> But to think that beauty is only sleek or wavy
> Is crazy.

Because whether we choose to wear it relaxed or natural
Every strand is testimony to *our* history.
That makes us stronger.
And strong is beautiful.[30]

P&G presents itself here as being familiar enough with the audience to be able to articulate their inner thoughts. Still, it is unclear from the commercial alone whether the company has taken efforts to change anything beyond how it speaks to Black women. The Pantene Gold Series commercial offers no information about products. This campaign demonstrates a focus on selling dignity, not hair care. In an attempt to appeal to Black women, the brand imbues consumption with a purpose far deeper than healthy hair. Even their take on racial bias is wanting in that the advertisement focuses on interpersonal insults and avoids the social hierarchies that impede equity. P&G is not concerned with justice here; rather, it is fixated on choice. For sure, it is wise to debunk the notion that certain styles—that is, those achieved through chemical straightening—are less culturally authentic than others. Still, this commercial gestures away from the product's efficacy and assumes that Black women will prioritize flattery over function. Pantene expects that consumers will accept their affirmations as a form of power and show appreciation for Pantene's attention through spending.

As is typical for contemporary multi-platform marketing campaigns, Pantene published supplementary promotional content via their YouTube channel. In "Pantene Gold Series: The Scientists Behind It" P&G works to amplify its projected identity as a force that helps Black women shine. The video features brief commentary from five Black scientists—four of them women—who articulate the significance of the new product line. The video presents the Gold Series as a promising resource for an underserved consumer group and as a symbol of achievement for the Black community. "I most recently had a little girl, and I can say mommy worked on a line that would help Black women to be able to care for their hair in a better way," Dr. Rolanda J. Wilkerson states in the recording.[31] Dr. Wilkerson's statement supports P&G's aim to showcase the Gold Series as a legendary feat; a notion that falls flat considering the numerous Black-owned companies that beat them to this particular marketplace. In an effort to present Pantene as a pioneer in recognizing Black women's value, the supplementary content excludes visuals of the actual products to highlight dignified images of Black women who carry PhD at the end of their names. As each scientist appears on screen, their name and credentials follow. Mimicking a sequence that one might observe in a story when a superhero is preparing for a grand rescue, the video shows each figure in close shots that emphasize valor (see figures 3.1–3.6). Several of the women are affixing or adjusting their white laboratory coats as the camera captures them from low angles,

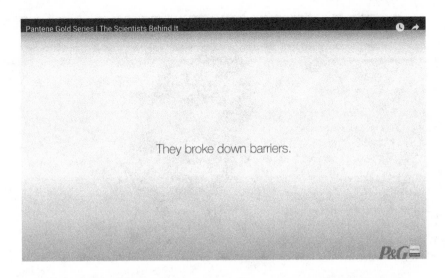

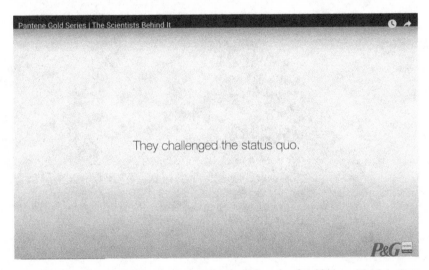

FIGURES 3.1 AND 3.2 Screenshots from a Pantene YouTube video, "Gold Series: The Scientists behind It." Credit: Pantene.

the kind of shots commonly used to incite awe. The jackets present as superhero capes in the monochrome mise-en-scène. "This consumer has been relegated to the back of hair care aisles," and "left off of clinical trials," the figures declare.[32] Using P&G's resources, these Black scientists have accepted the mission to rescue consumers from invisibility and undesirable hair. Despite lagging years behind competitors in an ever-growing marketplace focused on Black consumers, Pantene casts itself as "lead[ing] the way" by "challenging the status quo . . . deliver[ing] results . . . [and] break[ing] down barriers."[33]

FIGURES 3.3-3.6 Additional screenshots taken from a Pantene YouTube video entitled "Pantene Gold Series: The Scientists behind It." Posted March 22, 2017, the video was part of P&G's effort to appeal to Black women consumers through promotional texts that explicitly address racial bias. Credit: Pantene.

At face value, there is nothing dangerous about Procter & Gamble proclaiming Black women's beauty. The content published under the *MBIB* banner has largely lived up to the campaign's stated promise of glamorizing Black bodies of different complexions, hair textures, and sizes. However, the ideology that undergirds these images complicates the initiative. What does it mean for a

beauty brand to present itself as not only serving consumers through producing quality goods, but as redeeming consumers from their degraded status in the image economy? What does such a campaign ask the consumer to believe about herself and her mobility? As corporations like P&G continue to structure their commercial grammar around statements like "#RedefineBlack,"[34] they position themselves to dominate discourses about identity politics. As a consequence, they steer the conversation as they see fit. Regardless of how many campaigns they create to woo Black women, these mass-market firms will always be driven by profits as long as they remain in the business of beauty. This reality begs the question of where Black women will stand if corporations fail to realize the return on investment that spawned their enchantment with this consumer group in the first place.

In(Her) Vision: Ford Motor Company and the Black Women behind the Scenes

At its best, commercial empowerment grammar appeals to Black women's desire to be recognized and (re)presented in all the glory that the white gaze refuses to acknowledge. It is not empty flattery or superficial mimicry, but careful narrative imbued in a consciousness only accessible through personal experience. For this reason, Black women are often responsible for generating the most effective commercial expressions of Black Girl Magic. In addition to applying their cultural expertise to the visual and aural architecture of their respective advertising projects, Black women professionals become elements of the sales pitch. Whether they are industry insiders with a low public profile or celebrities lending their voices and images to the campaign, Black women marketers' capacity to embody Black Girl Magic is essential for facilitating the empowerment message that undergirds the texts. These women imbue the advertisements with an authenticity that makes the promotional campaign more relatable and the products more attractive. Angela Bassett, a beloved actor and filmmaker heralded for portraying characters as brawny as her physique, is one such example of how Black women leverage their racial community ties to legitimize advertising claims. Bassett partnered with Ford Motor Company for their 2019–2020 campaign, *Built Ford Proud*.

In addition to an alluring and distinct verbal intonation, Bassett's body of work made her an ideal partner for Ford's promotional strategy. Her most notable performances include magical Black women characters—both figuratively and literally—who conquer all manner of adversity. In 1994, Bassett received an Oscar nomination for her lead performance in the Tina Turner biopic *What's Love Got to Do with It*. Although she did not win the Academy Award, Bassett went on to captivate audiences in subsequent big and small screen projects. The most indelible scene of her career, one that has been crystallized in numerous memes and GIFs, occurred in the 1996 blockbuster *Waiting to Exhale*.[35] There Bassett portrayed Bernadine, one member of a quartet of professional Black women who seek solace in friendship as they approach middle age. Bernadine's particular challenge is grappling with marital trauma after her husband of more than ten years announces his desire for a divorce and plans to solidify a relationship with his white secretary. Struggling to cope with this upheaval, Bernadine decides to destroy the belongings that her husband left behind in his swift departure from their family home. After collecting as many items as she could carry in a tear-soaked rage, she loads them into his luxury sedan and incinerates the lot. The iconic scene features a satisfied Bernadine lighting a cigarette before using the same match to scorch her estranged husband's possessions. The camera watches Bernadine strut back toward her home, flames dancing behind her in the distance, as if to scream that this is how a woman scorned reclaims her power.

One viewing is enough to embed the scene into one's consciousness. Bassett's fierceness in that cinematic moment lingers over every subsequent performance, whether she is settling scores as a voodoo priestess in FX's *American Horror Story* or selling a Ford Explorer. Beyond her theatrical aptitude, that Bassett has produced numerous unforgettable performances without recognition from the major institutions of her field marks her as a magical Black woman. She has been denied her rightful praise and must therefore take it upon herself to celebrate her beauty and worth. Despite mostly limited recognition beyond Black institutions, Bassett has committed to animating noble African American figures—including Betty Shabazz, Coretta Scott King, Rosa Parks, and Ramonda, Queen of Wakanda (*Black Panther*, 2018). Her career reads as a cinematic encyclopedia attending to real and imagined subjects of great import to Black Americans. Nevertheless, these projects, some of which were television mini-series, have not been a certain path to the kinds of accolades that secure a position on power lists issued by the likes of the *Hollywood Reporter*. That Bassett is selective with her image and voice, even when the cost of her "no" is palpable, makes her inclusion in the 2019–2020 Ford campaigns more poignant. As one multicultural communications manager at the company stated, she was the "perfect fit" to advance the brand's marketing focus on "being a leader, serving your community, being proud of where you come from and passionate about the future."[36]

Black Girl Magic advertisements like the ones Bassett voiced for Ford rely on a coding system that allows the text to transcend the level of sales pitch and become an identity narrative. In these story worlds, designed to appeal to Black women's interior longings and anxieties, beauty products become political tools and cars become symbols of destiny. Each item is a building block to the ultimate object for sale: dignified and empowered womanhood. Ford Motor Company's advertisement for the 2020 Escape—"Built Phenomenally"— exemplifies this complex interplay between commodities and the notion of magical Black womanhood. The commercial presents the compact sport utility vehicle as a portal to a latent, better self and to a community of other empowered women.

Ford draws viewers into the commercial with an up-tempo drum beat exuding equal parts techno and hip-hop, a fuchsia neon sign announcing the "2020 ESCAPE," and rhythmic prose that, in Angela Bassett's voice, meets the ear more like poetry than a commercial voiceover: "Phenomenal doesn't just happen. It's designed with intention. Assembled with care. And even still to bring it all to life, takes a sprinkling of magic. Introducing the unmistakably new 2020 Ford Escape. Built phenomenally."[37] The script urges viewers to recall Maya Angelou's acclaimed poem, "Phenomenal Woman," first published in the 1978 collection *And Still I Rise*. Although those who interact with her cannot help but succumb to her allure, the key subject in the poem is an unlikely figure to dote upon. Yet, she is confident in her identity as "a woman/ Phenomenally/ Phenomenal woman/ That's me," as the recurrent verse declares. Because she is "not cute or built to suit a fashion model's size," the key to her phenomenal nature is a secret. Like Angelou's narrator, the Ford advertisement also alludes to an "inner mystery" that Black women possess. It is an inherent magic that must nevertheless be cultivated, rigorously planned, and precisely executed. According to the commercial, phenomenal women—much like phenomenal cars—do not emerge by chance. Rather, they are always premeditated and carefully constructed. Being a phenomenal woman, a magical Black woman, requires the right material resources, a car for example, as well as disciplined labor.

The advertisement was staged as a production shoot, showcasing the behind-the-scenes process of creating a commercial for the Ford Escape. Beginning with a shot of a director rising from her chair to offer guidance to an actor seated in the driver's position of the vehicle on set, the camera travels the entire sound-stage, briefly pausing on various women completing their contribution to the production. Captions identify different women by name and role—Kanyessa McMahon (director), Lola Okanlawon (makeup artist), Dibrie Guerrero (Ford marketer), Raj Register (Ford marketer), Marci Rodgers (stylist), and N'jeri Nicholson (copywriter)—signaling to the target viewer that the women responsible for promoting the product are members of their community, people like them or who they aspire to become. One of the concluding shots in the commercial features the full production team, all women of color, mostly Black, crowded around the automobile. Since the car is only partially visible behind the women, this scene amplifies their centrality to the text. Ford is not only presenting an updated vehicle, but the company is also highlighting the Black women they partnered with to market the Escape.[38]

"A main goal of our 'Built Phenomenally' campaign is to honestly represent African American females.... Ford is confident the campaign is a true celebration of [B]lack women," said Raj Register, in a press release.[39] Register is the company's head of brand strategy and growth audience marketing and one of the women featured in the commercial. The advertisement shores up its authenticity factor by showcasing women of different complexions, body sizes, hair textures, and professions. Stark contrasts in the colors adorning the women in the commercial—bold pinks, reds, yellows, greens, oranges, black and white—reinforce diversity. Since the cast consisted mostly of noncelebrity women and not professional models, the idea that almost any Black woman viewer could place herself within this imaginary setting is evident; so apparent, in fact, that this magical world could begin to seem less like a fabrication and more like a reachable goal. While the campaign tagline "Built Phenomenally" refers to the automobile, it more importantly describes the team of Black women responsible for selling the product. More than managing a single advertisement, these women are co-constructing an image of womanhood that other Black women may draw from to make sense of themselves and their place in the world.

The companion commercial for the "Built Phenomenally" project features the same theme song, cast and crew, with voiceover narration by Angela Bassett. "Own It" is the finished production that viewers witnessed being designed and executed from behind the camera in the previous advertisement. While upgraded models of the 2020 Ford Escape maintain center stage in this commercial more than in the companion piece, self-actualization remains fundamental to the script. "What makes you different is what makes you, you. Unique and unrepeatable inside and out. When you get comfortable with that, destiny's yours to navigate."[40] The intention behind the piercing color palette is more evident in this text, given its emphasis on uniqueness. The stylist featured in the previous "Built Phenomenally" advertisement, who has vitiligo, occupies the driver's seat in one scene. In light of the condition, something that could easily be read as a defect, her power positioning communicates that one need not fully conform to a mold to progress. The traits that external arbiters interpret as imperfections are the very factors that make Black women magical. Under this logic, an internal failure to appreciate our unique magic is what most threatens to hinder Black women from realizing our potential rather than external, structural forces.

Ford further extended its empowerment objective for the *Built Phenomenally* campaign through digital content featuring middle and high school–aged Black girls. The company invited select participants from Girls Make Beats, a music production mentorship program, to visit with Bassett as she recorded the voiceover for the campaign. Ford taped the experience and published the final video package on their YouTube channel. In addition to sharing some of their own work and ambitions, the girls listened to Bassett's stirring oration of the advertising script: "What makes you different is what makes you, you. Unique and unrepeatable, inside and out."[41] The script doubles as sales pitch and mantra, heralding the updated Ford Escape as an exemplary vehicle in its class and guiding girls of color in how they should similarly view themselves as uniquely powerful beings. Bassett enunciates the empowerment ethos in her own words of encouragement to the girls: "Sometimes they say that Black and Brown girls' images don't travel, you know. They'll try to make you believe in the world and life that you're less than, when actually, you're on top. You're the head, not the tail. You're above and not beneath. You're phenomenal. You're built phenomenally."[42] Sponsored experiences like this are common in the Black Girl Magic era where empowerment exists as a commercial project. They normalize the conflation of consumption and dignity by drawing brands and products out of the marketplace and into the self-improvement sphere.

Taken together, the *Built Phenomenally* campaign offers potential customers more than the opportunity to buy into a brand: additionally, it offers admission into a colorful world where Black women (and girls) occupy director's chairs and driver's seats, wielding the power to design their lives on their terms. While Ford seeks to maintain brand visibility here, the particular car is less significant. Rather than preserve some mystery about their sales plan, the company sought to distinguish itself in this campaign through transparency about their aim to "celebrate the defiance, transformation, and versatility of [B]lack women as creators, marketers, and performers who own their uniqueness and live phenomenally."[43] Such an approach is common within Black Girl Magic advertisements where product descriptions are secondary to audience exaltation.

In another strategy to woo their target market, Ford Motor Company has designed advertising campaigns around nonfictional narratives of high-achieving Black women. Kellee Edwards, a self-described adventure journalist and host of the Travel Channel's *Mysterious Islands*, sat in the driver's seat for the company's 2019 Explorer campaign. While this advertisement highlighted the vehicle more prominently than other sales pitches, the empowerment motif persisted through details of Edwards' personal journey. The Chicago native's hometown served as the setting for a commercial centered on community pride and upward mobility. The advertisement opens on a bust of Jean Baptiste Point du Sable, the African American man lauded as the city's founder, and Angela Bassett's distinctive narration: "When this explorer [Jean Baptiste Point du Sable] founded this city [Chicago] he couldn't possibly have imagined that this explorer [Kellee Edwards] would be born here. And this Explorer [the vehicle], would be built here. Imagine that. When exploration is what you do, this is what you drive."[44] After driving through the city and passing various historic sites, Edwards finally arrives at a hangar where she trades her sport utility vehicle for a private propeller plane. Not even the sky is the limit for her success. The commercial presents her as a magical Black woman who has managed to conquer the world while maintaining a connection to her roots.

The 2019 Explorer campaign followed a tactic that Ford had previously used in their 2018 *Born to Roll* project. There the brand spotlighted three different Black women in separate advertisements for their Escape, Explorer, and Fusion models: Georgie Nakima, a muralist, Dr. Kirstie Cunningham, an obstetrician-gynecologist and clinical professor, and fire department lieutenant Nikkoel Gilmore. The commercials feature each of the women at work in their respective professional settings. Nakima navigates through an urban setting to her workplace, an empty warehouse, in a Ford Escape. The overall-clad artist bounces across the grungy shop floor with an aerosol can, splashing color on its walls. Dance is more fitting for this campaign spot because it most clearly features the theme song for the campaign.

> Every day the unstoppable / Do the impossible / We the undeniable / Royalty undefinable / Don't need the perfect day for my victory to be had / The rain is just clearing my path / We roll on.[45]

Without directly mentioning Black Girl Magic, the lyrics enunciate the primary characteristic that distinguishes Black women in the contemporary image economy: our ability to triumph over adversity and ultimately achieve what should be unfeasible. In this and many other advertisements that promote the Black Girl Magic ethos, the script doubles as a celebratory anthem and set of commandments for empowered living. The song both narrates the lives of the exemplary women in the commercials and presents viewers with guidelines for how they can realize their own greatness.

Dr. Kirstie Cunningham's commercial chronicles a typical day that begins with her and her husband traveling to an unknown destination. The doctor, of course, is in the driver's seat. A phone call interrupts the couple's calm drive through the vehicle's integrated Bluetooth apparatus, seemingly alerting Cunningham to the fact that a patient has gone into labor. In the next scene Dr. Cunningham enters a hospital to attend what appears to be a safe vaginal delivery. Finally, the Ford Fusion commercial follows Lieutenant Nikkoel Gilmore and her team as they hustle out of the fire station to respond to a call. After successfully extinguishing the fire, Gilmore drives a Ford Fusion to the home where her child is enthusiastically awaiting her return. Importantly, the latter two advertisements enunciate women's roles outside of their careers, indicating the various relationships and elements that constitute a full life. This touch of reality makes the women appear more relatable to the target audience. The choice not to rely on actors or marketing professionals to animate these pitches shows how brands who exploit this commercial grammar have positioned themselves to market dignity alongside their products. Unlike advertisements that hinge on desire by offering potential customers access to an unattainable ideal, these campaigns hinge on affirmation. Placing non-celebrity women at the center of this imagery increases the potential for audience resonance and provides an opportunity for Ford to communicate that they see Black women the way that the target audience sees themselves.

Like the vehicles that they promote, the automobile advertisements analyzed here demonstrate the promises and limitations of commodified empowerment.

Just as "the car facilitates movement among different locations, both physically and figuratively," mediated rhetoric creates a story world where Black women travel unbound by pejorative stereotypes and ill-fitting scripts.[46] The power and authority that figures wield in this commercial imagery, however, is akin to the conditional agency that automobiles have offered otherwise restricted owners. In her history of women motorists in twentieth century America, Deborah Clarke theorizes automotive citizenship as a mode of agency for marginalized groups who are otherwise suppressed from asserting themselves as free, dignified beings. The open road is no respecter of persons, accessible to whomever finds themselves behind the wheel. And while early automobile manufacturers may have infused American car culture with their unrelenting beliefs about gender and race, they could not ultimately prohibit unintended markets from attaining the machines and whatever privilege accompanied them.

Yet, automobile access did not equate to full freedom. Clarke explains that since one cannot "drive into the mainstream . . . automotive citizenship does not construct an idyllic space, [rather] it does offer an alternative to those denied access to American civic culture."[47] Ford Motor Company's contemporary advertisements extend Black women a similar offering: a substitute empowerment tethered to consumption. Furthermore, these promotional texts evade any discussion of the dangers that await Black motorists in the new millennium. The dark side of the automobile explosion was its facilitation of the car as a weapon or instrument in transporting racist perpetrators to their victims. Accounts of Black people being tied to automobile bumpers and dragged to meet death, harassed by white passersby while halted roadside by car trouble, and run out of town by road ragers in so-called sundown towns punctuate America's love story with cars. Thus, the open road has been just as much a symbol of freedom as it has been a hotbed for the brutalization of Black bodies. These horrors cannot be dismissed as past relics; twenty-first century motorists encounter an equally troubling reality at the hands of law enforcement. In an analysis of roughly 95 million police stops that occurred in the United States between 2011 and 2018, researchers found that police stopped Black drivers more often than those identified as white or Latinx.[48] The study also indicated that police subjected Black and Latinx drivers to searches more frequently than white motorists during traffic stops. Beyond arrest, such roadside encounters carry the risk of a worse fate, as materialized through the headline-grabbing deaths of Sandra Bland and Philando Castille.[49]

Evading the dangers of driving while Black, Ford's marketing campaigns script a world where the driver's seat is the foremost position of control. In accordance with the Black Girl Magic ethos, they claim that Black women's capacity to achieve, produce, and succeed is inherent because we are "built phenomenally" and "born to roll." This logic charges us to resist discouragement and shift our perspective of the hindrances and annoyances we encounter on the road to fulfilling our destiny. Rain, or whatever other unexpected circumstances we confront, are accelerants, not obstacles. The most important thing women can do to realize greatness is embrace our inner magic and press forward, resolved to the belief that victory is inevitable. While this commercial grammar succeeds in recognizing Black women's beauty, strength, and agency, it disappears threats lurking just beyond the production set. Certainly, the Black women working behind-the-scenes at Ford are aware of this reality and sought to close the gap between the cocoon they designed for the marketing campaigns and the injustices that shape the material world. Insisting on a majority Black woman–led cast, crew, and strategic team, and inviting pre-teens and teenagers from Girls Make Beats and Made in Her Image to witness the taping were significant acts. The girls likely left the experience inspired but still no less likely to face increased surveillance and disciplinary action in lesser-resourced academic environments. Wage inequity and discriminatory hiring practices may not have impeded some forty-plus Black women from executing the *Built Ford Proud* and *Born to Roll* campaigns, but those issues will not dissipate simply because a woman has decided to "own" her uniqueness.

The Burden of Affirmation

Black women consumers inhabit a world where a Ford Escape is not just a reasonable purchase but one that drives her to fulfill entrepreneurial ambitions. And Pantene's Gold Series not only strengthens hair; it challenges the status quo. It is in these ways that corporations appropriate Susan L. Taylor's practice of enlightened consumption—only giving one's power to companies that deserve it—for contemporary beauty and automobile advertisements. These commercial campaigns offer Black women figurative crowns that have long been withheld. The cost of that recognition, however, is our agreement to deploy that capital in prescribed ways: through purchases and lifestyle choices that bolster profits for Black media and their corporate sponsors.[50] While the commercial grammar analyzed here affords Black women the (spending) power to transform our lives and impact the world, it leaves little room to critique the institutions that structure that world.

I interviewed multiple women who mediate between Black women consumers and white industry gatekeepers to better understand how these professionals manage the ambiguity bred from their "outsider-within" status—members of marginalized communities who inhabit the culture industry's situation rooms.[51] I found that these women self-identify both as industry combatants and community authorities. While they advocate on behalf of a mishandled audience, they also work to police a consumer market that sometimes fails to act or spend responsibly—that is, in alignment with corporate profit models. These professionals make peace with their entangled status by conceptualizing their target audience as a powerful bloc who wield more control over images and dollars than we tend to admit. In their rush to amplify everyday consumers as influential agents, however, they minimize Black women's vulnerability. Ironically, it is the very condition of being perceived as powerful that stifles Black women's movement within the media landscape. Having ascended to the level of prized target audience in this moment, the logic of Black Girl Magic demands that these media citizens sacrifice personal preferences to prove that we are indeed a worthwhile investment.

Actress, entrepreneur, and *Red Table Talk* web series creator Jada Pinkett Smith enunciated this point at the 2017 Essence Festival. Pinkett Smith and co-star Queen Latifah were at the event promoting their film *Girls Trip*. Both media figures participated in the "Strength of a Woman" panel where they defined Black Girl Magic and discussed how it translates into power in the broader image economy. Pinkett Smith's words capture the sentiments that other content creators have expressed regarding the responsibility that accompanies the increased attention Black women consumers are receiving: "You might think that these [cultural producers] on this stage have a lot of power, but you actually have far more power than we do because you are the ones that are consuming the product. You are the ones that are dictating what is going to be made. . . . Even if it's a project that might not pull your passion, just know that as a people we always have to support diverse personalities, diverse stories in our communities. . . . I don't care *what* we do; you gotta support it."[52] Pinkett Smith's charge to the audience confirms that commercial (self-)empowerment is not free, especially for Black women. Whatever affirmation we receive by way of expanded cultural representation must be earned, in perpetuity, through unconditional support. It cannot be true that Black women consumers have absolute power to dictate the marketplace available to us *and* that we risk losing rank if we do not consume whatever the industry presents us. And yet, these are the parameters we must navigate at a time when, we are told, things are the best they have ever been.

So which Black women, if any, stand to gain from the commercial empowerment project that has unfolded in the first decades of the twenty-first century? Marketing professionals at Ford answered this question in a panel discussion about their *Built Phenomenally* campaign by underscoring how the promotion bolstered traditionally underrepresented cultural producers. In addition to selecting a Black woman to direct both commercials, a rarity, they employed an almost exclusively Black and female cast and crew. Women who worked on the campaign described the production set as a safe space and familiar community where Black consciousness ruled. "At one point I turned to the stylist and I said, no Black girl would wear that. And she was like, correct, I'll be right back," explained ad director Kanyessa McMahon.[53] "I didn't have to explain myself or show pictures and give a history lesson. It was really, really empowering to have that shorthand."[54] These victories are important, but singular. That Ford values an insider's perspective enough to rely on members of the target market in their multicultural programs reflects business acumen more than advocacy. Furthermore, corporate America's history with Black consumers indicates that courtship periods like the one unfolding in the era of Black Girl Magic are fleeting. Seeing women of color in executive positions at Ford today does not mean that the same can be expected for tomorrow. When those women occupy roles specifically connected to diversity programming (or what Ford refers to as "growth audiences"), which is inherently dynamic and fickle, it is all the more challenging to hold out hope that the company is invested in lasting, structural change. While it is true that this period in history has witnessed a proliferation of dignified images through campaigns such as *Built Phenomenally* and platforms such as *My Black Is Beautiful*, it is also true that dignity is not power.

Nevertheless, the 2010s has also seen cultural producers leverage their visibility and elevated status as media citizens to delegitimate the positive-negative dichotomy often used to assess Black images. There is no doubt that the culture industries perceive these women as magical, but the creative decisions that they have made with their power point toward a conception of Black womanhood beyond magic. If the media frame of Black Girl Magic privileges fierceness, infallibility, and self-discipline, these writer-producers seem devoted to an anti-magic framework. Mara Brock Akil, Issa Rae, and Lena Waithe have each used cable television to advance Black women characters that are unapologetically messy. Importantly, Black Entertainment Television (BET)'s *Being Mary Jane* (2013–2019), HBO's *Insecure* (2016–2021), and BET/Showtime's *Twenties* (2020, ongoing), do not relegate their flawed characters to the margins; rather, they center these women in lead roles. These television programs reveal what is possible when minoritized media citizens marshal commercial resources to serve their own agendas. In the following chapter, I explore how Akil, Rae, and Waithe deploy vulnerability and consider what their strategy does for the project of Black womanhood that Black Girl Magic does not.

4

Beyond Magic

Black Women Content
Creators and
Productive Vulnerability

Mara Brock Akil had been helping a classmate write the script for a student showcase at Northwestern University when she realized that in addition to being skilled at entertaining an audience with her words, she preferred this creative labor over the advertising work she had been planning to pursue. Others would later encourage her to seek a path toward the front of the camera, citing her marketable look as evidence that she would thrive as an actress. But the young Mara Brock had fallen in love with the art of dreaming up characters, writing them to life, and shepherding her vision from page to screen. She did not have the luxury of looking like the white men whose names most often appeared next to credits like creator and executive producer, but she was nonetheless committed to using all the resources she could access to pursue her dream, behind the camera.

After honing her skills on Black sitcoms including *The Jamie Foxx Show* and *Moesha*, the United Paramount Network (UPN) approached Akil about creating her own series. *Girlfriends* premiered in the Fall of 2000. The show thrust four college-educated Black women into a televisual space dominated by the likes of the mini-skirt-styled lawyer, Ally McBeal, and the Manolo Blahnik-obsessed women of *Sex in the City*. Not only were her characters disrupting the culture, but so too was their creator. Women made up less than a quarter of the professionals producing primetime network television in the 2001–2002 season, Akil's sophomore year as showrunner for her own series. So, she approached the project as much more than just a half-hour sitcom starring Black women. It was a chance to have a conversation with her audience and to exhibit Black humanity.

Two future Black women series creators were watching Akil's rise, one up close as a showrunner's assistant on *Girlfriends*, the other from her living room, both receiving lessons that they would later apply to their own work. Within the next twenty years, Akil would create and produce three more series showcasing a spectrum of Black femininities, including Black Entertainment Television (BET)'s first original dramatic program, *Being Mary Jane*. By 2019, Lena Waithe would create a series loosely based on the time she spent working for Akil. *Twenties* became the first television comedy centering a masculine-presenting Black lesbian after finding a somewhat unlikely home at BET. The network had never had a show with a queer protagonist until Waithe's series.[1] And Issa Rae would not only have the honor of meeting the woman whose nuanced depiction of Black women's friendship inspired her, she would share a magazine cover with Akil for *Essence*'s May 2015 issue spotlighting television producers whom the magazine considered "game changers."

Unlike the image economy that Akil negotiated to make space for complex Black female characters at the dawn of the twenty-first century, the mediascape of the late 2010s that she shared with creators like Rae and Waithe had become enchanted with Black women. They were, Akil joked, "the flavor of the month."[2] She was convinced, though, that Black women producers like her could use this visibility like a "secret weapon."[3] In other words, these content creators could exploit Hollywood's renewed interest in Black women consumers to cement a place for Black narratives that would outlive the latest surge of investment. For Akil, Rae, and Waithe, those narratives would be built around multidimensional subjects whose complexity did not threaten their dignity, characters that they would make intentionally messy.

Mara Brock Akil, Issa Rae, and Lena Waithe demonstrate how media citizens who have access to Black Girl Magic can leverage their capital to advance Black womanhood at a larger scale. Magazine covers for titles as diverse as the *Hollywood Reporter*, *Essence*, *Out*, and *Vanity Fair*, as well as programming deals with companies such as HBO, Warner Bros. TV, Showtime, and Netflix attest to their star power. These women have managed to galvanize a following not just for their content, but also for their personal brands. They are seen as embodying Black excellence, beauty, resilience and wokeness—key qualifiers for being magical. Yet, they have used commercial visibility not only for individual gain, but for a more collective mission. Each content creator's approach to Black female subjectivities broadens contemporary understandings of dignified Black womanhood beyond the limiting frame of magic.[4] In addition to emphasizing imperfection through narratives centered on relationships and sexuality, the creators also position themselves as the arbiters of their own work by routinely intervening in audience discourses. Thus, central to this inquiry are the numerous interviews and public discussions in which Akil, Rae, and Waithe have participated, offering unique insights into their artistic consciousness.

While Mara Brock Akil, Issa Rae, and Lena Waithe have contributed to various scripted projects, I focus on their series which unsettle the notion that Black women must be magical to be visible: *Being Mary Jane, Insecure*, and *Twenties*. These three writer-producers have strategically deployed vulnerability in their cable television series to reframe Black women as human, countering the Hollywood convention of representing these raced and gendered bodies in extremes, either superhuman or subhuman. Casting their protagonists as vulnerable is an intentional maneuver that reflects active resistance to the "respectability/irreverence binary" that constrains most depictions of Black women in popular culture.[5] This political agenda is clear from the interviews, speeches, and social media content that Akil, Rae, and Waithe have used to reinforce the conceptions of dignified Black womanhood presented in their respective series.

These content creators have located Black female subjectivity in a theoretical space where erotic desire and features of Black ladyhood are not mutually exclusive. The lead characters of *Being Mary Jane, Insecure*, and *Twenties* are college-educated professionals. Rather than treat their social standing as a preemptive shield against sexual exposure and potential distortion, however, Akil, Rae, and Waithe highlight the ways in which their protagonists blur traditional understandings of dignified or middle-class Black womanhood. More than the capacity to fail or possess weaknesses, these writer-producers operationalize vulnerability as a fundamental quality of humanness that accommodates contradictory attitudes, actions, and desires within their Black female subjects without compromising their personhood.

Since the lexicon of Black womanhood has always been bound to sexuality in the American imagination, any assertion of Black women's humanity must always be read in relation to sexual politics. Thus, how Akil, Rae, and Waithe express their characters' sex lives is essential to understanding how their creative work points to a form of womanhood beyond magic. Indeed, they are recouping a space for playful exhibitions in excess and indulgence of the *Sex in the City* variety, a debt accrued from the erasure of Black female voices from third wave feminist treatises that pervaded the televisual sphere beginning in the 1990s.

Efforts to degrade Black women to the level of inferior Others have been facilitated through legal, economic, and ideological discourses that either desexualize or hypersexualize. America's attempts to render the Black female body void of fundamental human capacities and emotions can be read through the caricatures of the asexual Mammy and her derivative, the emasculating Matriarch, who are both uninterested in the erotic and necessarily undesirable. On the other side of this dichotomy, Black women have been rendered criminally promiscuous and likely to wield their bodies as destructive forces against innocent men and the state. A singular idea undergirds each of these repressive images: that Black women are the antithesis of ideal white ladies and are therefore not quite human. Through representing healthy sexuality as a fragment of the larger self, the content creators who animate this chapter script Black women as full human beings whose erotic capabilities are an extension of their humanity. It is in this way that they approximate what CaShawn Thompson, the originator of the Black Girl Magic motto, envisioned when she crafted the declaration. Thompson believed that all Black women were dignified and worthy of honor, regardless of their proximity to respectable ladyhood. By compelling viewers to attend to characters whose complicated erotic lives either fail to align with their perceived social status or otherwise exclude them from being worthy of visibility, Akil, Rae, and Waithe, challenge elitist assumptions of who deserves to be seen and heard.

Flawed by Design: The Construction of Mary Jane Paul

Being Mary Jane's entrance into the media landscape in 2013, shepherded by creator and executive producer Mara Brock Akil, prompted critics and viewers to compare the lead character with another primetime Black leading lady, Olivia Pope of ABC's *Scandal*. Like Pope, Mary Jane is an elite college–educated woman who, despite her professional success and alignment with normative beauty standards, finds herself unmarried in her late thirties. Falling into the gendered dichotomy that pits romance against career, both characters lead deviant love lives initially marked by affairs with married men. Many viewers that grew to embrace Olivia, whose transgressions occur in a lily-white fantasy world, refused to give equal pardon to Mary Jane.[6] Unlike Pope, Mary Jane mostly lives in the heterogeneous Black mecca of Atlanta. She often uses sex and alcohol to cope with disappointments, and although she fails to live up to the ideals that she espouses, is often critical when those around her deviate from Black bourgeois conventions. The lead character's imperfections "hit too close to home," as one blogger explained, and pierced the performance of strength attached to magical Black womanhood.[7]

Although the protagonist publicly embodies the ideal of the empowered Black woman and seems well-poised to complete the Black lady image by becoming a wife and mother, her private persona reveals that the projected self is a fragile façade. Akil makes this tension between the two selves apparent by giving the lead character two names. Mary Jane Paul is the name that appears on her professional resumé and the moniker that her friends use. Pauletta

Patterson is the character's given and family name, reserved for intimate settings with the other Pattersons. Mary Jane presents herself as composed and capable, regardless of the context. She is an excellent journalist who goes to work early and stays late to get the story right. She is a heroine to family and friends, willing to sacrifice anything to support those she loves. She is a hopeful romantic who understands Black, heterosexual marriage to be the basis for racial uplift. Conversely, Pauletta is often unhinged. She isolates herself from others out of fear that her flaws will be exposed. She is envious of those who enjoy the things that she believes she deserves, and she tends to express her frustration in heinous and irresponsible acts. Combining behaviors associated with respectability and deviance in a single character is an intentional strategy that Akil uses to expose Black women's complex nature. "I love to draw the viewers in with images that they think they know already, and I like to sort of dismantle them," she said in a 2015 interview.[8] The less easily her characters fit into extremes, the more they can be appreciated as fully human.

While Mary Jane's unfulfilling love life enhances the dramatic appeal of the series, her labor as a journalist and a family nurturer complicates the character. As the host of her own cable news show, *Talk Back*, Mary Jane imbues her work with a critical race consciousness often lacking in mainstream news. Her fictional show has a format similar to MSNBC's *The ReidOut*. Like Joy Reid, Mary Jane uses her show as a vehicle to explore racially charged issues in all of their nuances and is unrelenting in her critique of guests who espouse thinly veiled racist views.[9] Although the talented tenth ethos that pervaded her childhood home tends to impede Mary Jane's capacity to interrogate her own class privilege—her father was the first African American executive for an Atlanta-based airline, her mother a school principal and member of Jack and Jill of America—she continuously reaches for a Black feminist framework to enlighten her viewers.

Furthermore, the lead character is perpetually attempting to enlighten, inform, or otherwise uplift someone in her intimate circle of family and friends. An older brother who is a recovering drug addict, a niece who is a young, single mother, a younger brother in college who moonlights as a marijuana dealer, a suicidal best friend, and a mother battling lupus trade places as Mary Jane's charity targets. Although she complains about her family's expectations, it is clear that the protagonist garners validation from playing the rescuer. Focusing on other people's dysfunction distracts Mary Jane from the reality of her own. Beneath the veil of respectability that her degrees and salary have afforded her, she struggles with the same flaws she attempts to correct in others.

While the first season of the series offers the audience an interior view of Mary Jane's life, the second season draws the character's shortcomings into public settings where her vulnerability becomes more glaring through the constant juxtaposition of Mary Jane and Pauletta. In the premiere episode's opening scene, Mary Jane strips down to her underwear and shatters the floor-to-ceiling window that flanks the front of her house. Here, Mara Brock Akil foreshadows the dismantling that awaits the protagonist throughout the season. Although Mary Jane is herself the cause of the broken glass, as the season unfolds it becomes clear that she is reluctant to relinquish her facade of magical Black womanhood.

For a moment, the window shattering reads as a move toward freedom. The object Mary Jane uses to facilitate the breaking—a small, cubical fish tank strikingly similar in design to the architecture of the main character's mid-century modern home—contains a solitary fish that represents her own existence as a discontented, unmarried woman. As a television journalist and the daughter of well-connected parents, she too lives her life on display, entrapped by the very ideal that is supposed to afford her greater social capital. Just before shattering the glass Mary Jane addresses the fish: "Hey Starsky, you still looking for Hutch?"[10] Having just returned home from a fraught visit to her ex-boyfriend's house, which he now shares with another woman who is pregnant with his child, the wounded woman appears eager to finally unshackle herself from the need to continue pursuing her own "Hutch." She is releasing herself from the yoke of old desires and unmet expectations.

In the very next scene, two weeks have passed, and Mary Jane is hosting a dinner party for her equally accomplished upper-middle class social circle. As she and her guests muse over Walter Mosley's *Life Out of Context* and debate the vicissitudes of African American experiences during and after the Jim Crow era, it becomes clear that Mary Jane's self-transformation has been thwarted. Just as she has repaired the broken window of her home, she also attempts to reclaim a life of bourgeois respectability which she believes is her birthright. Reaching back to old tactics of self-aggrandizement, Mary Jane proceeds to do something the audience has seen many times before, scrutinize others to assuage her own feelings of inadequacy and shame. The rant that precipitates at her dinner party, however, is more malicious than previous speeches Mary Jane has given under the guise of tough love. Beginning with an essentializing critique of the Black poor in which she borrows from Bill Cosby's logic of the underclass to make her point, she eventually aims her contempt at her own two brothers and the only married couple in attendance at the party.[11]

Through this failed attempt at progression, Mara Brock Akil makes it clear that Mary Jane is not only unable to move on from her immediate past, but that she is also tethered to a larger history of repressive images of Black womanhood. By infusing the scene with the rhetoric of twenty-first century debates about respectability, Akil situates Mary Jane's romantic struggles within the context of gendered notions of racial uplift. She lashes out at others to deflect attention away from herself and what she perceives as her own inability to perform ideal Blackness. Her unspoken angst is finally revealed when her brother responds to the verbal attack with a jab of his own: "Wow, now I see why David doesn't want you. Now I see why he's with that white chick."[12] In alignment with historical discourses, Mary Jane has been excluded from the conception of true womanhood because she is emasculating, and therefore undesirable. Meanwhile, a white woman has effortlessly taken her place. Since Mary Jane invests in a neoliberal ideology of success that points to "wanting more," as the most important factor for achievement, she gives herself little room to deviate from the model of respectability embodied by her parents. Mary Jane reads her singleness as a form of racial delinquency, as the result of her own brokenness, and as the cause of her unhappiness.

The unfiltered humanity that Mary Jane embodies initially repelled some viewers, but gratified others. In an article penned for *TheAtlantic.com*, Enuma Okoro reads Mary Jane as a more authentic and relatable Black woman figure because "unlike Olivia Pope, Mary Jane does not pretend to be an unbreakable force unto herself."[13] Indeed, Mary Jane's abundant shortcomings are the result of one Black woman creator's effort to disrupt images of professional Black women as flawless, invincible, and non-sexual, and to replace them with images imbued with the messiness of everyday life. When asked to describe the character in one word during a promotional interview that aired on BET.com, Mara Brock Akil responded with two: beautifully flawed.

> It was our tagline, I think, for last season, but really, she's beautifully flawed.
> I think we need to start embracing that part of our humanity, especially Black women. We're trying to sort of correct the wrongness that has been done to us, so we want positive images to combat all these negative stereotypes. And I really feel like positive images can be just as damaging as negative images. . . .
> We're human beings. We're going to make mistakes. The strong Black woman is going to mess up. She is not strong all the time.[14]

The motive behind exposing Mary Jane's vulnerability, then, is to encourage Black women to envision the worst of themselves alongside their best qualities, and to make peace with the tension.

Locating Black Women's Sexuality in the Between

Recuperating Black women's sexuality is among Akil's key objectives in *Being Mary Jane*. She breathes life into her characters by treating them as human beings whose sexuality is a given, rather than a mystery that must be explained to the audience. Akil aims for enlightenment through familiarity. Seeing Mary Jane urinate and masturbate in the first episode of the series reminds the audience of what is already known, while also beaconing toward a more profound truth. Black women's sexuality, like the urge to empty the bladder, is not a

marker of bestiality but a marker of humanity. The complexity of that sexuality demands no further justification than does the basic functions of the human
urinary system. Since the bathroom is a gendered space, on and off screen, Mary
Jane's urination scene is itself a critique of "normal humanness" as defined by
Hollywood.[15]

Taking its cues from the philosophical project of whiteness that Sylvia Wynter refers to as the "invention of Man2," mainstream cinema and television
have framed the bathroom as a place where men participate in the self-relieving,
biological process of peeing, and where women take up the coerced act of primp-
ing.[16] By breaching conventional notions of masculinity and femininity, Akil
and the other series writers direct viewers to engage Mary Jane as a human,
not an Other. Rather than contributing to an apologetics of Black womanhood, Akil imbues her protagonist with the right to simultaneously embody
and express modes of being that seem at once to be incompatible. Mary Jane,
like her creator, is cognizant of the stereotypes that threaten every move of the
Black female body; such an awareness is yoked to Black female consciousness.
Nevertheless, in Akil's story world, the constraints of public perception fail to
subjugate the untidy nature of human desire.

Indeed, the complexity of Mary Jane's sexuality is most vivid through messy
moments—when the reality of her sexual nature bubbles up around the elements of her life that more easily yield to self-management. Mary Jane's vulnerability exists alongside of her strength. The capacity to be seducible and
dominant, and the tension that arises from those qualities, further distinguishes
the protagonist from Black woman archetypes. The show's sophomore season
explores Mary Jane's ambiguous relationship with pleasure as she moves across
a spectrum of agency. Even as she avows her right to engage her sexuality as she
pleases, she struggles to make peace with the limitations of her control over the
body. In episode six, entitled "Pulling the Trigger," tensions around bodily
autonomy and perception come to the fore when Mary Jane experiences an
inadvertent orgasm.

Early in the sophomore season the lead character is faced with the awareness that she may have forever lost her one true love. Following the classic formula for redemption narratives, Mary Jane attempts to redesign her life around
new dreams that appear to be more firmly within her grasp. Inclusive of this
attempt to reconstruct her reality is securing a career-enhancing interview, and
undergoing the process of oocyte cryopreservation, or egg freezing. Her goals
to advance her career and subvert the biological clock collide when she is finally
granted an interview in a subject's home.

In the midst of debating the gendered nature of racial oppression with Shelton Blake, a prominent attorney who has targeted Mary Jane with increasingly overt romantic advances and has promised to offer information for a story,
Mary Jane pauses the conversation to visit the bathroom. Although suspicious

of visiting the source in his home, the appeal of an exclusive compels her to agree to the meeting. The conversation pivots toward the sexual when Shelton comments on her physique.

> MARY JANE: Truth be told, not only has society tried to smother Black women, we've also been smothered by the very Black men who claim to defend our honor. But at least you guys have someone to go home to, chit chat with, talk out your troubles. But who the hell takes care of us? Who's left to love the Black woman? [. . .]
>
> SHELTON: Yeah, you're sexy.
>
> MARY JANE: Ok, see that's the belittling that I was just talking about. Why is it that men automatically have to reduce us down to our sexuality? Why can't you, excuse me, hear me, and not try to minimalize me down to a pair of tits and ass? I thought you were a little smarter than that.
>
> SHELTON: I do hear you, Mary Jane. That's why I think you're sexy. . . . You know what I find most attractive about you, is your passion, your wit, your, your perceptions on life. That's why I called you. Not because of your full lips, your high cheekbones, or those soulful brown eyes that you have. I called you because you are the absolute best person to share this story with the world.
>
> MARY JANE: Can you show me which way to your powder room please?[17]

Upon entering the bathroom and finding physical evidence of what she suspects may have been prompted by her hormone treatment, Mary Jane telephones her gynecologist.

> I'm one of Dr. Morris' patients and I just experienced like a, like a discharge. No, more of like a massive orgasm. [inaudible response] Uh, no, like totally out of the blue. [inaudible response] I just took it this morning. [inaudible response] Oh so it's totally normal. [inaudible response] Ok, ok.[18]

The fierce timbre in Mary Jane's voice as she presents her argument to Shelton reveals that she is speaking to an interior battle between fulfilling the self and capitulating to external forces, a struggle both specific to her own present circumstances and known to Black women generally. While she acknowledges that her desires matter and can be no more eradicated than those of any man, she has become exhausted from the public assault on that truth. Each step she takes toward an autonomous femininity is met with an impediment—a man who fails to love her the way she wants to be loved, a reproductive system that fails to align with her ideal life sequence, a public that rejects her nonconformity to gendered restrictions of desire. Collectively, these oppositions fray her sense of self. Nevertheless, Akil's use of tensions in this scene demonstrate that while Mary Jane's dignity—and that of all Black women—may be under attack, her humanity has not been undone.

Under the barrage of caricature and other calamitous tactics, Mary Jane's capacity to fully embrace her humanity and stand in the complexity of Black womanhood is constrained. Although she seeks to correct the falsehoods and impossible expectations that smother Black women, she also absorbs them to some degree. Her response to Shelton's initial statement about her sexual appeal reveals a reading of the body as being in opposition to the mind. The challenge, as presented by the writer(s), is to understand intellect, soul, and body as mutually constitutive, rather than yielding to a societal standard that seeks to compartmentalize these components of self. The burden that society assigns to Black women's bodies obscures what Shelton intends as a compliment and prohibits Mary Jane from reveling in this moment of potential gratification. Shelton's corrective re-presentation of his thoughts hints at the preferred definition of Black female sexuality that Akil invites the audience to exchange for the lady-whore dichotomy.

Through the conversation between Shelton and Mary Jane, Akil communicates that her efforts to place Black women's humanity beyond pristine and negative images is not an indication that she ignores their durability. She acknowledges the distortions and invites the audience to transcend them. In this case, the invitation is to accept Shelton's assertion that his appreciation of Mary Jane's lips, cheekbones, and eyes are bound up with his attraction to her mind and rhetorical abilities. By defining Shelton's spectatorial pleasure and Mary Jane's unpredictable physical pleasure as "totally normal," the writer(s) render the *denial* of sexuality as the abnormal practice. This episode communicates that Black women can be vulnerable to erotic desire without being hypersexual. And that we need not shoehorn our sexuality into the narrowing confines of magic or any other external mold.

In a sponsored conversation published on the network website following the "Pulling the Trigger" episode, Akil explains her rationale behind these unorthodox scenes of everyday life where female sexuality obtrudes the ordinary. The creator's aim is to render Black female desire as unremarkable and habitual as the mundane moments that it seems to disrupt: "Women need to own their sexuality. Otherwise, if we don't, then it kind of sends the message that we're really only here for a man's convenience. And I think for women, but specifically for women of color, if you are owning your sexuality, somehow, you're a whore or a stripper, or otherwise you need to be pious. And it's like no, no, no . . . I'm a lot in between here."[19] These words reiterate that the emphasis on sexuality in Akil's female-centered work is an intentional component in her larger narrative strategy. Leaning into the subject matter that is typically neglected or framed in ways that elicit shame is part of her creative mission. The sexually themed stereotypes that haunt Black female images do not repel her, in fact, they seem to inspire her. In the aforementioned interview, as in her fictional work, Akil taps into a shared code of anxieties in order to hail an intended viewership. Once she has captured their attention, she offers an alternative way of relating to the sexual self—"own[ing]"—and an alternative language of being—"in between."

While the television creator's ethos runs close to the philosophical edge of the commercial empowerment enterprise, Akil's emphasis on sexuality and choice is grounded in an ethic of care, not a profit agenda. "When women are empowered by their own sexuality, by their choice, they will be responsible," she said in a September 2020 interview. "They will buy the condoms, they're not going to wait for a man. They will take care of themselves."[20] High HIV infection rates among African American women was one of the issues that Akil wanted to address in her shows by exploring sexuality. Black women in America led in new infections for the virus during the period when the showrunner was working on her first series, *Girlfriends* (2000–2008). With that reality in mind, she aimed to write a world where it was normal for college-educated Black women to not only have orgasms, but to talk about having them.

The resistance that Akil often met in her quest to normalize Black women's sexuality and collapse the mammy-jezebel dichotomy further evidences the extent to which her creative maneuvers have upset enduring logics. On several occasions she defeated corporate executives who did not share her vision for Black womanhood. She recalls that in one such meeting, her combatants were so angered by her insistence that her women characters be allowed to verbalize their sexual desires, like their male counterparts, that they "turned red."[21] "I said, *so, what you're telling me is, jokes about sex, when it's for the pleasure of men, they're ok. But when women have their own choice of pleasure, then that's not ok.*"[22] The writer-showrunner anticipated these battles and fought them strategically, at times claiming victory through persistence alone. By framing these struggles in political terms, that is as institutional conflicts about the terms under which Black women would be defined and reflected, Akil reveals the profound agenda that has guided her work in an industry focused on frivolity.

In addition to her strategic use of scripts and paratexts, Mara Brock Akil also uses public lectures as a mechanism for steering the interpretation of her content and disrupting restrictive logics of representation in general. The demand for positive portrayals is a recurring theme in her talks that she typically uses as an entry point to expound on her rationale for writing Black women's sexuality into her work. At a 2015 conference held at Rutgers University, Akil challenged the metrics used to police Black bodies on-screen and explained their destructive capacity: "I can't write positive images because that would be buying into fixing an image I never believed in. . . . Participating in rewriting the wrongs keeps me chasing behind something already done, or better yet, validating the lie by trying to offer a counter experience. It doesn't allow me to just simply tell the story of our humanity and not apologize for the rough edges."[23] Her speech proposes an artistic framework that reads sex scenes and other dramatic tools as more than customary conveniences devised as scene enhancers. Mary Jane's "rough edges," and those of other characters Akil creates, are interventions that envision Black womanhood through vulnerability, not magic.

Mainstreaming (Awkward) Black Female Consciousness in *Insecure*

One of the things that sets writer-producer Issa Rae apart from her counterparts is her emergence within the television landscape. Beginning her career as a digital storyteller with the online series *The Mis-Adventures of Awkward Black Girl*, Rae initially conceptualized her brand through a multi-series catalogue offered exclusively through her YouTube channel. Her distinct authorial voice, and undoubtedly the millions of millennial consumers drawn to her content, garnered interest from Hollywood executives.[24] Struggling to locate her own personality and quirks within the parameters of Blackness normalized among her peer group, Rae used her content to imagine a hybrid identity that could accommodate her experience. Her embodiment of awkward Blackness ruptured the instinctively cool and fierce Black Girl Magic image, replacing it with something more grounded and self-referential. When pressured to mute the racial specificity of her original Awkward Black Girl narrative, Rae resisted. "The Black part is what makes it special," she stated in a 2017 interview. "We don't get to be those characters. . . . That is an identity that we're not allowed to have."[25]

Following a failed project with ABC where Rae claimed she struggled to negotiate industry standards while maintaining her cultural fluency, she recommitted to her own rhetoric of messy Black womanhood.[26] The outcome of her internal artistic reckoning is *Insecure*, a series focused around two young adult professionals, Issa and Molly, who are best friends. Together they confront romantic and professional breakthroughs and perils as they work to define themselves. Issa and Molly's friendship began in college and has strengthened over time as they work through various challenges and triumphs, together. They give each other permission to be painfully honest, even as they keep secrets from lovers and other women in their larger friendship group. Given the depth of their sisterhood, Issa and Molly are also capable of hurting each other with their words. Nevertheless, this is a relationship that survives intense arguments. Through their friendship Rae invites the audience into an intimate area of Black women's experiences, that space that they may only share with one or two others in the span of a lifetime. The friendship is a critical gateway to Rae's particular vision of vulnerable Black womanhood. The juxtaposition of each character's actions, alongside of her perceptions of herself and of her interpretations of the other, constitute a range of intersecting and competing ideas of Blackness, friendship, sexuality, and respectability.

Importantly, *Insecure* is rooted in a cipher of Blackness. The consciousness that shapes the show materializes in the visual, sonic, and psychic elements that connect each episode. Landmarks of South Los Angeles, such as Randy's Donuts, that punctuate each scene locate the characters in an urban terrain just beginning to succumb to the stampeding demands of 21st century gentrification. Although the lead character, Issa, is required to engage the Black and brown domains of Los Angeles for her work at an educational nonprofit (she resigns from the organization in season two), she travels these areas as a native. Her white coworkers routinely look to Issa to clarify the peoples and places of an urban experience that befuddles them as outsiders. She occupies a dual positioning. Issa's coworkers envision her as one of *us*, but also as one of *them*. Her status as a degree-holding professional has not stripped her of cultural consciousness, it has only heightened her frustrations with the colorblind ethos that pervades the white world around her. Furthermore, the music that Issa listens to on her car radio and the subtle code switches she enacts when transitioning from her white liberal office setting to social settings emphasize her Blackness.[27]

One of the most profound maneuvers that Rae makes toward establishing Black women's humanness through *Insecure* is in situating character narratives as widely accessible, while simultaneously emphasizing their particularities. Rae redeems her main characters' subjecthood from the peripheral function of representing a foil to normative white womanhood. Her story world situates Black women as both an entry point to universal discourses of relationships, career, and self-concept, and as exhibitions of a pointedly Black feminist aesthetic.[28]

In many episodes reflective surfaces function as portals that transport viewers into the soul circuit of the main character, revealing patterns between external triggers and the emotional reactions they provoke. Viewers also have access to the stream of self-dialogue that lives in the protagonist's—Issa's—head through voice-overs and her iconic, self-centered rap performances. Taken together, Rae's series inhabits the complex realm of Black female interiority. Nevertheless, she envisions the show as an expansive project that dislocates culturally specific experiences from the margins of public discourse and drives them to the center. Rae promotes her series as universally entertaining for all viewers who value comedic performance, even if they cannot access her specific consciousness.

Establishing *Insecure* as mainstream televisual content requires persistent and deliberate intervention from the creator. Such was the case in a 2016 interview conducted by Gayle King for *CBS This Morning* prior to the show's premiere.

> KING: Are you concerned that people will think it's only relatable to Black people or Black women?
>
> RAE: No. I mean, I'm concerned with the people who are open-minded enough to watch and who feel like, [they] want to know more about this.
>
> KING: You've been compared to *Curb Your Enthusiasm*.
>
> RAE: Which is an honor because I love Larry David's work. [In] that show there were a lot of Jewish references and you know I would either look them up or just . . . figure them out by context clues and still laugh. And . . . you know, that wasn't an issue for me. I didn't see a show about like, oh a Jewish guy, an old Jewish guy, what am I supposed to do with that, that's not for me.[29]

Rae counters the critique that her series is not mainstream by articulating a revised logic of the relationship between Black artistic expression and mass culture. She refuses to sanitize the aural, verbal, and visual rhetoric of the show, or dislocate racial markers from their Black cultural context. Instead, she insists that viewers meet the text on her terms. Rae's response ruptures hegemonic discourses which define normalcy through whiteness, and therefore require artists to dilute ethnic signifiers to appeal to white, arguably more desirable, audiences. Furthermore, by pointing to her own amusement with another comedy series outside of her experiential reality, Rae both refutes the invisibility of whiteness and the presumed inferiority of Black female audiences. If shows with all-white casts that reflect exclusive perspectives and sensibilities are still accepted as mainstream, ghettoizing content from Black artists that is similarly oriented to reflect a particular aesthetic is irrational. In this and other interviews Issa Rae directs audiences to register the strangeness of whiteness, and the commonality of Blackness.

Even when interviewed for a hip-hop audience on nationally syndicated radio show *The Breakfast Club*, Rae continued to emphasize the value of *Insecure* as a text that frames Black characters as ordinary people managing dilemmas and successes, rather than magical figures. "We're just trying to remind people that Black people are human at the end of the day," she asserted. "And we're not shunning the fact that we are Black, like that is very clear."[30] On the one hand, Rae presents her show as an educational tool for white audiences that normalizes Blackness without diluting it. Conversely, her project also draws on and assuages the angst of representing marginalized populations by offering expanded notions of dignity. Rather than force her characters to justify their presence in the televisual sphere through pristine behavior, she frees them to be awkward, untidy, and vulnerable without compromising their Blackness. By satisfying network ratings expectations and attracting a racially mixed viewership across its first four seasons, *Insecure* demonstrates the capacity of Black art to convey mainstream, mundane stories.[31]

Insecure as the "Prequel to Black Girl Magic"

Much like with her web series, *The Mis-Adventures of Awkward Black Girl*, Issa Rae constructed *Insecure* as an intervention into the universe of magical Black women characters that Hollywood had become so fond of in the mid-2010s. Even the name of the series, as she discussed on Twitter prior to Insecure's premiere, was intended to guide viewers toward a more expansive view of Black womanhood less grounded in excellence and sophistication. "A lot of you have asked why I decided to call the show *Insecure*, and it's because there's this like narrative going around, that's awesome, that Black women are fierce; they're strong, they're flawless. And I don't know that life. And my friends definitely don't know that life. So, I wanted to center a show around like weak Black women and the uncertainty that they feel on that journey to get to greatness. It's like the prequel to Black Girl Magic."[32]

Despite being college-educated professionals the lead characters of *Insecure* consistently face complications in their careers, friendships, and romantic lives. Some dilemmas, such as the significant salary gap between Molly and her white male counterpart, reflect structural inequities and exhibit the characters' resistance strategies and coping mechanisms. The relationship struggles that animate the series, however, are more often consequences of impulsive behavior and poor judgement. Although one member of the central friendship group presents as a class-conscious and respectable wife, Issa and Molly muddle through their love lives with little finesse or wisdom. Through relationship failures, Rae invites the audience to reconsider "weak Black women," and, consequently, interrogate their gendered expectations of strength and restraint.[33]

Rae's most generative use of vulnerability was an act of infidelity perpetrated by Issa in the first season of *Insecure*. At the time of the transgression, Issa was in the midst of a years' long relationship with Lawrence, her unemployed boyfriend. Despite cohabitating, the couple's intimacy had eroded under the strain of individual frustrations and miscommunication. Disenchantment with her career, exhaustion from Lawrence's professional drought, and the angst of approaching her thirties culminate in the premiere episode, compelling Issa to confront her biting discontentment. While giving a presentation about her foundation's offerings at a predominantly Black and Latinx high school, the students target Issa with questions about the areas of her life where she is most confused and dissatisfied: work, her relationship status, her adornment choices, and her vocal inflections, which they read as contrived and racially inauthentic.

Frustrated with the interrogation, Issa offers the students a brief summary of her life in the hopes that their interest will shift to the after-school program that she is there to discuss.

> ISSA: Ok! Since you guys are so interested in my personal life, here it is. I'm twenty-eight, actually twenty-nine 'cause today's my birthday. Uh, I came from a great family. I have a college degree. I work in the nonprofit world because I like to give back. I've been with my boyfriend for five years. And I did this to my hair on purpose. So, I hope that covers everything. Does anybody actually have any questions about We Got Y'all?
>
> DAYNIECE (STUDENT): Why ain't you married?
>
> ISSA: I'm just not, right now.
>
> DAYNIECE: My dad said ain't nobody checkin' for bitter ass Black women anymore.
>
> ISSA: . . . Tell your dad that Black women aren't bitter, they're just tired of being expected to settle for less.[34]

The intrusive line of questioning within the first few minutes of the series establishes Rae's method of exposure as a storytelling tool. Issa's attempts to deny or mute her emotions, to practice dissemblance in accordance with a fierce or magical Black woman image, is futile. Although the protagonist goes about shedding her "aggressively passive" demeanor, as Rae describes it, in imperfect ways, the writer-creator frames the character's development toward an empowered subjectivity as natural and ultimately healthy.[35] A spontaneous tryst with a former boyfriend is her first attempt to assuage the disappointment that haunts her interior life. In the season finale, Lawrence confronts Issa with suspicions of her unfaithfulness, prompting her to confess.

Rae anticipated that writing infidelity into her lead character's story would jolt viewers. Some Black publics expect cultural producers to generate stories that "protect or save [B]lack women, and [B]lack communities more generally, from narratives of sexual and familial pathology, through the embrace of conventional bourgeois propriety in the arenas of sexuality and domesticity."[36] Such a strategy of public containment is rooted in a valid anxiety of exposure and distortion that, as Candice M. Jenkins explains, is ultimately an effect of Black sexual exploitation during and after slavery. Jenkins argues: "In such an over-determined cultural framework, in which one's Black body is always already assumed to be signifying desire, the added vulnerability that comes with expressing something as personal and deeply felt as sexual attraction, filial affection, human tenderness, or need, takes exposure to a painful extreme."[37]

Thus, Rae knew she would be transgressing racial dictates of sexual denial and silence by daring to make her series' central character a cheater, something far beyond the bounds of Black Girl Magic. In fact, a desire to disrupt the prototype of female protagonists that has proven lucrative in Hollywood motivated Rae.[38]

Although Issa's weaknesses are accessible from the first episode, the character does not read as a profligate. She is guilty, yet also underserved within her relationship. She is eager to assert her right to pleasure, yet capricious in her pursuit to secure happiness. Rae explained in a blog post that she intentionally situated the act of infidelity in a more stable moment in the relationship to direct viewers away from assigning blame to Lawrence.[39] Instead, she invites the audience to consider the transgression as a critical juncture along a journey of self-discovery. It involves Lawrence, and impacts him, but ultimately, the experience does not revolve around him.

After months of avoidance and tension between Issa and Lawrence, the conversation that facilitates closure in the relationship brings Rae's vision of constructive vulnerability to the fore. The conversation unfolds in the finale episode of *Insecure*'s sophomore season.[40]

ISSA: Lawrence, I wanted to be better, for you, because of you. But, somewhere along the way I depended on you to be better for both of us. And when you were going through what you were going through, I just didn't know how to handle it.

LAWRENCE: I mean, what could you have done though?

ISSA: More! You know, that's when you needed me to be better for the both of us. And I didn't even know how to do that for myself.

LAWRENCE: That makes two of us.

ISSA: And you know, what I did—

LAWRENCE: You don't have to go through that.

ISSA: It was the worst thing I could have ever done to you. And I wish I could somehow convince you that it wasn't about you. You've only ever loved me and expected me to want the best for you. And I promise I did. I still do. Lawrence, I still love you so much.

LAWRENCE: I love you too.[41]

Although it has taken her an entire season to find clarity, Issa eventually reaches a point where she can own her shortcomings without allowing them to define her. Cheating, in this case, is not an indicator of some intrinsic pathology that demands a cleansing. Rather, infidelity is an outcome of Issa's immaturity and inexperience in managing the competing demands of her partner and herself. Without justifying the transgression, Rae guides the audience to read the act in conjunction with the rational frustrations and valid desires that inspired it. The act of betrayal is no small blemish, but it is also not the totality of Issa's story. Furthermore, Rae also frames the decision to cheat as a productive one in that it signals the character's choice to be "aggressively active for once."[42] Issa's flaws are simultaneously generative, irrefutable, and relatable.

The rhetoric of vulnerability that animates Rae's work on *Insecure* answers a third wave Black feminist call for Black women to be recognized as "fallible human beings and not women of mythical proportions," that is, to be visible without being magical.[43] As Kimberly Springer asserts, the fight against "strongblackwoman syndrome," or the notion that Black women possess superhuman capabilities to overcome adversity and therefore have no need of reasonable human allowances and protections, has been an ongoing concern for Black women intellectuals.[44] While Springer's study focused on literature, Rae's televisual work demonstrates that commercial media can also function as a site for resistance. Furthermore, by taking up Black women's vulnerability within the context of heterosexual romantic relationships, an arena where the Strong Black Woman trope is continuously invoked, Rae reinforces the feminist orientation of her work.

"Gay Black Girls Rock, Too": Lena Waithe's Ascension

By the time Lena Waithe ascended Beverly Bond's *Black Girls Rock! Awards* show stage to receive the "Shot Caller" honor in 2018, she had already received an Emmy for her writing on Netflix's *Master of None* and all of the fanfare that attends such an award. Unlike accolades from the Academy of Television Arts and Sciences, the Black Girls Rock! trophy was not likely to help the rising film and television star secure more lucrative deals or opportunities with prestigious studios or networks, but it would furnish her with a certain kind of cultural capital rare for a Black queer woman. Bond's awards show had become a unique space in the Black television landscape since BET began broadcasting it in 2010. Waithe's honor positioned her alongside Shonda Rhimes and Iyanla Vanzant, former "Shot Caller" award recipients; and given what Bond's awards show and broader enterprise had come to represent in Black commercial culture, this honor officially sanctioned Lena Waithe as an openly queer and masculine-presenting magical Black woman.

Waithe received her award in 2018 on a network that had been critiqued as hostile to LGBTQ+ figures and had yet to feature a queer character as a star in any of its original programming. The actor-writer-producer that Black Girls Rock! had just declared a "shot caller" would soon use her clout to fill gaps in BET's representation of Blackness, but her awards show speech was the beginning. Having recently shed her chest-length locks and the proximity to traditional femininity that they had afforded her, Waithe ascended the stage that night prepared to make a statement with her physical aesthetic and her words. Just before leaving her seat, she shared a kiss with her then fiancée, Alano Mayo—another first in BET awards-show history. Using a rhetorical strategy common in the Black Girl Magic era, Waithe leveraged her personal struggles with image and expectations to offer a broader homily about self-actualization. "I was holding onto a piece of myself that felt feminine," she remarked of her former hairstyle. "And that piece of femininity made people feel comfortable; but then I came to the realization that that's not my job. . . . So, I decided to get free. And tonight, I wanted to speak to you about getting free."[45]

She went on to encourage the audience to identify their own barriers to liberation, suggesting that they might be struggling to terminate a poor relationship, or an unfulfilling job, or to release a limiting self-narrative. The amen-punctuated applause the crowd offered in return suggested that Waithe's message fell on welcoming ears. In addition to encouraging her listeners to realize their dreams, regardless of whether their choices met external expectations, Waithe reminded the audience that she was actively modeling this mode of living before their eyes. She was a Black queer woman from the South Side of Chicago who had managed to garner recognition from a contemporary respectability institution, without betraying her truth. The symbolism of the moment was not lost on her. By accepting the award, Waithe was claiming her space within the Black Girl Magic enterprise and declaring that "gay Black girls rock, too."[46]

Publicly intimate moments like these, where she connects to her cultural community through vulnerability, are just as important to Waithe as the fictional scenes that she pours onto the page. Her well-decorated career has provided many such opportunities on award show stages, where she reveals the philosophies that guide her work. Waithe's stated intention is to transcend the typical platitudes and thank-you-mamas by offering provocative insights. Thus, whatever enhanced capital her accolades afford her, they are a means to an end. Her objective is to marshal the privileged status that accompanies magical Black womanhood to serve a greater political end. Waithe therefore considers herself an artist-activist who creates what she describes as protest art, content that is as politically insightful as it is entertaining. "I got to be a journalist," she said in a 2018 interview. "I want to write about the world the way it is so that way we can look at it and re-evaluate."[47] While her shows—*The Chi, Boomerang,* and *Twenties*—trouble various hegemonic notions, compelling viewers to re-evaluate Black gender norms and erotic expression is consistent throughout. In *Twenties*, Waithe dares the audience to see a reflection of themselves in a main character whose self-presentation and counterproductive habits place her outside the bounds of respectable magic.

"My Life Ain't That Messy": Queering the Black Woman Protagonist

Placing a young Lena Waithe within the character of Hattie, portrayed by Jonica T. Gibbs, is not a difficult task; neither is it challenging to understand

Mara Brock Akil as the inspiration for the Ida B. character. Beyond the physical resemblances—which is especially striking between Akil and Sophina Brown, the actor who performs Ida B.—each role carries traces of reality plucked from Waithe's lived experiences and massaged into the mold of a half-hour cable comedy. In fact, Waithe sees parts of herself at different time periods in each of the characters. "I am Ida now, you know, but I also used to be Hattie," she said in a promotional interview for *Twenties*.[48] "It's a very interesting thing to write scenes with them because I know what Ida means when she tells Hattie I spent so much time trying to make it; and now that I've made it, I realize that I was happier when I was struggling."[49]

This tension between visibility as a cherished prize and exposure as the price one pays for such a victory is one of the complicated truths that manifests in Waithe's series and in her life as a media figure. Like Hattie, she spent the better half of her twenties clawing for a platform in Hollywood but having reached her goal and launched her own production company, Hillman Grad, she strives to protect some form of private space beyond the screen.[50] "Once you've crossed over into a space of success, then your life is about maintaining it. . . . With more success and more, you know, money and attention, comes more stress. It actually becomes less fun."[51] Waithe's message bleeds through each character's nuances, like the fact that Hattie, who seems to overindulge in frivolousness, reads James Baldwin and articulates an informed critique of Ida B.'s show. Although the beloved television writer and creator, Ida B., seems to have arrived, she carries her own regrets and secrets, such as giving up a child for adoption when she was in college.

By writing a sense of discontent and desire into Ida B.'s character, which she juxtaposes with Hattie's recklessness and vivacity, Waithe demonstrates that neither woman lives free of disappointment or struggle. In the premiere episode of *Twenties*, the voice-over, performed by Lena Waithe, introduces Hattie as having "found a new and creative way to screw up her life."[52] Without consistent work, the 24-year-old Los Angeles transplant has been unable to maintain timely rent payments and comes home to find that she has been evicted. Her friends, Marie and Nia, who Hattie relies on for various kinds of support, come to the rescue. Marie eventually helps Hattie secure a job as an assistant at Ida B.'s company, You Go Girl Productions, and offers her living room as temporary housing while Hattie saves money to secure a permanent residence. Marie's assistance comes at a cost, however, as she constantly lectures Hattie to begin taking her career and life more seriously. Among the issues that Marie chides Hattie to correct is her romantic choices. Were it not for her tendency to exhaust herself in relationships with women who do not identify as queer or who are otherwise unwilling to commit to a public relationship with her, Marie scolds, Hattie would have more time to devote to her professional goals.[53] Although she dreams of becoming a television writer and creating her own series, the young hopeful lacks discipline and presents as simultaneously determined and distracted. She manages to complete most of the tasks that Ida B. demands with little guidance, even when they sometimes interfere with personal plans. Nevertheless, her immaturity persists when she takes one of Ida B.'s scripts without her permission and shares it with her friends.

In addition to a flawed work ethic, Waithe also writes Hattie as an imperfect queer role model. She is unabashed about her attraction to straight women, insisting, when Marie questions her on the matter, that sexuality is fluid. Even Hattie's mother is convinced that her latest romantic interest is not actually queer and is therefore an unsuitable choice for her daughter. Hattie resists their attempts to confine her relationship to a fixed label; and in a brief encounter at a drugstore later in the season, she demonstrates that she has little investment in gender and sexuality categories altogether. Ida B. sends Hattie to fetch feminine hygiene products and a stranger misgenders her while at the store.

> STRANGER: What up, bro.
> HATTIE: [quizzical stare]
> STRANGER: Oh, my bad. My apologies for misgendering you.
> HATTIE: All good.
> STRANGER: My brother's trans, so I should know better. You on hormones?
> HATTIE: Uh, I'm, I'm not trans.
> STRANGER: Non-binary?
> HATTIE: I still don't quite know what that means.
> STRANGER: Gender queer?
> HATTIE: You know what, this is a lot. I'm gonna go get in line.[54]

Hattie's calm response and the stranger's repeated, futile attempts to find the right name for her self-presentation show him to be more fixated on the politics of their exchange than Hattie. As someone unfamiliar with certain terminology, Hattie shows that despite a gender performance that is indeed nonconformist, she does not consider herself to be a queer activist. Her adornment choices and romantic interests are individual matters that give her pleasure; she resists the compulsion to defend or define them.

That is not to say that Hattie is unaware of her own marginalization. In one scene set at You Go Girl Productions, she urges the writers to script a queer Black woman as a central character. When the writers respond to Hattie's suggestion with the defense that they have already adequately covered "the Black lesbian thing," by including a single queer woman character in the series, Hattie presses them further.[55] "I must've forgot that she was a lesbian because I never saw her kissing a woman," she says.[56] The scene is one of several moments where Waithe appears to collapse her own frustrations as a Black woman media citizen with Hattie's imagined grievances. Even within a writer's room occupied and run by Black women, queer characters languish at the margins of the script. Hattie dares to speak up on this particular day in the room where magical Black womanhood is manufactured because of a pact that she made with Marie and Nia. The trio decided that they would take one day to act out the privilege that the white men around them wield as a birthright. So, Hattie's assertion is more of a one-time decision than an intentional move toward LGBTQ+ activism. In the end, she is uninterested in making her identity a political rallying cry.

Constructing Hattie as a Black woman who happens to be a lesbian is part of Waithe's strategy to queer the traditional Black female protagonist that mainstream television has traditionally offered its audience. "Even if you aren't queer, if you aren't a girl or masculine-presenting, you still can look at her and see yourself," Waithe said.[57] By mainstreaming a character like Hattie, she aims to gesture away from the ways in which she may read as foreign and emphasize the character's vulnerabilities as relatable for a broad audience. The erotic scenes in *Twenties* underscore the notion that Hattie is just another woman stumbling through the uncertainties of young adulthood. In the premiere episode, the camera opens on two naked Black bodies, one clearly feminine and the other ambiguous, engaged in sexual play. Later the audience learns that this is Hattie and her casual partner, Lorraine. In another erotic-themed opening montage for episode five, viewers witness Hattie and Marie engage in intercourse with their respective partners and the celibate Nia pleasure herself with a vibrator. Rather than exploit Hattie's erotic life as something bizarre or needing an explanation, the writers see to it that each Black woman finds her pleasure along a spectrum of sexual practices. The fact that Hattie has sex with other women is not what makes her flawed; but the fact that she must engage partners in the middle of someone else's living room makes her juvenile.

Hattie's messy life, which a friend later muses could be the outcome of her absentee father, is obvious, but Ida B.'s drama is much better cloaked under a magical Black woman persona. The latter enjoys the clout of being able to walk into a production company that she owns where oversized posters commemorating her magazine covers and production successes adorn the walls. When she leaves work, the Hollywood mansion that she retreats to offers another reminder of all that she has achieved. Yet, it is also a bitter symbol of what professional success, becoming a force in Hollywood, has cost. She expresses her grief to Hattie one night while the two are watching a documentary together at Ida B.'s home.

HATTIE: One day I'm gone buy a house just like this.

IDA B.: Just make sure you don't live in it by yourself. [. . .] When I first moved out here, I slept on a bunk bed with a toothless girl from Ohio.

HATTIE: Damn! Thanks for making me feel better about my situation.

IDA B.: I was your age. All I wanted to do was make it. I made it, realized I was happier when I was struggling.

HATTIE: Wow. I'm so confused right now.

IDA B.: Enjoy the journey.

HATTIE: The journey sucks.[58]

The good life, that is life as a magical Black woman, is not all that Hattie imagines. Ida B. corrects her fantasy by exposing the tradeoffs that she herself confronts daily, the most significant of which is a failed marriage and a life without the child that she gave birth to but chose not to raise. Throughout the show's first season Hattie learns that despite her success, Ida B. must still curry favor with gatekeepers in Hollywood and negotiates the demands of corporate executives and Black women viewers. In a sense, the aspiring television writer is less inhibited than her boss because she faces fewer outside expectations. Ida B.'s desire to grasp the uninhibited posture that comes naturally to Hattie bubbles over in the season one finale when she kisses an unexpecting Hattie. For all the power and poise that she exudes in the fictional mass media ecosystem of *Twenties*, Ida B., like Hattie, is still a flawed woman capable of succumbing to the urges that deviate from the magical Black woman image. Like her television predecessor, Mara Brock Akil's Mary Jane, she is a multidimensional character humanized in her most vulnerable moments. By juxtaposing a 24-year-old Hattie with an equally flawed version of what she could one day become after she realizes her dream, Waithe affirms Hattie's declaration that her life "ain't that messy," or at least no less imperfect than those women deemed magical.[59]

Negotiating the Mandates of Magic

Mara Brock Akil, Issa Rae, and Lena Waithe's strategic deployment of vulnerability in *Being Mary Jane*, *Insecure*, and *Twenties* creates a pathway to humanity that does not require Black women to capitulate to hegemonic scripts to be visible. These writer-producers hold space for their characters and audiences to make peace with, and even delight in, the tensions that we embody. They have used their television series, press interviews, and social media channels to build counter-narratives that challenge the dichotomies that dehumanize Black female subjects. Their cable television programs are Black feminist expressions derivative of earlier articulations of anxiety, delight, fantasy, and fallibility. Reading these media texts into a larger tradition of subversive cultural creation—including the work of 1920s blues singers, and eighties and nineties era female MCs—facilitates a way of imagining Black women's televisual presence beyond the specters of Mammy and Jezebel, and the mandates of magic.

Since sustaining programming that centers Black women's narratives requires the capacity to maneuver cultural expectations and institutional conventions that threaten the creative spirit, these cable series represent no small triumph. Cable television, especially premium networks like HBO, defines itself as an alternative space equipped to produce raced and gendered "counterprogramming" otherwise nonexistent in network series.[60] The proliferation of caricature-laden (un)scripted shows, however, demonstrates that even projects created by Black producers often fall into hegemonic modes of representation to appeal to white audiences. Jennifer Fuller argues that Black narratives function as a branding tool that cable networks use to demonstrate that they are "on the vanguard of television programming," a quality that plays well among their target demographic of white, urban, young professionals.[61] At the same time, Black shows are expected to attract a loyal audience of African American consumers. Surviving the competing demands of industry and culture as a Black woman auteur, that is, authoring projects that fit within network logics of "edge" and "hipness," that appeal to white audiences, and that meet the televisual expectations of authentic Blackness is a complicated endeavor.[62] While they have not succeeded in producing characters completely disentangled from the baggage that enshrouds representations of marginalized bodies, the three writers of focus in this chapter have offered one template for subversive programming in a commercial medium.

Given that their series are situated within the rigid infrastructures of elite media corporations, I read Akil's, Rae's, and Waithe's creative labors, both within and beyond fictional programming, as part of their approach to navigating the Hollywood establishment as outsiders, within. Carving out an additional platform beyond their scripted series allows the auteurs to simultaneously maintain status as commercially viable producers and enunciate counterhegemonic ideas that might otherwise be obscured or diluted. For sure, the fact that Akil, Rae, and Waithe fall within the parameters of magical Black womanhood ensures them access to the mass media infrastructure that their series disrupt. These women comply with the mandates of magic, to varying degrees, so that their characters can circulate throughout popular culture uninhibited by this yoke.

There is a cost to wielding the status of magical Black woman, however; one that each series creator confronts in some form. As one of the first queer Black women with access to major studios and networks in twenty-first century Hollywood, Waithe carries the dual burden of satisfying overlapping communities with often conflicting expectations. For her, representing Black life in a way that resonates with residents from her native South Side Chicago neighborhood is just as important as making space for LGBTQ+ narratives. Yet, it is not just her productions that certain publics measure by their own standards of authenticity; they also expect Waithe's persona to meet their expectations. "When I walk out into the world, I'm a property of the public," the writer-producer-actor said in a 2018 interview.[63] When her marriage to Alana Mayo failed mere months after the couple announced their union, some members of Waithe's audience assessed that loss in the same way that they would evaluate a character's performance. It is not just the fictional figure Hattie that must shoulder public aspirations and anxieties, it is Waithe herself.

Similarly, when accusations of harassment, coercion, and infidelity began circulating around Mara Brock Akil's husband and longtime collaborator, Salim Akil, the writer-producer's career sustained a major blow. The Oprah Winfrey Network, which had enthusiastically welcomed *Love Is__*, a drama loosely based on the couple's love story, to their programming lineup, cancelled the previously scheduled second season amid the allegations. The show's termination suggests that because Akil's personal life may have deviated from the confines of Black excellence, her platform as a media citizen would suffer. Such outcomes are inevitable under the conditional agency that Black Girl Magic provides. Nevertheless, Akil and her counterparts accept the downside of visibility in order to write and attend to that which has been invisible.

Epilogue

Even before her record-shattering book release in 2018, subsequent tour in 2019, and the Netflix special and podcast that followed in 2020, Michelle Obama's status as a magical Black woman had been secured. Surviving eight years in the White House as a member of the first Black family to ever do so had already proven her to be a phenomenon. She may have occasionally emerged within the interior fantasy worlds of the most audacious among us, but undoubtedly, those who framed America on paper never envisioned Michelle Obama. Betraying the ethos of inclusion expressed in certain seminal declarations, the nation has depended upon a hierarchy that positions Black femaleness as a foil to white womanhood. This reality emerged time and time again as her husband's popularity rose and with it a barrage of rants aimed to neutralize the woman who had briefly been considered an asset to his historic campaign. And yet, after being caricatured in nearly every shade of Black trope, from ape to afro-donning anarchist, Michelle Obama persisted. More than that, she thrived—at Easter Egg Rolls on the south lawn and in conversation with the likes of Oprah Winfrey at the United States of Women Summit, on Democratic National Convention stages and on Hollywood soundstages in push-up contests against talk show hosts. Before the publishing feat she was already a privileged media citizen.

Americans across racial backgrounds generally embraced Michelle Obama. According to Gallup polls published in the *Washington Post*, 72 percent of people surveyed held favorable views of the First Lady when her family entered the White House.[1] Positive assessments of her dropped slightly to 64 percent upon the family's exit in 2016, but she sustained approval ratings often above those of the President from 2009 through 2016. For white Americans seeking admission to a world beyond the entanglements of racialized sexism, Michelle Obama functioned as the necessary proof that someone could be born both female and the descendent of slaves and effectively navigate the world if she capitulated to hegemonic modes of self-presentation. Her persona functioned as something more important than a substantiation of the claims of meritocracy. One of the quintessential elements of post-racial and postfeminist rhetoric is not to deny that racism and sexism have ever existed, but to recognize these forces as obstacles that have been eliminated through collective effort. Obama was therefore a case study of magical Black womanhood in the supposedly new, "post" America.

In public, she appropriately embraced Blackness as an element—and not the sum—of her identity. She leveraged her upbringing on the South Side of Chicago to achieve resonance with the African American publics she frequently addressed. Each time she referenced the struggles she faced during her professional and social ascent, she lauded hard work, resilience, and education as the resources that would counter every opposition. Her brand of self-empowerment became clearer with each address to the nation. She told the 2018 *Black Girls Rock! Awards* show audience to be strong in the face of adversity because "when things get hard, that's not always a sign that you're doing something wrong, it's often a sign that you're doing something right."[2] She encouraged those of us who were listening to expect and embrace resistance as evidence of our potential for greatness. And perhaps her best-known single phrase—"when they go low, we go high"[3]—communicated that the best way to manage one's detractors was to weather and overcome their blows. For a nation undergoing a reconstruction of sorts, the Michelle Obama brand made for a convenient resource that could be used to help rewrite the narrative about what America was becoming and how Black people, and Black women specifically, fit into that future.

Of course, the global cyclone of glory surrounding Obama's memoir, *Becoming*, helped solidify her brand and cement her status as a figure it would be impossible to get through a book on Black womanhood, visibility, and power without mentioning. In less than three weeks of her story existing in the marketplace it had become the best-selling literary product of the year. According to the online retail giant Amazon, *Becoming* surpassed a sales record that had previously been held by the new millennium erotica franchise, *Fifty Shades of Grey*. Even the packaging managed to somehow exude the demure sexiness, sophistication, and grounded confidence that constituted the icon's signature aesthetic. The book jacket's soft white modern font and the mocha brown hue of Obama's bare right shoulder played well against a glossy, teal background that rested somewhere in the middle of Tiffany blue and aqua blue. Looking at her warm gaze reminded me of another magical Black woman whose smile lived on the cover of a book prominently displayed in my childhood home: Susan L. Taylor.

When mass media was becoming enchanted with women like Obama, some staffers at the dominant platform for Black women were experiencing a less glamourous reality. A new Black man had taken control of *Essence* and instigated a company culture that many found untenable. When Black beauty entrepreneur Richelieu Dennis first announced that he would be buying the legacy brand, the enthusiasm was palpable. Edward Lewis and Clarence Smith had sold the company to the publishing conglomerate Time, Inc. in 2005, ending its three-decade run as a Black-owned business. By returning *Essence* to Black ownership his admirers declared that Dennis had "saved" it from white control.[4] Ironically, just months before critics had taken issue with the fact that Dennis's Shea Moisture, a product line that had become successful by marketing its products to Black women, would no longer be Black-owned. Selling the beauty company to Unilever is what put Dennis in a position to acquire Essence Communications Inc. (ECI). What those celebrating the acquisition dismissed is that Dennis's purchase still put *Essence* and the images of Black womanhood that it monetized in the hands of a Black man.

The company made seismic changes under its new commander: it reduced the magazine to a bimonthly printing schedule, fired the editor-in-chief, eliminating the position altogether, and reassigned Michelle Ebanks, who had been crucial in the Time Inc. deal some thirteen years prior, from CEO to board member for the new parent company Essence Ventures. The new owner's wife, Martha Dennis, also assumed the role of human resources director. During this transition, a group calling themselves Black Female Anonymous started a petition urging Dennis, Ebanks and two other executives to resign. The coalition of unnamed active and former employees bemoaned that the "once exalted media brand" had been "hijacked by cultural and corporate greed and an unhinged abuse of power."[5] They published an open letter on June 28, 2020, airing their grievances and challenging long-time corporate sponsors (i.e., AT&T, Coca-Cola, Ford, Procter & Gamble, Walmart) to suspend their relationships with the company until their concerns had been addressed:

> Historically a haven for Black female media professionals who couldn't get roles at major publishers like Hearst and Condé Nast due to racial bias, the magazine's very first cover in May 1970 boldly presented a Black woman in a natural afro with a tantalizing cover line asking Black men, *do you love me?* Today, the company's predominately Black female workforce is asking Essence itself, *do you love us like we love you?* For past and present Black female talent once lucky enough to walk its prestigious halls, Essence is the most deceptive Black media company in America. Why? Essence aggressively monetizes #BlackGirlMagic but the company does not internally practice #BlackGirlMagic. The company's longstanding pattern of gross mistreatment and abuse of its Black female employees is the biggest open secret in the media business.[6]

Richelieu Dennis stepped down as CEO within days of the letter's release, but he refuted claims that he had facilitated a toxic workplace culture and continued to chair the board for the parent company. Save for one woman who had reportedly already had plans to resign, all other executives named in the open letter maintained their leadership positions after an independent internal investigation did not yield evidence that substantiated the claims made in the June statement. The lack of proof does not mean that the anonymous claims regarding pay inequity and harassment were "false and egregious," as ECI's interim CEO would claim in September 2020, only that these assertions did not meet the legal standard for truth.[7]

ECI announced an undisclosed number of staff furloughs weeks after a rhetorical victory lap through social media boasting the results of the internal investigation. Economic hardship from the COVID-19 pandemic had forced the company to adjust its financial strategy. Using his personal Instagram profile, Dennis alluded to the consolidation as a challenging but necessary part of his "transformation plan" for the company.[8] It is also possible, however, that the pandemic presented the owner with a window of opportunity to restructure his company without skepticism. COVID-19 could have provided just enough cover for Dennis to rid himself of Black women employees who refused to be silent in their discontent without risking a retaliation lawsuit. In the online post he reminded his followers that while purchasing "Essence may not have been the most profitable decision," it was worthwhile because of his devotion to what the company represents to Black women around the world.[9] The message positions him once again as the brand's savior and compels Black women to see him as community servant, rather than profiteer. History will judge the veracity of Dennis's presentation of himself as a benevolent actor. Yet, even if his motives are pure and his record is clean, he will always be a Black man who ascended to a position of authority over Black women's images. We will never know what would have become of *Essence* had Black women been afforded a seat at the founder's table back in 1969.

In the decades since the magazine's founding Black women have become more visible but we have not necessarily become more powerful. Yes, the level of cultural enfranchisement that the other sovereigns of this moment have achieved has fractured the image economy such that those who were once left to make do with scraps of spotlight are more and more center stage. By infiltrating a system that was not designed to honor our humanity we do indeed become harder to ignore. And a few, like Michelle Obama, and Issa Rae, and Lena Waithe, and Beverly Bond, even translate this cultural currency into other forms of capital. The magic that iconic Black women figures possess is useful for transactions: for selling out arenas, for moving books and magazines off store shelves at record speed, and for drawing audiences and their dollars to old and new marketplaces. It is not a transformational property; it will not save us from the forces that are sustained through our oppression. Believing otherwise requires that we dismiss a recent history where corporations built ephemeral, rhetorical monuments to our beauty and strength which only offered temporary gains. These affirmation campaigns can emerge rapidly because they are not built to last. They are not permanent disruptions to the commercial infrastructure, but indeed are designed to fit within the existing capitalist framework.

I now turn to one of the most accessible personifications of magical Black womanhood in the twenty-first century to underscore the limitations of a people becoming a brand, and to expound on what is at stake if we overestimate the benefits of visibility. As an elite athlete, entrepreneur, wife, mother, occasional performer in Beyoncé music videos and an enterprising subject who promotes products like the Lincoln Navigator, Serena Williams is a titan in the modern image economy. She has encountered misrepresentation and heightened scrutiny as a Black woman media citizen, but she has also capitalized on her visibility to advance a vision of herself that aligns with strength, resilience, and other affirmative traits. Williams's documentary series *Being Serena*, which mediates her first pregnancy, shows how the cultural figure participates in strategic exposure to solidify her self-defined brand.

From footage of Williams's twenty-third Grand Slam win, which she achieved during her first trimester of pregnancy, to interviews detailing the champion's relentless drive to become "the best tennis player in the world and the best mother in the world," *Being Serena* promised viewers a look into the interior life of a magical Black woman.[10] Beyond detailing the star's anxieties, hopes, and athletic superiority, the series reproduced a narrowing gaze often deployed in public narratives about Black women—a framework that normalizes the effects of structural inequities. For example, in the first episode—entitled "Fear"—Williams discussed an anxious childhood in an economically-depressed city as a crucial impetus for her success: "I had to worry about all kinds of things growing up: gangs, robberies, murders, gunshots right outside our door. There was a lot to be afraid of. There was a lot to run away from. But ultimately, that fear, it drove us forward."[11] In this distorted context fear, pain, and trauma are not hindrances but constitutive elements of the environment from which magical Black girls emerge.

In addition to subjecting an already public life to greater exposure, the series reinforces the notion that magical Black women are not merely individuals, but carefully crafted brands. The series suggests an alignment between Williams, the tennis champion, and Williams, the private individual. Fierceness and discipline not only enable her to dominate the court, but also translate to her intimate experiences, including the danger she found herself in after medical professionals did not provide adequate care after the birth of her first child. Serena Williams was one of two icons—Beyoncé was the other—to catapult the news media narrative on the precarity of Black birthing into the popular realm when she testified to her experiences for *Vogue* and *In Style* magazines. While public discourse had already hailed Williams a superior being for continuing to compete (and win) during her first trimester, news of the trauma that ensued after an unplanned cesarean birth added credence to her so-called magic.

While Williams has a history of blood clots, she had not been taking her normal anticoagulant (which is typical for someone who has undergone major surgery). Given her past health experience she knew to alert medical personnel when she began experiencing shortness of breath. She suspected that blood clots had formed in her lungs. According to Williams, her nurse assumed she was confused and did not proceed with the CT scan and heparin drip she requested. Despite the severity of this experience, in an interview for *In Style*'s "Badass Woman" issue, editor Laura Brown classified the near-death encounter as just another example of Williams's innate capacity to accomplish feats that would subdue the average woman. The editor likened her physical trauma to her athletic accomplishments, presenting both as credits that landed Williams on the cover of the magazine's issue celebrating high-achieving women.

SERENA WILLIAMS: If I weren't working, I'd already be pregnant. I hear everyone's different, but I had a really easy pregnancy until the birth. Not even birth—after.

LAURA BROWN: You and your blood clots! You've got to just do everything hard-core, don't you?[12]

Even if the editor's response was intended as a playful gesture, her amused reaction fits neatly within mass media's broader logic which perceives all Black women as "hard-core" and therefore more tolerant of physical pain.[13]

Black Girl Magic's frame directs us to view this experience as triumphant, rather than typifying of the ways in which Black women across economic levels confront fatal risks for what should be a routine procedure. Under this lens, Williams's capacity and strength become the focus while the medical personnel's failure and the psychic cost of the ordeal fade from clear view. Furthermore, the unreasonable task of managing one's own health emergency while recovering from surgery becomes acceptable within Black Girl Magic's frame. In fact, Williams jokingly referred to herself as "Dr. Williams"[14] in an interview with *Vogue* magazine and praised the "incredible medical team of doctors and nurses" who "knew exactly how to handle this complicated turn of events" in an opinion piece for *CNN.com*.[15]

Emphasizing how medical personnel failed to familiarize themselves with Williams's medical history and their delayed reaction to her petitions for intervention would not have aligned with the frame of magic through which we understand the star's brand. Thus, articles published after the ordeal used

Williams's own words to prop up the U.S. medical system and legitimize the notion of Black women as master self-regulators. Within this twisted discursive framework, what would otherwise be presented as cause for alarm is instead offered up as evidence of personal merit. Rather than use Williams's story as an example of the ways in which medical racism is a reality that transcends class, the *CNN* essay points to lower-income Black women as vulnerable because they cannot afford the level of treatment she received. Following the command that magical Black women uplift others, Williams used the essay and her near-death encounter to draw attention to others who lack her financial means, requiring that she deny her own fragility. Like a magical Black woman prototype, she channeled her innate superpowers to rise above adversity and lived to talk (and joke) about it for two commercial fashion magazines.

Numerous tensions regarding magical Black women's increased visibility abound in Williams's story. First, while the media figure uses the HBO series to humanize herself, she also capitulates to a frame that challenges her humanity. Williams operates in an image economy unlike that which Black women elite athletes who precede her navigated. Hungry for marketable magical Black women narratives, the culture industries afford Williams room to tell her own story and present herself in a dignified manner. Nevertheless, Williams's narrative still conforms to parameters that belie systemic injustice. Being presented as magical offers Black women subjects the privilege to align public representation with our inner vision, to a degree. Yet magic also eclipses the parts of our narrative that unsettle a neoliberal conception of citizenship. Magic allows us a path to cultural enfranchisement that is self-managed and self-maintained, but not self-defined.

Finally, and most importantly, Serena Williams's story makes clear that the veneer of magic does not prevent us from seeing Black women's pain; on the contrary, it directs us to fixate on such suffering with a normalizing gaze. It begs us to look until the horror we are seeing loses its sting and fades into just another part of the Black female form. Coverage of Williams's birth story drew attention to her iconicity, while simultaneously ignoring the structural factors that contribute to increased health risks for Black mothers. Since she is read as a magical figure, her survival becomes a personal triumph and her vulnerability as a Black woman birthing in the United States during a period of elevated maternal mortality fades beneath her glow. She is presented as all things strong and beautiful and excellent, but she is not treated as a full (medical) citizen. She is a worthy pop culture icon, but she is not a credible witness to her own bodily experience. She must eschew some matter of vulnerability to be magical, but she must be magical to be visible.

In the end, Black Girl Magic matters because it is one process through which a constrained public can access media citizenship. Despite its limitations as a form of enfranchisement bound to certain affirming images, which the Serena

Williams case illustrates, this framework offers Black women a pathway to a kind of everyday empowerment. Recognition and cultural belonging are valuable because we do not experience citizenship purely or primarily as a legal subjectivity defined by a nation-state. We also experience it through mundane social interactions at the doctor's office, in the beauty aisle at a big box retailer, in the pages of a magazine, and on our screens. Representation matters, and it always will, but endorsing the notion that being *presented* as beautiful, or magical, is synonymous with *being* powerful, is detrimental if it supersedes the other things that matter, such as access to adequate healthcare, political representation, and knowing that one's life and well-being have value.

Acknowledgments

Branding Black Womanhood is the book that I had been searching for throughout my graduate school and postdoc years but could not quite grasp. Robin Means Coleman always believed I would find it. Thank you, Robin, for being the kind of champion that I needed at every stage. I will be forever grateful to Janis Mayes for helping me to see myself as a scholar and to Patricia McFadden for encouraging me to pursue my doctorate. Thank you for your vision.

I am grateful to the community who helped me sharpen my ideas at the University of Michigan, especially Shazia Iftkhar, Megan Sweeney, Paddy Scannell, Brandi Hughes, Kyera Singleton, Akila Wise, Marvin Chochotte, David Green, Amanda Cote, Dam Hee Kim, Kitior Ngu, Lia Wolock, Monique Bourdage, Sarah Erickson, Katherine Weathers, Jessica Moorman, Faithe Day, André Brock, Aswin Punathambekar, and Megan Ankerson.

This project came into focus more clearly at the end of an hours-long workshop with Alex Fattal, Michelle Rodino-Colocino, Beretta Smith-Shomade, and Noliwe Rooks. Thank you for your feedback and for encouraging me to return to my original spark. I found the gumption to start over after an emergency pep talk with Amira Rose Davis, Dara Walker, and J. Marlena Edwards. Thank you for being there when I needed you most.

I am blessed to work among brilliant and generous colleagues in the College of Liberal Arts and the Bellisario College of Communications at Penn State, specifically in the department that I call home, African American Studies. This book was also improved through conversations I had during my fellowship term at the Humanities Institute. Many thanks to all who made the fellowship possible, even in the midst of a pandemic. I appreciate Cynthia Young and Deborah Atwater for your kindness and mentorship. And to the spectacular women whom I have written alongside of and collaborated with over these past few years thank you for your support and collegiality. Ashleigh Wade, thank you for seeing the beauty in every rough draft that you read.

Thanks to the editors and anonymous readers who have supported this book and helped me make it better, especially Nicole Solano and Sara Appel. I am grateful to the helpful librarians at the Schomburg Center for Research in Black Culture who made my archival work much easier. And to the women who participated in interviews that informed this project, thank you for your time and candor.

To my mom and dad, thank you for teaching me what I am made of and for reminding me when doubts emerged. Your sacrifices will never be forgotten. To my brothers, Michael and Kelvin, aunts, uncles, cousins, and in-laws, thank you for the cheers and prayers and good times. This book would not have been completed without the soul-nourishing moments I shared with my dear church families, sorority sisters, and friends along the way. Special thanks to Benita, Chantel, Janel, Jessica, Khadija, Nicole, Nyrie, Sharisse, and Tasha for being sounding boards.

Chris, I have leaned on your love as support when the book felt like it was slipping away from me and as comfort when the writing process was kicking my butt. Thank you for being my partner in all things. And to Cairo, Mommy loves you. I hope that I have written something that you will one day read, learn from, and be proud of.

To God be the glory.

As a last, but not least, editorial note, portions of chapter 4 appeared in "Productive Vulnerability: Black Women Writers and Narratives of Humanity in Contemporary Cable Television," *Souls* 20, no. 3 (2018): 304–327, and are reprinted here with permission from Taylor & Francis.

Notes

Introduction

1 Her idea was not novel. More than a decade prior, hip-hop feminist Joan Morgan had encouraged Black women to recognize and own their magic in her memoir, *When Chickenheads Come Home to Roost: My Life as a Hip-Hop Feminist* (New York: Simon & Schuster, 1999).

2 Thompson reported that she sold ten times as many shirts as she thought she would in her first run. She sold three thousand shirts between January 2014 and September 2015, including to celebrities who posted images of themselves in the paraphernalia on social media.

3 In an interview with *The Glow Up*, Bond asserted that she did not learn of CaShawn Thompson's use of the term "Black Girls Are Magic" until after she filed the trademark application. Maiysha Kai, "Who Benefits from 'Black Girl Magic'? Google's Latest Ad Reignites Enduring Issues of Erasure," *The Root*, March 10, 2019, https://theglowup.theroot.com/who-benefits-from-black-girl-magic-googles -latest-ad-r-1833144103. Nevertheless, Thompson maintains that she was the first person to use the phrase on Twitter as an assertion of Black women's dignity, not simply their beauty. Other early Twitter users have corroborated her claim. Feminista Jones, *Reclaiming Our Space: How Black Feminists Are Changing the World from the Tweets to the Streets* (Boston: Beacon Press, 2019), 89.

4 For Harriet, "How the Creator of #BlackGirlMagic Got Erased from the Movement She Started," YouTube video, 37:47, April 11, 2020, https://www .youtube.com/watch?v=y2Ko-mgo1DU.

5 Franchesca Ramsey and Nefetari Spencer, writers, *Black Girls Rock! Awards* show, directed by Sandra Restrepo, featuring Niecy Nash, aired September 8, 2019, on BET.

6 Roland S. Martin, "New Nielsen Report Measures the Impact of Black Women on Culture & Consumer Spending," YouTube video, 6:37, February 9, 2017, https://youtu.be/TlncMgR1GgA.

7 The primary distinction between how magic functions within Black Girl Magic and the "magical Negro" trope is who stands to benefit from the Black subject's superpowers. In popular texts, especially film, characters who play the role of the

"magical Negro" use their other-worldly capabilities to support white protagonists. Conversely, the magic in Black Girl Magic is primarily self-centered.

8 Julia S. Jordan-Zachery and Duchess Harris, "We Are Magic and We Are Real: Exploring the Politics of Black Femmes, Girls, and Women's Self-Articulation" in *Black Girl Magic beyond the Hashtag: Twenty-First Century Acts of Self-Definition*, ed. Julia S. Jordan-Zachery and Duchess Harris (Tucson: University of Arizona Press, 2019), 15.

9 Conversely, the use of "girl" instead of woman further sanitizes the term and simultaneously erases the particularities of Black girlhood. CaShawn Thompson was forty years old when she coined the phrase and it has since been most often applied to adult females.

10 Jordan-Zachery and Harris, "We Are Magic and We Are Real," 15.

11 Nielsen Company, *African American Women: Our Science, Her Magic*, September 21, 2017, https://www.nielsen.com/wp-content/uploads/sites/3/2019/04/nielsen-african-american-diverse-intelligence-report-2017.pdf, 2–5.

12 In her study of the psychic and physical consequences of strong Black womanhood, Tamara Beauboeuf-Lafontant, quoting Betty Friedan, describes the concept as a "mystique" tethered to the idea of America as a meritocracy where the only valid obstacle to success is one's own will power. Tamara Beauboeuf-Lafontant, *Behind the Mask of the Strong Black Woman: Voice and the Embodiment of a Costly Performance* (Philadelphia: Temple University Press, 2009), 3.

13 The consequences of deviating from this code of racial authenticity can be perilous, especially when Black women appear to critique Black men. For example, Gayle King experienced a severe backlash, including death threats, after a portion of an interview where she references the sexual assault allegations against basketball legend Kobe Bryant went viral in February 2020. The clip appeared days after a fatal helicopter crash killed Bryant and his daughter Gianna. Among the most vehement critics was hip-hop star Snoop Dogg who posted a message to social media warning King to "back off . . . before we come get you." Matthew Impelli, "#IStandWithGayle Trends After Gayle King Received Death Threats for Raising Kobe Bryant Rape Allegations in Lisa Leslie Interview," *Newsweek*, February 10, 2020, https://www.newsweek.com/istandwithgayle-trends-after-gayle-king-receives-death-threats-raising-kobe-bryant-rape-1486548.

14 Ramsey and Spencer, *Black Girls Rock! Awards*.

15 Ibid.

16 Ibid.

17 Essence, "Queen Latifah and Jada Pinkett Smith Join Ladies Panel on Strength," YouTube video, 28:46, July 23, 2017, https://www.youtube.com/watch?v=fBEMZktTvG4&t=129s.

18 Ibid.

19 Ibid.

20 Herman Gray, "Subject(ed) to Recognition," *American Quarterly* 65, no. 4 (2013): 771–798; Kristen J. Warner, "In the Time of Plastic Representation," *Film Quarterly* 71, no. 2 (2017): 32–37.

21 Beretta Smith-Shomade, *Pimpin' Ain't Easy: Selling Black Entertainment Television* (New York: Routledge, 2008); Robert E. Weems Jr., *Desegregating the Dollar: African American Consumerism in the Twentieth Century* (New York: New York University Press, 1998).

22 Gray, "Subject(ed) to Recognition," 772.

23 Sarah Banet-Weiser and Inna Arzumanova, "Creative Authorship: Self-Actualizing Individuals and the Self-Brand," in *Media Authorship*, edited by Cynthia Chris and David A. Gerstner (New York: Routledge, 2013), 164–65. Conversely, other theorists argue that twenty-first century technologies of exposure have offered a new pathway whereby "women have been able to enter as full participants into a late modern culture of the self that endorses self-invention, autonomy and personal responsibility alongside key competences of reflexivity, self-observation and personal biographical narration." Shelly Budgeon, "The Contradictions of Successful Femininity: Third-Wave Feminism, Postfeminism and 'New' Femininities," in *New Femininities: Postfeminism, Neoliberalism and Subjectivity*, ed. Rosalind Gill and Christina Scharff (London: Palgrave Macmillan, 2011), 284.

24 Sarah Banet-Weiser, *Empowered: Popular Feminism and Popular Misogyny* (Durham: Duke University Press, 2018), 27.

25 Sarah Banet-Weiser, *Kids Rule!: Nickelodeon and Consumer Citizenship* (Durham: Duke University Press, 2007), 20.

26 Joseph Turrow, *Breaking Up America: Advertisers and the New Media World* (Chicago: University of Chicago Press, 1997), 3.

27 Turrow, *Breaking Up America*, 6.

28 Banet-Weiser, *Kids Rule!*, 12.

29 As Gregory T. Carter explains, the Naturalization Act of 1790 "excluded indentured servants, slaves, free blacks, and American Indians" from being able to become legal citizens, but these parameters would be redrawn multiple times over the coming centuries. Gregory T. Carter, "Race and Citizenship," in *The Oxford Handbook of American Immigration and Ethnicity*, ed. Ronald H. Bayor (Oxford, England: Oxford University Press, 2016), 166.

30 Ann S. Holder has mapped the move to race-based citizenship in the U.S. and illuminated how this reconfiguration required white supremacists to fabricate distinct racial boundaries that did not reflect America's demographic reality. Ann S. Holder, "What's Sex Got to Do with It? Race, Power, Citizenship, and 'Intermediate Identities' in the Post-Emancipation United States," *The Journal of African American History* 93, no. 2 (2008): 153–173.

31 Derrick R. Spires, *The Practice of Citizenship: Black Politics and Print Culture in the Early United States* (Philadelphia: University of Pennsylvania Press, 2019), 3.

32 The NAACP describes ongoing image activism as a distinguishing characteristic that sets the organization apart from other civil rights entities. Indeed, the organization has maintained a focus on Black representation since its earliest years. For example, Stephen Weinberger has chronicled how the NAACP's nationwide protest against the release of the film *The Birth of a Nation* bolstered the association's network by facilitating communication between local chapter leaders, the national team, and city government. Since the boycott occurred in 1915, just six years into the association's existence, it was crucial for helping the NAACP realize its mission to be a nationally relevant organization not limited to Southern issues. Stephen Weinberger, "*The Birth of a Nation* and the Making of the NAACP," *Journal of American Studies* 45, no. 1 (2011): 77–93. The association continued its image activism throughout the twentieth century and galvanized support from prominent Black actors in 1982 for its Fair Share Program which

aimed to "correct the false images of Blacks on the screen and to increase the number of Blacks in front of and behind the camera." Barbara Faggins, "Black Stars Join NAACP's Film Boycott," *Philadelphia Tribune*, July 20, 1982.

33 Harry Levette, "Walter White Asks Change in Picture Roles," *Atlanta Daily World*, July 27, 1942.

34 Herman Hill, "Change in Attitude of Hollywood Observed: Walter White Is Winning His Fight for Better Roles," *Pittsburgh Courier*, August 8, 1942.

35 Lindahl, Martin L. "The Federal Trade Commission Act as Amended in 1938." *Journal of Political Economy* 47, no. 4 (1939): 503.

36 Kaela Jubas, "Conceptual Con/fusion in Democratic Societies: Understandings and Limitations of Consumer-Citizenship," *Journal of Consumer Culture* 7, no. 2 (2007): 238.

37 The Aunt Jemima brand, known for its pancake mix and syrup, exemplifies how Black images have been integrated into U.S. marketing rhetoric in ways that appeal to the white gaze. The mammy caricature that Aunt Jemima was based on—bandanaed, jovially overweight, and content with her subservient place in the white household—was also presented as undesirable and asexual. Micki McElya, *Clinging to Mammy: The Faithful Slave in Twentieth-Century America* (Cambridge, MA: Harvard University Press, 2007), 15–37.

38 Jason Chambers and Judy Foster Davis offer expansive histories of Black men's and women's contributions to the U.S. advertising industry that I have drawn on to understand the connection between consumption and political progress. Jason Chambers, *Madison Avenue and the Color Line: African Americans in the Advertising Industry* (Philadelphia: University of Pennsylvania Press, 2008); Judy Foster Davis, *Pioneering African-American Women in the Advertising Business: Biographies of M.A.D. Black Women* (New York: Routledge, 2017).

39 Chambers, *Madison Avenue and the Color Line,* 21–22.

40 Brenna Wynn Greer, *Represented: The Black Imagemakers Who Reimagined African American Citizenship* (Philadelphia: University of Pennsylvania Press, 2019), 4.

41 John T. Connor, Alexander B. Trowbridge, and Forest D. Hockersmith, *A Guide to Negro Marketing Information* (Washington, DC: United States Department of Commerce, 1966), iv.

42 The census data only captured Black women of a specific age group, 25–29 years. When considering the percentage of Black women who have never been married up to the age of 55, the numbers decreased dramatically to 13 percent.

43 Yale University, "Marriage, Family on the Decline for Highly Educated Black Women," *Yale News*, August 8, 2009, https://news.yale.edu/2009/08/08/marriage -family-decline-highly-educated-black-women.

44 Steve Harvey authored back-to-back relationship strategy books aimed at Black women: *Act Like a Lady, Think Like a Man: What Men Really Think About Love, Relationships, Intimacy, and Commitment* (New York: Amistad, 2009) and *Straight Talk, No Chaser: How to Find, Keep and Understand a Man* (New York: Amistad, 2010). Screen Gems, a division of Sony Pictures, released the former as a film in 2012. Hill Harper published *The Conversation: How Men and Women Can Build Loving, Trusting Relationships*, an *Essence* Book Club Recommended Read (New York: Gotham Books, 2009).

45 Billionaire media titan Tyler Perry's work is also relevant here. Perry typically centers his films on Black women who are miserable and/or in the midst of a crisis.

In most cases the women are suffering at the hands of upper-class men (e.g., an attorney or investment banker), but blue-collar men (e.g., a bus driver or car mechanic) are the answer to their problems. In *Diary of a Mad Black Woman* (Grant, Darren, dir., *Diary of a Mad Black Woman*, 2005, Santa Monica, CA: Lionsgate Films, 2005, DVD), *Madea's Family Reunion* (2006, Santa Monica, CA: Lionsgate Films, 2006, DVD), *Daddy's Little Girls* (2007, Santa Monica, CA: Lionsgate Films, 2007, DVD) and *I Can Do Bad All By Myself* (2009, Santa Monica, CA: Lionsgate Films, 2009, DVD), Perry writes the female protagonists as the cause of their own pain because they have inappropriately prioritized wealth and status over character when selecting a romantic partner.

46 GlobalHue was a privately held multicultural marketing agency that operated from 1988 to 2016.

47 NBA star LeBron James founded SpringHill Entertainment with his friend and business partner, Maverick Carter. The production company is behind several products focused on African American life and culture, including the biographical series, *Self Made: Inspired by the Life of Madam C. J. Walker* (Netflix, 2020).

48 As an African American woman, Ross understood that the magazine's potential readers associated "sapphire" with an excessively angry character from the caricature-laden 1950s sitcom, *Amos N' Andy*.

Chapter 1   The Black Woman That *Essence* Built

1 Grace Lichtenstein, "Feminists Demand 'Liberation' In Ladies' Home Journal Sit-In," *New York Times*, March 19, 1970.

2 Susan L. Taylor, "In the Beginning," in *Essence: 25 Years Celebrating Black Women*, ed. Patricia Mignon Hinds, (New York: Harry N. Abrams, Incorporated, 1995), 41.

3 Carson was once quoted as stating that he was antiwhite. Furthermore, he insisted that the seven-year prison sentence he received for kidnapping in 1974 was retaliation for the work he was doing to protect the Black community. Marc Santora, "Sonny Carson, 66, Figure in 60's Battle for Schools, Dies," *New York Times*, Dec. 23, 2002.

4 Taylor, "In the Beginning," 41.

5 Daniel Patrick Moynihan published *The Negro Family: The Case for National Action* in 1965 while serving as Assistant Secretary of Labor under President Lyndon B. Johnson; it would become known as the Moynihan Report.

6 "Essence Magazine to Appeal to Black Woman," *Atlanta Daily World*, May 22, 1970, 2.

7 Stan Lathan, director, *The Essence of Essence* (1973; New York: Tony Brown Productions, 2013), DVD.

8 Edward Lewis and Audrey Edwards, *The Man from Essence: Creating a Magazine for Black Women* (New York: Atria Books, 2014), 9.

9 Robert E. Weems Jr. and Lewis A. Randolph, *Business in Black and White: American Presidents & Black Entrepreneurs in the Twentieth Century* (New York: New York University Press, 2009), 121.

10 Although popular histories of the sixties and seventies tend to suggest otherwise, the Black Power movement was less a singular crusade than a wide banner encompassing a range of political, religious, economic, and cultural ideas and initiatives. Lauren Warren Hill and Julia Rabig's anthology, *The Business of Black*

Power: Community Development, Capitalism, and Corporate Responsibility in Postwar America, explores various commercial and community-based projects that took root in the Black Power era.

11 Michael O. West explains that Black Power's most prominent progenitors were anti-capitalist and that those individuals who translated the movement's ideology into the commercial philosophy of Black capitalism were in the minority. Michael O. West, "Whose Black Power?: The Business of Black Power and Black Power's Business," in *The Business of Black Power: Community Development, Capitalism, and Corporate Responsibility in Postwar America*, ed. Lauren Warren Hill and Julia Rabig (Rochester, NY: University of Rochester Press, 2012), 276.

12 Bayard Rustin, "RUSTIN SAYS: Nixon-Agnew, Wallace Biggest Threat of Post-Reconstruction," *Afro-American*, August 31, 1968.

13 Sala Udin, "Serve the People," *New Pittsburgh Courier* (Pittsburgh, PA), January 25, 1975.

14 Chicago Defender, "Jackson Rejects Black Capitalism," *Chicago Defender*, February 18, 1969.

15 Jerry DeMuth, "'Breadbasket Full of Black 'Green Power',"" *National Catholic Reporter*, January 15, 1969.

16 The debate over whether Nixon's project was fulfilling its mission continued to unfold in the press. Writing for the *Michigan Chronicle*, Nadine Brown argued that because "Black people are great suckers for the power of suggestion" they had been fooled by Nixon's hollow words. Nadine Brown, "People, Places and Situations," *Michigan Chronicle*, January 9, 1971. Earl B. Dickerson, a Chicago businessman, said that Black capitalism amounted to "a plethora of unimaginative programs that have been overly generous in terms of promises and red tape but concomitantly very short on venture capital and management training programs that would create real wealth in the hands of [B]lack people"; see also Edward Lee, "Dickerson Hits Nixon's 'Black Capitalism'," *Chicago Tribune*, May 12, 1973. Conversely, some business owners believed the president's plan was working. The owners of Progress Manufacturing Company, a women's clothier in Philadelphia, considered their success a credit to Black capitalism. Trudy Prokop, "Black Capitalism Works in Philadelphia," *Women's Wear Daily*, February 25, 1969, 36.

17 Chicago Defender, "Class in 'Soul Food' as Small Business Offered at College," *Chicago Defender*, February 22, 1969.

18 Public Broadcasting Service (PBS), "Tom Burrell on Revolutionizing Advertising," PBS, WTTW Archive, June 28, 2018, video, 9:11, https://www.pbs.org/video/tom-burrell-revolutionizing-advertising-6u42gm/.

19 Nina S. Hyde, "The Beautiful Billion-Dollar Business of Black Cosmetics," *Washington Post*, July 9, 1977.

20 Essence Communications Inc. "Advertisement: Flori Roberts," *Essence*, May 1970, 12.

21 Weems Jr. and Randolph, *Business in Black and White*, 115.

22 Dan Dorfman, "The Bottom Line: Black Broker Blasts Big Board," *New York Magazine*, July 15, 1974, 11.

23 Phillip (Tony) Janniere, a salesman for the *New York Times*, was also present at the initial meeting and selected as the initial president of their business, The Hollingsworth Group. At a meeting in early 1969, the men discussed the terms of the partnership, specifically that they would need to vacate their positions elsewhere in order to devote their energies to the magazine full time. Janniere would not

agree to those terms and left the partnership. Lewis and Edwards, *The Man from Essence*, 19–20.

24 Lewis and Edwards, 11.

25 These titles dominated the magazine industry in profits for much of the twentieth century until 1979 when an economic recession upset their business model. Ellen McCracken, *Decoding Women's Magazines from Mademoiselle to Ms.* (New York: St. Martin's Press, 1993), 174.

26 McCracken, *Decoding Women's Magazines*, 196.

27 Ibid.

28 Ibid.

29 Lewis and Edwards, *The Man from Essence*, 103.

30 Ibid.

31 Gordon Parks directed *Shaft* (1971), starring Richard Roundtree and featuring a soundtrack by soul legend Isaac Hayes. The low-budget film was a box office hit for MGM, grossing about $80 million in 2019 dollars and is credited for helping to pioneer a new genre in Black cinematic representation known as blaxploitation. Aimed at African American audiences, blaxploitation films were inexpensive productions typically set in urban areas that carried "extra heavy doses of the film industry's unholy trinity of sex, violence, and crime." Weems Jr., *Desegregating the Dollar*, 83.

32 In 1977, Parks joined Jonathan Blount and Cecil Hollingsworth in a legal scheme to gain controlling shares of ECI. James L. Hicks, "Fight On for Control of Essence Magazine," *New York Amsterdam News*, April 23, 1977.

33 Marcia Gillespie, *For You . . . Black Woman*, interview by Nell Bassett, Gerber/Carter Communications, 1978, https://browse.nypl.org/iii/encore/record/C_ _Rb11253064__SMarcia%20Gillespie__Po%2C1__Orightresult__U__X3?lang =eng&suite=def.

34 Lathan, *The Essence of Essence*.

35 In August 1831 Nat Turner, a minister and Southampton County, Virginia, native, led what is known as the most violent and successful revolt of enslaved peoples in American history.

36 Marcia Gillespie, "Getting Down," *Essence*, August 1971, 32.

37 Ibid.

38 Lathan, *The Essence of Essence*.

39 Ibid.

40 Marjorie Moore, "The Essence Woman: Lydia Cade," *Essence*, October 1971, 18.

41 The empowered Black woman that the magazine constructed would have also been considered heterosexual by default. *Essence*'s first significant discussion of queer sexuality occurred in September 1979 with Chirlane McCray's seven-page personal essay on coming to terms with her identity as a lesbian. At the time McCray, a former editorial assistant at *Redbook*, was a freelance writer. Fifteen years after the article was published McCray married Bill de Blasio. He was elected mayor of New York City in 2013. Chirlane McCray, "I Am a Lesbian," *Essence*, September 1979, 90–91, 157, 159, 161, 164, 166.

42 Marjorie Moore, "The Essence Woman: Hulan Watson," *Essence*, December 1971, 11.

43 Marjorie Moore, "The Essence Woman: Janice Terry," *Essence*, November 1971, 7.

44 Ibid.

45 Essence, "Essence Women: We've Come This Far By Faith!," *Essence*, May 1980, 32.

46 Moore, "The Essence Woman: Lydia Cade."

47 Moore, 18.

48 Bonnie Allen, "Essence & Other Thoughts on the 70's," *Essence*, May 1980, 95.

49 Moore, "The Essence Woman: Lydia Cade," 18.

50 Ibid.

51 Lathan, *The Essence of Essence*.

52 Ibid. In a 1976 interview on the show *Woman*, Gillespie explained that she took a "Sojourner Truth" approach to the women's movement, whereby she supported the thrusts that could be beneficial to all women, while rejecting elements exclusive to white, middle-class women. Marcia Gillespie, "Woman," interview by Sandra Elkin, WNED, January 16, 1976.

53 Sheila F. Younge, "Essence Woman: Vy Higginsen," *Essence*, December 1972, 28.

54 Marjorie Moore, "Essence Woman: Barbara Fouch," *Essence*, March 1972, 22.

55 Thelma Jackson Stiles, "Essence Women," *Essence,* May 1975, 27.

56 Ibid.

57 Pearl Lomax, "Point of View: Black Women's Lib?," *Essence*, August 1972, 68.

58 Marjorie Moore, "The Essence Woman: Delores James," *Essence*, April 1972, 25.

59 Jimi Lawrence, "Essence Women," *Essence*, October 1975, 10.

60 Marjorie Moore, "Essence Woman: Fern Stanford," *Essence*, July 1972, 11.

61 Jane Sumner, "Essence Woman: Eddie Johnson," *Essence*, September 1975, 20.

62 Marjorie Moore, "Essence Woman: Michele Freeman," *Essence*, June 1972, 24.

63 Lathan, *The Essence of Essence*.

64 McCracken, *Decoding Women's Magazines*, 14.

65 In a 1969 essay for *Ebony* magazine, Black Arts Movement leader Larry Neal wrote, "For a Sister to wear her hair natural asserts the sacred and essentially holy nature of her body. The natural, in its most positive sense, symbolizes the Sister's willingness to determine her own destiny. It is an act of love for herself and her people. The natural helps to psychologically liberate the Sister." Larry Neal, "Any Day Now: Black Art and Black Liberation," *Ebony*, August 1969, 58.

66 Susan L. Taylor, interview by James Briggs Murray, May 5, 1987, video recording, Moving Image and Recorded Sound collection, Schomburg Center for Research in Black Culture.

67 Ibid.

68 This article drew criticism from one reader who thought it "read as if it were geared toward white women." She took issue with the tips about tanning and recommendations for "a deeper rosier blush, a vibrant-er lip color, and more intense eyeshadow colors." The reader viewed the beauty and fashion pages as posing a particular threat to the Black affirmation agenda that *Essence* claimed. Sandra R. Taylor, "Write On!," *Essence*, May 1973, 85 and 104.

69 Pan-Africanism is a Black resistance praxis established on the belief that African descendants around the world share a racial condition and therefore a political reality. Although men have been most credited for developing Pan-Africanism, Blain et al. point to several women who have been instrumental in shaping various iterations of this movement. Keisha N. Blain, Asia Leeds, and Ula Y. Taylor, "Women, Gender Politics, and Pan-Africanism," *Women, Gender, and Families of Color* 4, no. 2 (2016): 139–145.

70 Tanisha C. Ford, *Liberated Threads: Black Women, Style, and the Global Politics of Soul*, (Chapel Hill: University of North Carolina Press, 2015), 4.

71 Susannah Walker, *Style & Status: Selling Beauty to African American Women, 1920–1975* (Lexington: The University Press of Kentucky, 2007), 174.

72 Susan Taylor, "A Beautiful New You!," *Essence*, July 1971, 35.

73 Susan Taylor, "Shape 'N' Up," *Essence*, March 1972, 57.

74 Ibid.

75 Ibid.

Chapter 2   Self-Branding Black Womanhood

1 Bishop Arthur M. Brazier, head pastor of Apostolic from 1960 to 2008, had increased the congregation to more than eighteen thousand members. The *Chicago Tribune* described the church as "an obligatory campaign stop for politicians." It hosted Senator Barack Obama during his 2008 presidential run. Margaret Ramirez, "Bishop Arthur M. Brazier, 1921–2010," October 22, 2010, *Chicago Tribune*, https://www.chicagotribune.com/lifestyles/ct-xpm-2010-10-22 -ct-met-brazier-obit-1023-20101022-story.html.

2 See Valerie Norman introducing Susan L. Taylor in November 1995, at the Apostolic Church of God, Chicago, Illinois. Kevin Kitchen, "Susan L Taylor Speaks!," YouTube video, 29:42, n.d., https://www.youtube.com/watch?v =n9EmSueycGk, 0:01.

3 See Susan L. Taylor speaking on the topic of "The Power Is Within" in November 1995 at the Apostolic Church of God, Chicago, IL. Kitchen, "Susan L Taylor Speaks!," 4:48.

4 Ibid.

5 Joyce White, "Susan Taylor on Beauty," *Essence*, January 1978, 48.

6 Susan Taylor, "Haiti Chéri," *Essence*, March 1973, 39.

7 Sandra R. Taylor, "Write On!," 104.

8 White, "Susan Taylor on Beauty," 49.

9 Ibid.

10 Ibid.

11 Taylor, interview by James Briggs Murray.

12 Susan Taylor, "Beauty Lookout," *Essence*, January 1977, 26.

13 Micki McGee, "From Makeover Media to Remaking Culture: Four Directions for the Critical Study of Self-Help Culture," *Sociology Compass* 6, no. 9 (2012): 686.

14 British Prime Minister Margaret Thatcher was another political leader who championed small government, free enterprise, and personal responsibility in the 1980s.

15 In an August 1987 speech President Reagan proposed federal changes to the Aid For Dependent Children policy that would require women to work, and bolstered the power of individual states to "locat[e] absent parents, [establish] paternity, and [collect] child support on behalf of AFDC recipients." In this way, a philosophy that was associated with smaller government and increased individual liberties justified legislators' intrusion into the most intimate aspects of poor—and mostly Black—people's lives. Reagan Foundation, "President Reagan's Radio Address to the Nation on Welfare Reform—8/1/87," broadcast August 1, 1987, Washington, DC, YouTube video, 5:33, August 20, 2010, https://www.youtube.com/watch?v =MjnTQ8b6byY.

16 Nikolas Rose, *Governing the Soul: The Shaping of the Private Self* (London: Routledge, 1990), 215.

17 Self-help philosophies have been debated as a barrier and aid to political agency. Gayle McKeen, "Whose Rights? Whose Responsibility? Self-Help in African-American Thought," *Polity* 34, no. 4 (2002): 410; Natalia M. Petrzela and Christine B. Whelan, "Self-Help Gurus Like Tony Robbins Have Often Stood in the Way of Social Change," *Washington Post*, April 13, 2018.

18 Susan L. Taylor, *In the Spirit: The Inspirational Writings of Susan L. Taylor* (New York: HarperCollins, 1993), 14.

19 Taylor, *In the Spirit: Inspirational Writings*, 29.

20 Taylor, 47.

21 Taylor, 56.

22 Ibid. "In the Spirit" is also the title of Taylor's well-known *Essence* column which she penned as editor-in-chief and as editorial director.

23 Laurie Ouellette and Julie Wilson, "Women's Work: Affective Labour and Convergence Culture," *Cultural Studies* 25, no. 4–5 (2011): 556.

24 Susan Taylor, "Critical Issues Affecting Black Women," C-SPAN video, 1:19:32, July 8, 1994, https://www.c-span.org/video/?58537-1/critical-issues-affecting-black-women.

25 Janice Hamlet analyzed 228 "In the Spirit" columns published between 1981 and 2000, ultimately concluding that Taylor's writings were rooted in womanism and Afrocentric philosophy. Janice D. Hamlet, "Assessing Womanist Thought: The Rhetoric of Susan L. Taylor," *Communication Quarterly* 48, no. 4 (2000): 420–436.

26 Susan L. Taylor was not the only author to exploit self-help rhetoric in the name of women's liberation. Even feminist authors such as bell hooks have adopted this format to appeal to a broader public. Wendy Simonds, "All Consuming Selves: Self-Help Literature and Women's Identities," in *Constructing the Self in a Mediated World*, edited by Debra Grodin and Thomas R. Lindlof (Thousand Oaks: SAGE Publications, 1996), 15.

27 Alice Walker, *In Search of Our Mothers' Gardens: Womanist Prose* (San Diego: Harcourt Brace Jovanovich, 1983), xi–xii.

28 Theorists have debated use of the term womanism since it first began circulating in American scholarly discourse in the 1980s. This argument is at once a debate about language and epistemology. The impulse to specify Black women's struggles for justice and distinguish a political arena that prioritizes Black women's oppression has yielded various approaches. While some who choose womanism do so in resistance to the white and patriarchal leanings of other social justice movements, they do not all acquiesce to the theological appropriation of the term. Indeed, some who identify or would identify as womanists read the exclusionary dogma espoused in certain Christian denominations as antithetical to the spirit of Alice Walker's words in the 1983 release, *In Search of Our Mothers' Gardens*. Others have assessed womanism as an unnecessary splintering of those who labor in the name of freedom for Black women and embrace Black feminism as a strategic choice. Still others have described womanism as an accessible framework intended to reach those who eschew the more radical tenets of feminism. The aforementioned arguments assume that a substantive difference exists between womanism and Black feminism and fail to accommodate still another camp of scholars who use the terms interchangeably.

29 Monica A. Coleman, "Must I Be Womanist?," *Journal of Feminist Studies in Religion* 22, no. 1 (2006): 93.

30 Taylor, interview by James Briggs Murray.

31 Taylor, *In the Spirit: Inspirational Writings*, xvi–xvii.

32 Georgia Dullea, "Getting to the Essence of Black Women's Lives," *Chicago Tribune*, April 19, 1985.

33 Mona Gable, "Author Alice Walker Discusses 'The Color Purple'," *Wall Street Journal*, December 19, 1985.

34 Notable Essence Books projects by the Editors of Essence Magazine include *Making It Happen: Creating Success and Abundance* (New York: Essence, 2004); *The Black Woman's Guide to Healthy Living: The Best Advice For Body, Mind + Spirit in Your 20s, 30s, 40s, 50s + Beyond* (New York: Essence, 2009); and *Your Faith Walk: Wisdom and Affirmations on the Path to Personal Power* (New York: Essence, 2015).

35 Iyanla Vanzant and Bebe Moore Campbell, "The Powers That Free," *Essence*, October 1989, 82.

36 Diane Weathers, "At Home with Iyanla Vanzant," *Essence*, July 1996, 106.

37 Taylor, "In the Spirit: Our Achievements," 69.

38 Taylor, "Critical Issues Affecting Black Women."

39 Essence, "Yes, Girl Podcast: Iyanla Vanzant Doesn't Hold Back When It Comes to R. Kelly," YouTube video, 33:21, January 18, 2019, www.youtube.com/watch?v=yKw6B-1kNJo.

40 *Essence* is one of the few magazines that continued to secure Oprah Winfrey for cover shoots after she started her own magazine in 2000; *Vogue* is another. This is a significant fact given that *O: The Oprah Magazine* and *Essence* occupy the same niche in women's magazines and compete for some of the same consumers. The major difference between the two periodicals is that one specifically targets Black women while the other creates content for a multiracial audience.

41 Susan L. Taylor, "An Intimate Talk With Oprah," *Essence*, August 1987, 57.

42 Janice Peck points to 1994 as a critical juncture in the life of the Oprah Winfrey empire. Amid declining ratings and increased scrutiny of sensational afternoon talk shows, Peck argues that Winfrey carved a new identity as a "soul brand," which is "an unstable, contradictory union of commercial calculation and spiritualized altruism." Drawing on bestselling self-help author Marianne Williamson's aura, Winfrey announced her departure from salacious afternoon television during a broadcast that featured Williamson as a guest. Janice Peck, *The Age of Oprah: Cultural Icon for the Neoliberal Era* (Boulder, CO: Paradigm Publishers, 2008), 209.

43 Taylor, "An Intimate Talk with Oprah," 113.

44 Essence Fest is part of a longer tradition of public spectacles of Black consumption which link power to capital. A notable predecessor of such an exhibition is Jesse L. Jackson's Black Expo, which he established during his tenure at the Southern Christian Leadership Council and continued under the banner of his own Operation PUSH (People United to Save Humanity) from 1969 to 1972. Like Jackson's Black Expo, ECI framed its festival as a function of its mission to empower and serve Black women.

45 The COVID-19 pandemic forced ECI to conduct the festival virtually in 2020 and 2021.

46 Daytime events at the Essence Festival have typically been underwritten by corporate sponsors and offered for free, while the nightly concerts have always been ticketed events. In 2019 the festival was under new ownership and included

fee-based daytime programming. While certain events remained free and open to the public, others such as the mini-business conference, Essence E-Suite, and the Essence Fashion House, a new addition, required an additional fee. Tickets for admission to a single nightly concert started at approximately $120 on the low end. Attendees would need to upgrade to an all-inclusive package or buy additional tickets in order to attend more than one concert. When added to travel, lodging, and food costs, these fees make Essence Fest a four-figure investment.

47 Quoting Michelle Ebanks. "AT&T Humanity of Connection Celebrates Essence: 25 Years of the Culture," video presentation at AT&T, New Orleans, LA, July 5, 2019.

48 The media kit (a promotional brochure of sorts aimed at advertisers) that *Essence* released in 2020 highlights "a full calendar of multi-platform programs and experiential opportunities that provide a deep consumer connection," while minimizing its reduced editorial calendar. In 2019 the publisher announced that the magazine would scale back from twelve to six print issues a year. This shift reflected the growing importance of events like the festival and a desire to more effectively monetize the company's digital platforms. See Essence, "Essence 2020 Media Kit," Accessed November 10, 2020, https://www.essence.com/wp-content/uploads/2019/10/ESSENCE-MEDIA-KIT-2020-9.24.pdf.

49 Lewis and Edwards, *The Man from Essence*, 248.

50 Iyanla Vanzant and Oprah Winfrey have each been featured as keynote speakers at Essence Fest in 2018 and 2016, respectively.

51 Julian Mitchell, "Michelle Ebanks Talks Essence Fest Expansion and New Vision for the Media Brand," *Forbes*, June 8, 2018, https://www.forbes.com/sites/julianmitchell/2018/06/08/michelle-ebanks-talks-essence-fest-expansion-and-new-vision-for-the-media-brand/?sh=28e590ba4fca.

Chapter 3 Marketing Dignity

1 Kelly is the pseudonym for a Black woman marketing professional interviewed for this book. Certain identifying characteristics have been obscured to maintain confidentiality.

2 Essence Communications Inc. listed Walmart and *My Black Is Beautiful* (*MBIB*) as two of the six major sponsors for the 2013 festival.

3 Three years prior to the *MBIB* launch P&G acquired Johnson Products Company. A pioneering haircare manufacturer, it was the first Black business to be traded on the American Stock Exchange. Johnson Products returned to Black ownership in 2009. Grio Staff, "Johnson Products Back in Black Hands," *The Grio*, July 16, 2009, https://thegrio.com/2009/07/16/johnson-products-the-company-behind/.

4 Beverly Bond's Black Girls Rock! and the United Negro College Fund collaborated with P&G to produce the documentary.

5 Even when brands adjust their advertising rhetoric, a change in tone does not necessarily signify an ideological shift. In her analysis of personal care brands that primarily sold skin-bleaching creams well into the middle of the twentieth century, Simone Puff concluded that these companies had not significantly altered their product formulas or function decades later. For example, Puff found that while Ambi relaunched their skin-lightening product as "a 'fade' cream" in 2011, they continued to use the same chemical ingredient, hydroquinone, which functions as a lightening agent. Ambi's product marketing, Puff argues, "implied

that there is something wrong with Black women's skin which needs to be fixed." Simone Puff, "Writing (about) the Black Female Body: An Exploration of Skin Color Politics in Advertising within *Ebony* and *Essence*," in *Black Women and Popular Culture: The Conversation Continues*, eds. Adria Y. Goldman, Vanatta S. Ford, Alexa A. Harris, and Natasha R. Howard (Lanham, MD: Lexington Books, 2014), 225–246.

6   Weems Jr., *Desegregating the Dollar*, 1.

7   Jason Chambers has shown that the attention Black Americans began to receive from major corporations after World War II is in part the result of the work of early advertising professionals like Claude Barnett. Barnett founded and contributed to numerous efforts to sell ad space in Black media and amplify the value of Black spending power prior to 1930. Chambers, *Madison Avenue and the Color Line: African Americans in the Advertising Industry* (Philadelphia: University of Pennsylvania Press, 2008).

8   Elsie Archer, "How to Sell to Today's Negro Woman," *Sponsor* 20, no. 15 (July 25, 1966): 49.

9   Domestic workers who served in white homes also influenced purchases within those specific white contexts.

10 Chambers, *Madison Avenue and the Color Line*, 45.

11 Beginning in the 1960s, members of the Student Nonviolent Coordinating Committee (SNCC) adopted Black Power as the rallying cry for their Black liberation movement. This practice marked a departure from the less radical ideals that were at the center of earlier Civil Rights struggles and a move toward a Black nationalist ethos. Neither Black Power nor Black Nationalism were singular efforts in philosophy or praxis, however, the diverse factions who identified with the movement shared an appreciation for cultural expression as central to Black freedom struggles. Brands appropriated the myriad artistic, linguistic, sartorial, and visual elements that emerged in this era as signifiers of resistance to white supremacy in order to sell products to Black consumers. William L. Van Deburg, *New Day in Babylon: The Black Power Movement and American Culture, 1965–1975* (Chicago: University of Chicago Press, 1992), 9.

12 "Advertisement: L & M-Super Bad," *Essence*, September 1972, 84.

13 "Advertisement: Johnson Products Co., Inc.," *Essence*, August 1971, 3.

14 "Advertisement: Flori Roberts," *Essence*, May 1970, 12.

15 "Advertisement: Essence," *Essence*, March 1971, 73.

16 The blaxploitation era in Hollywood began and ended in the 1970s when gatekeepers, seeking to compensate for decreasing revenues, invested in low-budget, urban action films starring Black figures. These productions fell under the umbrella of what Robert E. Weems refers to as the "soul market" and tended to center excessive Black characters in roles such as pimps, prostitutes, and drug dealers. Despite their deviance, the protagonists in Blaxploitation films also made for compelling heroes for those Black moviegoers who sought a reprieve from the "nonthreatening" and passive portrayals common in more respectable films. Weems Jr., *Desegregating the Dollar*, 67–88.

17 "Advertisement: Honey & Spice," *Essence*, February 1983, 51.

18 "Advertisement: Posner Laboratories," *Essence*, September 1996, 75.

19 "Advertisement: Roux Laboratories, Inc.," *Essence*, October 1992, 3.

20 "Advertisement: Carson Products Co," *Essence*, September 1996, 93.

21 "Advertisement: Motorola, Inc.," *Essence*, September 1996, 155.

22 My Black Is Beautiful, "My Black Is Beautiful at Essence Festival 2016," YouTube video, 1:00, July 18, 2016, https://www.youtube.com/watch?v=U_BiDjzwxvs.

23 Ibid.

24 My Black Is Beautiful, "About Us."

25 *MBIB* partnered with Healthy Roots—a toy company committed to empowering girls of color—to create the Zoe doll. In 2021 the toy retailed for $79.99. According to the manufacturer's website, the doll is a "positive representation intended to promote 'self-love' and to be used for 'educational hair play.'" Zoe is more than a self-esteem tool; however, she is also a marketing tool. Her shirt—emblazoned with the *MBIB* logo—reminds Black girls and their mothers that they must manage their natural beauty with the right products. Healthy Roots Dolls, "Meet Zoe," Healthy Roots, accessed June 29, 2021, https://healthyrootsdolls.com/pages/meet-zoe.

26 Swaminathan et al., "Branding in a Hyperconnected World," 39.

27 Ibid.

28 Ukonwa Ojo, a Nigerian-American, is responsible for developing the campaign for Cover Girl and adding two Black female celebrities—Ayesha Curry and Issa Rae—to the company's roster of brand ambassadors. Gianina Thompson, "The Woman Behind CoverGirl's 'I Am What I Make Up' Marketing Campaign," *The Undefeated*, March 20, 2018, https://theundefeated.com/features/ukonwa-ojo-covergirl-ayesha-curry-issa-rae-i-am-what-i-make-up-marketing-campaign/.

29 Georgina Caldwell, "Procter & Gamble Targets African-American Women with New Ad Campaign for Pantene Gold Series," *Global Cosmetics News*, March 28, 2017, https://www.globalcosmeticsnews.com/procter-gamble-targets-african-american-women-with-new-ad-campaign-for-pantene-gold-series/.

30 Tierra Benton, "Tierra Benton Joins Pantene Gold Series Celebrating Strong, Beautiful African American Hair," YouTube video, 1:01, March 24, 2017, https://www.youtube.com/watch?v=oaXNHxAVQ4w.

31 Pantene, "Pantene Gold Series: The Scientists Behind It," YouTube video, 1:04, March 22, 2017, https://www.youtube.com/watch?v=pPVo_LQozLU.

32 Ibid.

33 Ibid.

34 P&G partnered with DoSomething.org to launch #RedefineBlack in 2019. The initiative targets dictionary publishers in its aim to "dismantle negative associations with the word 'Black'." Jennifer Ford, "Procter and Gamble's My Black Is Beautiful Platform Launches Initiative to #RedefineBlack," *Essence*, June 5, 2019, https://www.essence.com/beauty/procter-and-gambles-my-black-is-beautiful-platform-launches-initiative-to-redifineblack/.

35 The film is based on Terry McMillan's 1992 novel of the same name.

36 Ford Motor Company, "New Ford TV Ads, 'Built Ford Proud: We Lead' and 'Ode to the Builders' Narrated by Actress Angela Bassett—Showcases Ford F-150, Fusion, Mustang, Explorer and Expedition," *PR Newswire*, February 5, 2019, https://www.prnewswire.com/news-releases/new-ford-tv-ads-built-ford-proud-we-lead-and-ode-to-the-builders-narrated-by-actress-angela-bassett----showcases-ford-f-150-fusion-mustang-explorer-and-expedition-300790183.html.

37 Leggat Discovery Ford, "Introducing the New 2020 Ford Escape: Built Phenomenally," YouTube video, 0:35, February 7, 2020, https://www.youtube.com/watch?v=2f_XPAG7YUo.

38 Ford produced this campaign in compliance with two media industry initiatives aimed at broadening exposure for underrepresented content creators and

misrepresented groups: Free the Work and #SeeHer. The Association of National Advertisers (ANA) launched SeeHer in 2016. They describe the initiative as an apolitical movement that aims to "accurately portray all women and girls in marketing, advertising, media, and entertainment, so they see themselves as they truly are and in all their potential." ANA has created and trademarked the Gender Equality Measure, or GEM score, to offer companies specific feedback on how their content registers among women consumers. While SeeHer promotes female representation in broad terms, it singles out gender as a context for addressing inequity while excluding intersectional realities. Alma Har'el, an Israli-American filmmaker, developed Free the Work as a database to help marketers and other media companies secure talent from underrepresented groups to diversify their production teams. The architects behind SeeHer and Free the Work have coupled the social justice considerations that drive their initiatives with financial motives; each project promises that their diversity strategy yields a better return on investment. SeeHer, "Our Mission," ANA SeeHer, Association of National Advertisers, accessed October 24, 2021, https://www.seeher.com/about/; Alexandra Jardine, "Alma Har'el's Free the Bid Expands to Free the Work In Effort to Diversity All of Filmmaking," *Ad Age*, June 25, 2019, https://adage.com /creativity/work/alma-harel-free-work/2178311.

39 Ford Motor Company, "Ford Celebrates Black Women with 'Built Phenomenally' Ad Campaign for Debut of the All-New 2020 Ford Escape," *PR Newswire*, January 21, 2020, https://www.prnewswire.com/news-releases/ford-celebrates -black-women-with-built-phenomenally-ad-campaign-for-debut-of-the-all-new -2020-ford-escape-300989027.html.

40 Leggat Discovery Ford, "Introducing the New 2020 Ford Escape: Own It," YouTube video, 0:35, January 21, 2020, https://www.youtube.com/watch?v=S -ceo6I3l5Q.

41 "#WomenInAuto #WomenInAutomotive #WIA | Ford Motor Company | Girls Make Beats," Women in Automotive, August 1, 2020, video, 2:33, https://www .youtube.com/watch?v=jDFzW4BELgU.

42 Ibid.

43 Ford Motor Company, "Ford Celebrates Black Women."

44 "The 2020 Ford Explorer Kellee Edwards Explores Chicago Joe Cotton Ford Your Local Ford Dealer," Joe Cotton Ford Carol Stream, September 17, 2019, video, 0:35, https://www.youtube.com/watch?v=DkqJPfeGgAM.

45 Matt Kuttan, "Born2Roll," YouTube video, 1:36, September 18, 2018, https://www .youtube.com/watch?v=5TysnvhxnuU.

46 Deborah Clarke, *Driving Women: Fiction and Automobile Culture in Twentieth- Century America* (Baltimore, MD: Johns Hopkins University Press, 2007), 166.

47 Ibid.

48 Emma Pierson et al., "A Large-Scale Analysis of Racial Disparities in Police Stops across the United States," *Nature Human Behaviour* 4, (2020): 736–745, accessed June 23, 2021, https://doi.org/10.1038/s41562-020-0858-1.

49 A *Washington Post* report concluded that in 2015 one in three people killed during a traffic stop were Black, including individuals who were passengers in a vehicle that had been stopped. Wesley Lowery, "A Disproportionate Number of Black Victims in Fatal Traffic Stops," *Washington Post*, December 24, 2015.

50 Dove's CROWN (**C**reating a **R**espectful and **O**pen **W**orld with **N**o Racism) campaign is one of few commercial efforts that offers a more substantive political

outcome. The CROWN coalition is a "Black beauty alliance" between Dove, lawmakers, and civil rights groups that lobbies for anti-discrimination legislation to protect Black women and girls' right to select a hairstyle without fear of professional or academic penalty. The CROWN Act (SB 188) first passed in California in July 2019. The law addresses "dress code and grooming policies . . . [that] have a disparate impact on Black individuals." Dove, which is a property of Unilever, announced the CROWN Act campaign against hair bias under the guidance of Esi Eggleston Bracey, a Black woman who serves as Executive Vice President and Chief Operating Officer of beauty and personal care for Unilever North America.

51 Black feminist theorist Patricia Hill Collins uses the term outsider-within to describe Black women intellectuals' experiences as those who are present, yet marginalized, within academic settings. Patricia Hill Collins, "Learning from the Outsider Within: The Sociological Significance of Black Feminist Thought," *Social Problems* 33, no. 6 (1986): 14–32.

52 Essence, "Queen Latifah and Jada Pinkett Smith."

53 Essence, "Ford Presents #SeeHer and Ford," Facebook, February 2020, video, 35:17, https://www.facebook.com/essence/videos/1494857987357918.

54 Ibid.

Chapter 4   Beyond Magic

1 In addition to *Twenties*, Waithe partnered with Ben Cory Jones for the BET series, *Boomerang*, which premiered in 2019. The series is loosely based on the 1992 film featuring Eddie Murphy and Halle Berry and includes two queer characters in its ensemble cast.

2 Cori Murray, "(Un)Scripted," *Essence*, May 2015, 88.

3 Ibid.

4 While there are several other content creators whose work disrupts repressive tropes, Akil, Rae, and Waithe are of interest for this analysis for multiple reasons. First, they have occupied comparable positions as auteurs focused on Black women's narratives at cable television networks that are not Black-owned. Platform ownership, which is thought to guarantee creative autonomy, persists as a dependent variable of interest in explorations of the progressive potential of commercial media. Second, these content creators share a similar artistic sensibility regarding Black women's sexuality and articulate humanity through explicit scenes of the erotic. Although their artistic approaches are imperfect, their series ultimately advance the discourse around race, gender, and (commercial) visibility.

5 Valerie Chepp, "Black Feminist Theory and the Politics of Irreverence: The Case of Women's Rap," *Feminist Theory* 16, no. 2 (2015): 207.

6 Hillary Crosley Coker, "Why I'm Already Breaking Up with *Being Mary Jane*," *Jezebel*, January 9, 2014, https://jezebel.com/why-im-already-breaking-up-with -being-mary-jane-1497463330.

7 Amy Juicebox, "I Have Every Reason Not to Like *Being Mary Jane*," *Blavity*, February 22, 2015, https://blavity.com/every-reason-not-like-mary-jane?category1 =life-style&category2=opinion.

8 APB Speakers, "Mara Brock-Akil: Chicago Ideas Week," interview by Dan Harris, YouTube video, 18:18, January 7, 2015, https://www.youtube.com/watch?v =cwVr6Wp6xVM.

9   The myth of Black women as undesirable romantic partners, immigrant rights, human trafficking, and the disposability of Black bodies are among the topics that Mary Jane confronts on her show, *Talk Back with Mary Jane Paul*.

10   Mara Brock Akil, writer, *Being Mary Jane*, season 2, episode 1, "People in Glass Houses Shouldn't Throw Fish," directed by Salim Akil, featuring Gabrielle Union, aired February 3, 2015 on BET.

11   During her rant Mary Jane references Bill Cosby's infamous musings on the deficiencies of the Black poor. See Thedarkroome, "Bill Cosby Pound Cake Speech," YouTube video, 3:40, July 9, 2015, https://www.youtube.com/watch?v=CG5r5ByCbMI&t=112s, 1:52.

12   Akil, *Being Mary Jane*, season 2, episode 1.

13   Enuma Okoro, "*Being Mary Jane* Is No *Scandal*—and That's a Good Thing," *The Atlantic*, January 16, 2014, https://www.theatlantic.com/entertainment/archive/2014/01/-i-being-mary-jane-i-is-no-em-scandal-em-and-thats-a-good-thing/283118/.

14   Tai Beauchamp, "Color Commentary Aftershow with Mara Brock Akil—Episode 201," BET, February 3, 2015, video, 3:19, https://www.bet.com/video/being-mary-jane/season-2/color-commentary/episode-201-aftershow-with-mara-brock-akil.html.

15   Sylvia Wynter, "Unsettling the Colonial of Being/Power/Truth/Freedom: Towards the Human, After Man, Its Overrepresentation—An Argument," *CR: The New Centennial Review* 3, no. 3 (2003): 257–337.

16   Wynter, "Unsettling the Colonial of Being," 321.

17   Mara Brock Akil and Adam Giaudrone, writers, *Being Mary Jane*, season 2, episode 6, "Pulling the Trigger," directed by Salim Akil, featuring Gabrielle Union, aired March 10, 2015 on BET.

18   Ibid.

19   Beauchamp, "Color Commentary Aftershow."

20   Breakfast Club Power 105.1 FM, "Mara Brock Akil on Bringing 'Girlfriends' to Netflix, Conversations with Culture, History + More," YouTube video, 51:58, September 11, 2020, https://www.youtube.com/watch?v=vBejxZLJgio.

21   Ibid.

22   Ibid.

23   Mara Brock Akil, "Keynote Speech" (presentation, Digital Blackness Conference at Rutgers University, New Brunswick, NJ, April 22–23, 2016).

24   Rae was once slated to produce a loosely autobiographical series with Shondaland, the production company owned by Shonda Rhimes. According to Rae, the project failed because she lacked the confidence needed to address network petitions without compromising her creative vision. Roland S. Martin, "Issa Rae Talks 'Insecure,' Reactions to the HBO Series, the Importance of Timing & Catfishing," YouTube video, 10:02, February 9, 2017, https://youtu.be/TlncMgR1GgA.

25   Ibid.

26   Ibid.

27   Rae has described the music featured on *Insecure* as an essential component in communicating the intended meaning of each episode. During season two, she was particularly drawn to the work of R&B artist Sza, because of her focus on "women who make bad decisions" in the album *CTRL*. Genius, "A Genius Conversation with Issa Rae on the Music of 'Insecure'," interview by Rob Markman, YouTube video, 32:31, September 21, 2017, https://youtu.be/odrGmSpCxzI.

28 Kristen Warner, "[Home] Girls: Insecure and HBO's Risky Racial Politics," *Los Angeles Review of Books*, October 21, 2016, https://lareviewofbooks.org/article/home-girls-insecure-and-hbos-risky-racial-politics/.

29 CBS Mornings, "'Awkward Black Girl' Issa Rae brings unique spin to TV," interview by Gayle King, YouTube video, 5:52, October 5, 2016, https://youtu.be/jvfHL_Xcl_Q.

30 Breakfast Club Power 105.1 FM, "Issa Rae on Being an Awkward Black Girl, HBO's 'Insecure' and New Book," YouTube video, 35:35, October 28, 2016, https://www.youtube.com/watch?v=z26fq6EIL_w.

31 *Insecure*'s fifth season, which began taping in January 2021, was the show's last. Viewership throughout its original run was diverse. According to Nielsen data, 61.54 percent of *Insecure* viewers were not African American. Nielsen Company, "For Us By Us?: The Mainstream Appeal of Black Content," *Nielsen*, February 28, 2017, http://www.nielsen.com/us/en/insights/news/2017/for-us-by-us-the-mainstream-appeal-of-black-content.html.

32 Prior to the release of the trailer for the premiere season of *Insecure*, Rae explained her rationale for the name and premise of the show in a brief video posted to her Twitter account. Issa Rae (@IssaRae), text and video, Twitter, September 7, 2016, https://twitter.com/IssaRae/status/773586256039075840.

33 Ibid.

34 Issa Rae and Larry Wilmore, writers, *Insecure* season 1, episode 1, "Insecure as Fuck," directed by Melina Matsoukas, featuring Issa Rae, aired October 9, 2016 on HBO.

35 Ibid.

36 Candice M. Jenkins, *Private Lives, Proper Relations: Regulating Black Intimacy* (Minneapolis, MN: University of Minnesota Press, 2007), 14.

37 Jenkins, *Private Lives*, 20.

38 Issa Rae, "Issa Rae Recaps Season 1 Finale," *Entertainment Weekly*, November 28, 2016, http://ew.com/article/2016/11/28/insecure-blog-issa-rae-recaps-season-1-finale/.

39 Ibid.

40 The couple secretly reunites in season four.

41 Issa Rae, Jen Regan, and Christopher Oscar Peña, writers, *Insecure*, season 2, episode 8, "Hella Perspective," directed by Melina Matsoukas, featuring Issa Rae and Jay Ellis, aired September 10, 2017 on HBO.

42 Rae, "Issa Rae Recaps Season 1 Finale."

43 Kimberly Springer, "Third Wave Black Feminism?," *Signs* 27, no. 4, (2002): 1059–1082.

44 Springer, "Third Wave Black Feminism?," 1071.

45 Ashleigh Lakieva Atwell, "Lena Waithe Puts on for Black Gay Girls (Again) While Proudly Covered in Ava DuVernay's Smooches," *Blavity*, September 10, 2018, https://blavity.com/lena-waithe-puts-on-for-black-gay-girls-again-while-proudly-covered-in-ava-duvernays-smooches?category1=news&category2=race-identity.

46 Ibid.

47 Breakfast Club Power 105.1 FM, "Lena Waithe Talks Black Girls Rock, Humility, Liberation, New Projects + More," YouTube video, 25:52, August 28, 2018, https://www.youtube.com/watch?v=95W-LOZFSfU.

48 BET Networks, "Lena Waithe on Struggling in Her Twenties & Working on Last Season of 'Girlfriends'," YouTube video, 5:02, February 25, 2020, https://www.youtube.com/watch?v=9hwyrO9IXOg.

49 Ibid.

50 Hillman Grad is a tribute to Hillman College, the fictional Black institution that was the setting for the 1990s sitcom, *A Different World*. The series captivated Waithe and inspired her to pursue a career telling Black narratives. Susan Fales-Hill, who was a producer on *A Different World*, is also executive producer for *Twenties*.

51 BET Networks, "Lena Waithe on Struggling."

52 Lena Waithe, writer, *Twenties*, season 1, episode 1, "Pilot," directed by Justin Tipping, featuring Jonica T. Gibbs, aired March 4, 2020 on BET.

53 Hattie's isolation in a world of mostly straight characters is one of the critiques aimed at *Twenties*, making the show a somewhat hollow triumph for queer representation. Jordan Ealy, "Is 'Twenties' Really a Win for Black Queer Representation?," *Bitch Media*, June 10, 2020, https://www.bitchmedia.org/article/twenties -black-queer-representation-onscreen.

54 Kimiko Matsuda-Lawrence, writer, *Twenties*, season 1, episode, 4, "You Know How I Like It," directed by Juel Taylor, featuring Jonica T. Gibbs, aired March 18, 2020 on BET.

55 Patricia Ione Lloyd, writer, *Twenties*, season 1, episode 7, "What Would Todd Do," directed by Justin Tipping, featuring Jonica T. Gibbs, aired April 8, 2020 on BET.

56 Ibid.

57 Tre'vell Anderson, "Lena Waithe's 'Twenties' Signals LGBTQ+ Progress at BET and Beyond," *Zora*, March 4, 2020, https://zora.medium.com/lena-waithes -twenties-signals-lgbtq-progress-at-bet-and-beyond-ba819357197f.

58 Naomi Iwamoto, writer, *Twenties*, season 1, episode, 5, "Ain't Nothing Like the Real Thing," directed by Juel Taylor, featuring Jonica T. Gibbs, aired March 25 on 2020, BET.

59 Azie Dungey, writer, *Twenties*, season 1, episode 8, "Living the Dream," directed by Justin Tipping, featuring Jonica T. Gibbs, aired April 15, 2020 on BET.

60 Beretta E. Smith-Shomade, *Shaded Lives: African-American Women and Television*, (New Brunswick, NJ: Rutgers University Press, 2002), 19–20.

61 Jennifer Fuller, "Branding Blackness on US Cable Television," *Media Culture & Society*, 32, no. 2 (2010): 292.

62 Ibid.

63 Breakfast Club, "Lena Waithe Talks Black Girls Rock."

Epilogue

1 Scott Clement, "The Most Popular Obama Wasn't the President," *Washington Post*, December 12, 2016, https://www.washingtonpost.com/graphics/national /obama-legacy/michelle-obama-popularity.html.

2 Michelle Obama, "Remarks by the First Lady at BET's 'Black Girls Rock!' Event," The White House, Office of the First Lady, March 28, 2015, accessed October 23, 2018, https://obamawhitehouse.archives.gov/the-press-office/2015/03/28/remarks -first-lady-bets-black-girls-rock-event.

3 Will Drabold, "Read Michelle Obama's Emotional Speech at the Democratic Convention," *Time*, July 25, 2016, http://time.com/4421538/democratic -convention-michelle-obama-transcript/.

4 Such as Al Sharpton, "AT&T Humanity of Connection Celebrates Essence."

5 Black Female Anonymous, "The Truth About Essence," *Medium*, June 28, 2020, https://medium.com/@blackfemaleanonymous2020/the-truth-about-essence -532152b08051.

6 Ibid.

7 Business Wire, "ESSENCE Releases Statement Regarding Final Independent Review," *Business Wire*, September 8, 2020, https://www.businesswire.com/news /home/20200908006059/en/ESSENCE-Releases-Statement-Regarding-Final -Independent-Review-%E2%80%93.

8 Richelieu Dennis (@richelieudennis), text image, Instagram, September 29, 2020, https://www.instagram.com/p/CFvvFUeF45W/?utm_source=ig_embed.

9 Ibid.

10 *Being Serena,* season 1, episode 2, "Strength," produced by Mark Shapiro, featuring Serena Williams, aired May 9, 2018 on HBO, https://play.hbogo.com/episode /urn:hbo:episode:GXbNBkQdX-ZGYoAEAAAtd.

11 *Being Serena,* season 1, episode 1, "Fear," produced by Mark Shapiro, featuring Serena Williams, aired May 4, 2018 on HBO, https://play.hbogo.com/episode /urn:hbo:episode:GXbNBhwV-PoNiYAEAAAoO.

12 Laura Brown, "The Number 1," *In Style*, June 26, 2018, https://www.instyle.com /news/serena-williams-august-cover.

13 Narratives about Black maternal health are entangled in the systematic maltreatment of Black patients over centuries of racist practice within American medical institutions. Involuntary enrollment in abusive research experiments, exclusion from advanced medical education, and inadequate access to appropriate treatment and care facilities are some of the historic inequities that continue to fuel twenty-first century health disparities.

14 Rob Haskell, "Serena Williams on Motherhood, Marriage, and Making Her Comeback," *Vogue*, January 10, 2018, https://www.vogue.com/article/serena -williams-vogue-cover-interview-february-2018.

15 Serena Williams, "What My Life-Threatening Experience Taught Me about Giving Birth," *CNN*, February 20, 2018, https://www.cnn.com/2018/02/20 /opinions/protect-mother-pregnancy-williams-opinion/index.html.

Selected Bibliography

Advocate Staff Report. "Essence Breaks Attendance Records." *The Advocate*, August 16, 2013. https://www.theadvocate.com/baton_rouge/entertainment_life /article_30f1ec15-6051-537d-b83d-e91d7a348b13.html.

Akil, Mara Brock, writer. *Being Mary Jane*. Season 2, episode 1, "People in Glass Houses Shouldn't Throw Fish." Directed by Salim Akil, featuring Gabrielle Union. Aired February 3, 2015 on BET.

Akil, Mara Brock. "Keynote Speech." Presentation. Digital Blackness Conference at Rutgers University, New Brunswick, NJ. April 22–23, 2016.

Akil, Mara Brock and Adam Giaudrone, writers. *Being Mary Jane*. Season 2, episode 6, "Pulling the Trigger." Directed by Salim Akil, featuring Gabrielle Union. Aired March 10, 2015 on BET.

Allen, Bonnie. "Essence & Other Thoughts on the 70s." *Essence*, May 1980.

Amsterdam News. "Blacks Have Mixed Reaction to Nixon's Election." *New York Amsterdam News*, November 16, 1968.

Anderson, Tre'vell. "Lena Waithe's 'Twenties' Signals LGBTQ+ Progress at BET and Beyond." *Zora*, March 4, 2020. https://zora.medium.com/lena-waithes-twenties -signals-lgbtq-progress-at-bet-and-beyond-ba819357197f.

Andreeva, Nellie. "Mara Brock Akil Inks Overall Deal with Netflix as Streamer Sets Premiere Date for Her Series 'Girlfriends'." *Deadline*, September 9, 2020. https:// deadline.com/2020/09/mara-brock-akil-inks-overall-deal-netflix-girlfriends -premiere-date-1234573545/.

APB Speakers. "Mara Brock-Akil: Chicago Ideas Week." Interview by Dan Harris. YouTube video, 18:18, January 7, 2015. https://www.youtube.com/watch?v =cwVr6Wp6xVM.

Archer, Elsie. "How to Sell to Today's Negro Woman." *Sponsor*, July 25, 1966.

"AT&T Humanity of Connection Celebrates Essence: 25 Years of the Culture." Video presentation at AT&T, New Orleans, LA, July 5, 2019.

Atwell, Ashleigh Lakieva. "Lena Waithe Puts On for Black Gay Girls (Again) While Proudly Covered in Ava DuVernay's Smooches." *Blavity*, September 10, 2018. https://blavity.com/lena-waithe-puts-on-for-black-gay-girls-again-while-proudly -covered-in-ava-duvernays-smooches?category1=news&category2=race-identity.

Baker-Fletcher, Karen. *A Singing Something: Womanist Reflections on Anna Julia Cooper*. New York: Crossroad, 1994.

Banet-Weiser, Sarah. *Empowered: Popular Feminism and Popular Misogyny*. Durham: Duke University Press, 2018.

———. *Kids Rule!: Nickelodeon and Consumer Citizenship*. Durham: Duke University Press, 2007.

Banet-Weiser, Sarah and Inna Arzumanova. "Creative Authorship: Self-Actualizing Individuals and the Self-Brand." In *Media Authorship*, edited by Cynthia Chris and David A. Gerstner, 163–179. New York: Routledge, 2013.

Barbaro, Michael. "Once Alienated, and Now a Force in Her Husband's Bid for Mayor." *New York Times*, October 2, 2013.

BBC. "Russian Trolls' Chief Target Was 'Black US Voters' in 2016." *BBC News*, October 9, 2019. https://www.bbc.com/news/technology-49987657.

Beauboeuf-Lafontant, Tamara. *Behind the Mask of the Strong Black Woman: Voice and the Embodiment of a Costly Performance*. Philadelphia: Temple University Press, 2009.

Beauchamp, Tai. "Color Commentary Aftershow with Mara Brock Akil–Episode 201." BET video, 3:19, February 3, 2015. https://www.bet.com/video/being-mary-jane/season-2/color-commentary/episode-201-aftershow-with-mara-brock-akil.html.

———. "Color Commentary Aftershow with Mara Brock Akil–Episode 206." BET video, 3:15, March 10, 2015. https://www.bet.com/video/being-mary-jane/season-2/color-commentary/episode-206-aftershow-with-mara-brock-akil.html.

Being Serena. Season 1, episode 1. "Fear." Produced by Mark Shapiro. Featuring Serena Williams. Aired May 4, 2018 on HBO.

Benton, Tierra. "Tierra Benton Joins Pantene Gold Series Celebrating Strong, Beautiful African American Hair." YouTube video, 1:01, March 24, 2017. https://www.youtube.com/watch?v=oaXNHxAVQ4w.

BET Networks. "Lena Waithe on Struggling in Her Twenties & Working on Last Season of 'Girlfriends'." YouTube video, 5:02, February 25, 2020. https://www.youtube.com/watch?v=9hwyrO9IXOg.

Black Girl Magic–Trademark Details. Justia Trademarks. Accessed April 17, 2019. https://trademarks.justia.com/869/07/black-girl-86907838.html.

Black Female Anonymous. "The Truth About Essence." *Medium*, June 28, 2020. https://medium.com/@blackfemaleanonymous2020/the-truth-about-essence-532152b08051.

Blain, Keisha N., Asia Leeds, and Ula Y. Taylor. "Women, Gender Politics, and Pan-Africanism." *Women, Gender, and Families of Color* 4, no. 2 (2016): 139–145.

Breakfast Club Power 105.1 FM. "Issa Rae on Being an Awkward Black Girl, HBO's Insecure and New Book." YouTube video, 35:35, October 28, 2016. https://www.youtube.com/watch?v=z26fq6EIL_w.

———. "Lena Waithe Talks Black Girls Rock, Humility, Liberation, New Projects + More." YouTube video, 25:53, August 28, 2018. https://www.youtube.com/watch?v=95W-LOZFSfU.

———. "Mara Brock Akil on Bringing 'Girlfriends' to Netflix, Conversations with Culture, History + More." YouTube video, 51:58, September 11, 2020. https://www.youtube.com/watch?v=vBejxZLJgio.

Brown, Laura. "The Number 1." *In Style*, June 26, 2018. https://www.instyle.com/news/serena-williams-august-cover.

Brown, Nadine. "People, Places and Situations." *Michigan Chronicle*, January 9, 1971.

Budgeon, Shelly. "The Contradictions of Successful Femininity: Third-Wave Feminism, Postfeminism and 'New' Femininities." In *New Femininities: Postfeminism, Neoliberalism and Subjectivity*, edited by Rosalind Gill and Christina Scharff, 279–292. London: Palgrave Macmillan, 2011.

Business Wire. "ESSENCE Releases Statement Regarding Final Independent Review." *Business Wire*. September 8, 2020. https://www.businesswire.com/news/home/20200908006059/en/ESSENCE-Releases-Statement-Regarding-Final-Independent-Review-%E2%80%93.

Caldwell, Georgana. "Procter & Gamble Targets African-American Women with New Ad Campaign for Pantene Gold Series." *Global Cosmetics News*, March 28, 2017. https://www.globalcosmeticsnews.com/procter-gamble-targets-african-american-women-with-new-ad-campaign-for-pantene-gold-series/.

Cannon, Katie G. *Black Womanist Ethics*. Atlanta: Scholars Press, 1988.

Carter, Gregory T. "Race and Citizenship." In *The Oxford Handbook of American Immigration and Ethnicity*, edited by Ronald H. Bayor, 166–182. Oxford: Oxford University Press, 2016.

CBS Mornings. "'Awkward Black Girl' Issa Rae Brings Unique Spin to TV." Interview by Gayle King. YouTube video, 5:52, October 5, 2016. https://youtu.be/jvfHL_Xcl_Q.

Chambers, Jason. *Madison Avenue and the Color Line: African Americans in the Advertising Industry*. Philadelphia: University of Pennsylvania Press, 2008.

Chepp, Valerie. "Black Feminist Theory and the Politics of Irreverence: The Case of Women's Rap." *Feminist Theory* 16, no. 2 (2015): 207–226.

Chicago Defender. "Class in 'Soul Food' as Small Business Offered at College." *Chicago Defender*. February 22, 1969.

———. "Jackson Rejects Black Capitalism." *Chicago Defender*, February 18, 1969.

Clarke, Deborah. *Driving Women: Fiction and Automobile Culture in Twentieth-Century America*. Baltimore, MD: Johns Hopkins University Press, 2007.

Clement, Scott. "The Most Popular Obama Wasn't the President." *Washington Post*, December 12, 2016. https://www.washingtonpost.com/graphics/national/obama-legacy/michelle-obama-popularity.html.

Cobb, Janice. "The Essence Woman," *Sun Reporter*, August 1973.

Coker, Hillary Crosley. "Why I'm Already Breaking Up with *Being Mary Jane*." *Jezebel*, January 9, 2014. https://jezebel.com/why-im-already-breaking-up-with-being-mary-jane-1497463330.

Coleman, Monica A. "Must I Be Womanist?" *Journal of Feminist Studies in Religion* 22, no. 1 (2006): 85–96.

Collins, Patricia Hill. "Learning from the Outsider Within: The Sociological Significance of Black Feminist Thought." *Social Problems* 33, no. 6 (1986): 14–32.

Connor, John T., Alexander B. Trowbridge, and Forest D. Hockersmith. *A Guide to Negro Marketing Information*. Washington, DC: United States Department of Commerce, 1966.

Cox, Aimee Meredith. *Shapeshifters: Black Girls and the Choreography of Citizenship*. Durham, NC: Duke University Press, 2015.

Crawford, Margo Natalie. "Natural Black Beauty and Black Drag." In *New Thoughts on the Black Arts Movement*, edited by Lisa Gail Collins and Margo Natalie Crawford, 154–172. New Brunswick, NJ: Rutgers University Press, 2006.

Cuff, Daniel F. "Berkey Photo Replaces Its Longtime Chairman." *New York Times*, September 20, 1982.

Daily Beast. "Vanessa K. De Luca Dismissed As 'Essence' Restructures." *Daily Beast*, April 20, 2018. https://www.thedailybeast.com/vanessa-k-de-luca-dismissed-as -essence-restructures.

Davenport, Thomas H. and Jeanne Harris. "The Dark Side of Consumer Analytics." *Harvard Business Review*, May 2007. https://hbr.org/2007/05/the-dark-side-of -customer-analytics.

Dávila, Arlene. *Latinos, Inc.: The Marketing and Making of a People*. Berkeley: University of California Press, 2001.

Davis, Judy Foster. *Pioneering African-American Women in the Advertising Business: Biographies of M.A.D. Black Women*. New York: Routledge, 2017.

DeMuth, Jerry. "'Breadbasket Full of Black 'Green Power'." *National Catholic Reporter*, January 15, 1969.

Dennis, Richelieu (@richelieudennis). Text image. Instagram, September 29, 2020. https://www.instagram.com/p/CFvvFUeF45W/?utm_source=ig_embed.

Dorfman, Dan. "The Bottom Line: Black Broker Blasts Big Board." *New York Magazine*, July 15, 1974.

Drabold, Will. "Read Michelle Obama's Emotional Speech at the Democratic Convention." *Time*, July 25, 2016. http://time.com/4421538/democratic-convention -michelle-obama-transcript/.

Duffy, Brooke Erin. *Remake, Remodel: Women's Magazines in the Digital Age*. Urbana, IL: University of Illinois Press, 2013.

Dullea, Georgia. "Getting to the Essence of Black Women's Lives." *Chicago Tribune*, April 19, 1985.

Dungey, Azie, writer. *Twenties*. Season 1, episode, 8, "Living the Dream." Directed by Justin Tipping, featuring Jonica T. Gibbs. Aired April 15, 2020 on BET.

Ealy, Jordan. "Is 'Twenties' Really a Win for Black Queer Representation?" *Bitch Media*, June 10, 2020. https://www.bitchmedia.org/article/twenties-black-queer -representation-onscreen.

Editors of Essence Magazine. *Essence: Making It Happen!: Creating Success and Abundance*. New York: Essence, 2004.

———. *The Black Woman's Guide to Healthy Living: The Best Advice for Body, Mind + Spirit in Your 20s, 30s, 40s, 50s + Beyond*. New York: Essence, 2009.

———. *Your Faith Walk: Wisdom and Affirmations on the Path to Personal Power*. New York: Essence, 2015.

Edwards, Christina. "Michelle Obama's Memoir Is Already Becoming the Hottest Book Since 'Fifty Shades'." *Business Insider*, January 17, 2019. https://www .businessinsider.com/michelle-obamas-memoir-is-becoming-hottest-book-since -fifty-shades-2019-1.

Ember, Sydney and Andrew Ross Sorkin. "Time Inc. Sells Itself to Meredith Corp., Backed by Koch Brothers." *New York Times*, November 26, 2017.

Essence. "Essence 2020 Media Kit." Accessed November 10, 2020. https://www.essence .com/wp-content/uploads/2019/10/ESSENCE-MEDIA-KIT-2020-9.24.pdf.

———. "Essence Fest 2019." *Essence*. Accessed October 30, 2020. https://www.essence .com/essence-festival-2019/.

———. "Essence Women: We've Come This Far by Faith!" *Essence*, May 1980.

———. "Ford Presents #SeeHer and Ford." Facebook, February 2020, video, 35:17. https://www.facebook.com/essence/videos/1494857987357918.

———. "Party with a Purpose." *Essence*, October 1997.

——. "Queen Latifah and Jada Pinkett Smith Join Ladies Panel on Strength." YouTube video, 28:46, July 23, 2017. https://www.youtube.com/watch?v=fBEMZktTvG4&t=129s.

——. "Yes, Girl Podcast: Iyanla Vanzant Doesn't Hold Back When It Comes to R. Kelly." YouTube video, 33:21, January 18, 2019. www.youtube.com/watch?v=yKw6B-1kNJo.

Essence Magazine. "The 2013 ESSENCE Festival Presented by Coca-Cola Celebrates Fourth of July Weekend with Headline Performances by Beyonce, Maxwell, New Edition, Janelle Monae, Jill Scott, LL Cool J, Charlie Wilson, Trey Songz, Keyshia Cole, Solange, TGT and More!" *Cision PR Newswire*, July 5, 2013. https://www.prnewswire.com/news-releases/the-2013-essence-festival-presented-by-coca-cola-celebrates-fourth-of-july-weekend-with-headline-performances-by-beyonce-maxwell-new-edition-janelle-monae-jill-scott-ll-cool-j-charlie-wilson-trey-songz-keyshia-cole-solan-214356701.html.

Essence Staff. "Statement from ESSENCE Communications, Inc. Regarding Covid-19 Impact and Action." *Essence*, September 29, 2020. https://www.essence.com/business/statement-essence-covid-19-economic-impact-furlough/.

Faggins, Barbara. "Black Stars Join NAACP's Film Boycott." *Philadelphia Tribune*, July 20, 1982.

Farrell, Amy Erdman. *Yours in Sisterhood:* Ms. *Magazine and the Promise of Popular Feminism*. Chapel Hill: University of North Carolina Press, 1998.

Feldman, Dana. "Lena Waithe Inks Overall Deal with Amazon Studios." *Forbes*, July 27, 2019. https://www.forbes.com/sites/danafeldman/2019/07/27/emmy-award-winning-writer-creator-and-actor-lena-waithe-inks-overall-deal-with-amazon-studios/?sh=64366d1f3aed.

——. "New Ford TV Ads, 'Built Ford Proud: We Lead' and 'Ode to the Builders' Narrated by Actress Angela Bassett—Showcases Ford F-150, Fusion, Mustang, Explorer and Expedition." *PR Newswire*, February 5, 2019. https://www.prnewswire.com/news-releases/new-ford-tv-ads-built-ford-proud-we-lead-and-ode-to-the-builders-narrated-by-actress-angela-bassett----showcases-ford-f-150-fusion-mustang-explorer-and-expedition-300790183.html.

Ford, Jennifer. "Procter and Gamble's My Black Is Beautiful Platform Launches Initiative to #RedefineBlack." *Essence*, June 5, 2019. https://www.essence.com/beauty/procter-and-gambles-my-black-is-beautiful-platform-launches-initiative-to-redifineblack/.

Ford, Tanisha C. *Liberated Threads: Black Women, Style, and the Global Politics of Soul*. Chapel Hill, NC: University of North Carolina Press, 2015.

Ford Motor Company. "Ford Celebrates Black Women with 'Built Phenomenally' Ad Campaign for Debut of the All-New 2020 Ford Escape." *PR Newswire*, January 21, 2020. https://www.prnewswire.com/news-releases/ford-celebrates-black-women-with-built-phenomenally-ad-campaign-for-debut-of-the-all-new-2020-ford-escape-300989027.html.

For Harriet. "How the Creator of #BlackGirlMagic Got Erased from the Movement She Started." CaShawn Thompson, interview by Kimberly N. Foster. YouTube video, 37:47, April 11, 2020. https://www.youtube.com/watch?v=y2Ko-mgo1DU.

Fuller, Jennifer. "Branding Blackness on US Cable Television." *Media Culture & Society* 32, no. 2 (2010): 285–305.

Gable, Mona. "Author Alice Walker Discusses 'The Color Purple'." *Wall Street Journal*, December 19, 1985.

Garcia, Sandra E. "With Sale, Essence Is Once Again a Fully Black-Owned Maga-zine." *New York Times,* January 4, 2018.

Genius. "A Genius Conversation with Issa Rae on the Music of 'Insecure'." Interview by Rob Markman. YouTube video, 32:31, September 21, 2017. https://youtu.be /odrGmSpCxzI.

Gillespie, Marcia. "Getting Down." *Essence,* August 1971.

———. "Getting Down." *Essence,* February 1972.

———. *For You . . . Black Woman.* Interview by Nell Bassett. Gerber/Carter Commu-nications, 1978. https://browse.nypl.org/iii/encore/record/C__Rb11253064_ _SMarcia%20Gillespie__P0%2C1__Orightresult__U__X3?lang=eng&suite=def.

———. "Woman." Interview by Sandra Elkin. WNED, January 16, 1976.

Glenn, Cerise L. and Landra J. Cunningham. "The Power of Black Magic: The Magical Negro and White Salvation in Film." *Journal of Black Studies* 40, no. 2 (November 2009): 135–152.

Glenn, Evelyn Nakano. "Constructing Citizenship: Exclusion, Subordination, and Resistance." *American Sociological Review* 76, no. 1 (2011): 1–24.

Goings, Russell L. "Conversation: Russell L. Goings." *PBS NewsHour,* May 8, 2009. https://www.pbs.org/newshour/arts/to-sit-down-and-talk.

Goldberg, Daniel S. "Pain, Objectivity, and History: Understanding Pain Stigma." *Medical Humanities* 43, no. 4 (2017): 238–243.

Goldman, Robert. *Reading Ads Socially.* London: Routledge, 1992.

Grant, Darren, dir. *Diary of a Mad Black Woman.* 2005; Santa Monica, CA: Lionsgate Films, 2005. DVD.

Grant, Jacquelyn. *White Woman's Christ, Black Woman's Jesus.* Atlanta: Scholars Press, 1989.

Gray, Herman. "Subject(ed) to Recognition." *American Quarterly* 65, no. 4 (2013): 771–798.

Greer, Brenna Wynn. *Represented: The Black Imagemakers Who Reimagined African American Citizenship.* Philadelphia: University of Pennsylvania Press, 2019.

Grio Staff. "Johnson Products Back in Black Hands," *The Grio,* July 16, 2009, https://thegrio.com/2009/07/16/johnson-products-the-company-behind/.

Gross, Elana Lyn. "Essence Appoints New CEO Following Allegations Owner Richelieu Dennis Fostered Toxic Workplace Culture." *Forbes,* July 2, 2020. https://www.forbes.com/sites/elanagross/2020/07/02/essence-ceo-richelieu -dennis-resigns-following-allegations-of-a-toxic-workplace-culture/?sh =2d66912c22c5.

Gumbs, Alexis Pauline. "Black (Buying) Power: The Story of *Essence* Magazine." In *The Business of Black Power: Community Development, Capitalism, and Corporate Responsibility in Postwar America,* edited by Laura Warren Hill and Julia Rabig, 95–115. Rochester, NY: University of Rochester Press, 2012.

Hagerty, James R. "Flori Roberts Created a Cosmetics Line for Dark Skin." *Wall Street Journal,* December 22, 2020. https://www.wsj.com/articles/flori-roberts -created-a-cosmetics-line-for-dark-skin-11608649200.

Hamlet, Janice D. "Assessing Womanist Thought: The Rhetoric of Susan L. Taylor." *Communication Quarterly* 48, no. 4 (2000): 420–436.

Harper, Hill. *The Conversation: How Men and Women Can Build Loving, Trusting Relationships.* New York: Gotham Books, 2009.

Harper, Peter Alan. "Minorities Have It Tough on Wall St." AP News, February 19, 1999. https://apnews.com/231d8038683cb31b0ce0570d025dcfe3.

Harvey, Steve and Denene Millner. *Act Like a Lady, Think Like a Man: What Men Really Think About Love, Relationships, Intimacy, and Commitment.* New York: Amistad, 2009.

———. *Straight Talk, No Chaser: How to Find, Keep and Understand a Man.* New York: Amistad, 2010.

Haskell, Rob. "Serena Williams on Motherhood, Marriage, and Making Her Comeback." *Vogue*, January 10, 2018. https://www.vogue.com/article/serena-williams -vogue-cover-interview-february-2018.

Healthy Roots Dolls. "Meet Zoe." Healthy Roots. Accessed June 29, 2021. https:// healthyrootsdolls.com/pages/meet-zoe.

Henderson, Aneeka Ayanna. *Veil and Vow: Marriage Matters in Contemporary African American Culture.* Chapel Hill: University of North Carolina Press, 2020.

Henderson, Cydney. "Lena Waithe and Wife Alana Mayo Split Just Two Months after Announcing Marriage." *USA Today*, January 23, 2020. https://www.usatoday.com /story/entertainment/celebrities/2020/01/23/lena-waithe-wife-alana-mayo-split -months-after-announcing-marriage/4550535002/.

Herndon, Astead W. and Katie Glueck. "Biden Apologizes for Saying Black Voters 'Ain't Black' if They're Considering Trump." *New York Times*, May 22, 2020.

Hicks, James L. "Fight On for Control of Essence Magazine." *New York Amsterdam News*, April 23, 1977.

Hill, Herman. "Change in Attitude of Hollywood Observed: Walter White Is Winning His Fight For Better Roles." *Pittsburgh Courier*, August 8, 1942.

Holder, Ann S. "What's Sex Got to Do with It? Race, Power, Citizenship, and 'Intermediate Identities' in the Post-Emancipation United States." *Journal of African American History* 93, no. 2 (2008): 153–173.

Hope, Clover. "Beyoncé in Her Own Words: Her Life, Her Body, Her Heritage." *Vogue*, August 2018.

Impelli, Matthew. "#IStandWithGayle Trends after Gayle King Received Death Threats for Raising Kobe Bryant Rape Allegations in Lisa Leslie Interview." *Newsweek*, February 10, 2020. https://www.newsweek.com/istandwithgayle-trends -after-gayle-king-receives-death-threats-raising-kobe-bryant-rape-1486548.

Leggat Discovery Ford. "Introducing the New 2020 Ford Escape: Built Phenomenally." February 7, 2020. Video, 0:35. https://www.youtube.com/watch?v=2f _XPAG7YUo.

Iwamoto, Naomi, writer. *Twenties.* Season 1, episode, 5, "Ain't Nothing Like the Real Thing." Directed by Juel Taylor, featuring Jonica T. Gibbs. Aired March 25, 2020 on BET.

Jardine, Alexandra. "Alma Har'el's Free the Bid Expands to Free the Work in Effort to Diversity All of Filmmaking." *Ad Age*, June 25, 2019. https://adage.com/creativity /work/alma-harel-free-work/2178311.

Jeffries, Georgia Thomas. "Essence Women." *Essence*, April 1975.

Jenkins, Candice M. *Private Lives, Proper Relations: Regulating Black Intimacy.* Minneapolis: University of Minnesota Press, 2007.

Jolliffe, Lee and Terri Catlett. "Women Editors at the 'Seven Sisters' Magazines, 1965–1985: Did They Make a Difference?" *Journalism Quarterly* 71, no. 4 (1994), 800–808.

Jones, Feminista. *Reclaiming Our Space: How Black Feminists Are Changing the World from the Tweets to the Streets.* Boston: Beacon Press, 2019.

Jordan-Zachery, Julia S. and Duchess Harris. "We Are Magic and We Are Real: Exploring the Politics of Black Femmes, Girls, and Women's Self-Articulation." In *Black Girl Magic Beyond the Hashtag: Twenty-First Century Acts of Self-Definition*, edited by Julia S. Jordan-Zachery and Duchess Harris, 3–40. Tucson: The University of Arizona Press, 2019.

Joseph, Ralina L. *Postracial Resistance: Black Women, Media, and the Uses of Strategic Ambiguity*. New York: New York University Press, 2018.

Jubas, Kaela. "Conceptual Con/fusion in Democratic Societies: Understandings and Limitations of Consumer-Citizenship." *Journal of Consumer Culture* 7, no. 2 (2007): 231–254.

Juicebox, Amy. "I Have Every Reason Not to Like *Being Mary Jane*." *Blavity*, February 22, 2015. https://blavity.com/every-reason-not-like-mary-jane?category1=life -style&category2=opinion.

Kai, Maiysha. "Who Benefits from 'Black Girl Magic'? Google's Latest Ad Reignites Enduring Issues of Erasure." *The Root*, March 10, 2019. https://theglowup.theroot .com/who-benefits-from-black-girl-magic-googles-latest-ad-r-1833144103.

King, Maya. "Why Black Voters Never Flocked to Kamala Harris." *Politico*, December 4, 2019. https://www.politico.com/news/2019/12/04/kamala-harris-black -voters-2020-075651.

Kitchen, Kevin. "Susan L Taylor Speaks!" YouTube video, 29:42, n.d. https://www .youtube.com/watch?v=n9EmSueycGk.

Kuttan, Matt. "Born2Roll." YouTube video, 1:36, September 18, 2018. https://www .youtube.com/watch?v=5TysnvhxnuU.

Larson, Jennifer L. "A Rebellion to Remember: The Legacy of Nat Turner." Documenting the American South. Accessed November 2, 2020. https://docsouth.unc .edu/highlights/turner.html.

Lathan, Stan, dir. *The Essence of Essence*. 1973; New York: Tony Brown Productions, 2013. DVD.

Lawrence, Jimi. "Essence Women." *Essence*, October 1975.

Lee, Edward. "Dickerson Hits Nixon's 'Black Capitalism'." *Chicago Tribune*, May 12, 1973.

Levette, Harry. "Walter White Asks Change in Picture Roles." *Atlanta Daily World*, July 27, 1942.

Lewis, Edward and Audrey Edwards. *The Man from Essence: Creating a Magazine for Black Women*. New York: Atria Books, 2014.

Lewis, Edward, Clarence O. Smith, and Cecil Hollingsworth. "ESSENCE, the Real Story," *Essence*, August 1971.

Lindahl, Martin L. "The Federal Trade Commission Act as Amended in 1938." *Journal of Political Economy* 47, no. 4 (1939): 497–525.

Lloyd, Patricia Ione, writer. *Twenties*. Season 1, episode 7, "What Would Todd Do." Directed by Justin Tipping, featuring Jonica T. Gibbs. Aired April 8, 2020 on BET.

Lofton, Kathryn. *Oprah: The Gospel of an Icon*. Berkeley: University of California Press, 2011.

Lomax, Pearl. "Point of View: Black Women's Lib?" *Essence*, August 1972.

Love, James. "Mikki Taylor, Alva Chinn and Deborah Riley Draper on How a 1973 Fund-Raiser Broke Color Barriers for Black Models." *Essence*, July 9, 2019. https://www.essence.com/fashion/mikki-taylor-alva-chinn-deborah-riley-draper -versailles-73/.

Lowery, Wesley. "A Disproportionate Number of Black Victims in Fatal Traffic Stops." *Washington Post*, December 24, 2015.

Magee, Ny. "Essence Magazine to Furlough Staff amid Pandemic." *The Grio*, October 1, 2020. https://thegrio.com/2020/10/01/essence-magazine-to-furlough-staff-amid-pandemic/.

Martin, Roland S. "Issa Rae Talks 'Insecure,' Reactions to the HBO Series, The Importance of Timing & Catfishing." YouTube video, 10:02, February 9, 2017. https://youtu.be/TlncMgR1GgA.

———. "New Nielsen Report Measures the Impact of Black Women on Culture & Consumer Spending." YouTube video, 6:37, September 21, 2017. https://www.youtube.com/watch?v=2kwLWpUX94Q&t=317s.

Matsuda-Lawrence, Kimiko, writer. *Twenties*. Season 1, episode, 4, "You Know How I Like It." Directed by Juel Taylor, featuring Jonica T. Gibbs. Aired March 18, 2020 on BET.

McCracken, Ellen. *Decoding Women's Magazines from Mademoiselle to Ms*. New York: St. Martin's Press, 1993.

McCray, Chirlane. "I Am a Lesbian." *Essence*, September 1979.

McElya, Micki. *Clinging to Mammy: The Faithful Slave in Twentieth-Century America*. Cambridge, MA: Harvard University Press, 2007.

McGee, Micki. "From Makeover Media to Remaking Culture: Four Directions for the Critical Study of Self-Help Culture." *Sociology Compass* 6, no. 9 (2012): 685–693.

McKeen, Gayle. "Whose Rights? Whose Responsibility? Self-Help in African-American Thought." *Polity* 34, no. 4 (2002): 409–432.

Miller, Holly. "Interview with Nicole Wright, Producer/General Manager of Essence Music Festival in New Orleans." *New Orleans City Business*, June 14, 2004.

Miller, Stephen. "Street Veteran Who Sold Shearson, Hammill." *Wall Street Journal*, February 20, 2013. https://www.wsj.com/articles/SB10001424127887323864304578316523499875366.

Mitchell, Julian. "Michelle Ebanks Talks Essence Fest Expansion and New Vision for the Media Brand." *Forbes*, June 8, 2018. https://www.forbes.com/sites/julianmitchell/2018/06/08/michelle-ebanks-talks-essence-fest-expansion-and-new-vision-for-the-media-brand/?sh=28e590ba4fca.

Moore, Marjorie. "Essence Woman: Barbara Fouch." *Essence*, March 1972.

———. "The Essence Woman: Delores James." *Essence*, April 1972.

———. "Essence Woman: Fern Stanford." *Essence*, July 1972.

———. "The Essence Woman: Hulan Watson." *Essence*, December 1971.

———. "The Essence Woman: Janice Terry." *Essence*, November 1971.

———. "The Essence Woman: Lydia Cade." *Essence*, October 1971.

———. "Essence Woman: Michele Freeman." *Essence*, June 1972.

Morgan, Joan. *When Chickenheads Come Home to Roost: My Life as a Hip-Hop Feminist*. New York: Simon & Schuster, 1999.

Morris, Rachel. "Essence Woman: Ada Evans." *Essence*, July 1975.

Mujati, Thandeka. "Lena Waithe and Alana Mayo's Divorce Hit Me Like a Bus." *In Style*, August 25, 2020. https://www.instyle.com/celebrity/alana-mayo-and-lena-waithe-breakup-timeline.

Murray, Cori. "(Un)Scripted." *Essence*, May 2015.

My Black Is Beautiful. "About Us." Accessed October 29, 2020. https://www.mbib.com/en-us/about-us.

———. "My Black Is Beautiful at Essence Festival 2016." YouTube video, 1:00, July 18, 2016. https://www.youtube.com/watch?v=U_BiDjzwxvs.

Neal, Larry. "Any Day Now: Black Art and Black Liberation." *Ebony*, August 1969.

New York Times. "Shearson, Hammill Names Four as Vice Presidents." *New York Times*, December 9, 1964.

Nielsen Company. "African American Women: Our Science, Her Magic." *Nielsen*, September 21, 2017. https://www.nielsen.com/wp-content/uploads/sites/3/2019/04 /nielsen-african-american-diverse-intelligence-report-2017.pdf.

———. "For Us By Us?: The Mainstream Appeal of Black Content." *Nielsen*, February 28, 2017. http://www.nielsen.com/us/en/insights/news/2017/for-us-by-us-the -mainstream-appeal-of-black-content.html.

Nixon, Richard M. *Bridges to Human Dignity*. New York: The Nixon / Agnew Campaign Committee, 1968. https://digitallibrary.sdsu.edu/islandora/object /sdsu%3A39730.

Noel, Linda. "Essence Women." *Essence*, November 1975.

Obama, Michelle. "Remarks by the First Lady at BET's 'Black Girls Rock!' Event." The White House, Office of the First Lady, March 28, 2015. Accessed October 23, 2018. https://obamawhitehouse.archives.gov/the-press-office/2015/03/28/remarks -first-lady-bets-black-girls-rock-event.

———. *Becoming*. New York: Crown Publishing Group, 2018.

O'Connell, Mikey. "Lena Waithe Inks First-Look Deal with Showtime." *Hollywood Reporter*, July 24, 2018. https://www.hollywoodreporter.com/tv/tv-news/lena -waithe-extends-showtime-relationship-signs-first-look-deal-1129479/.

Okoro, Enuma. "*Being Mary Jane* Is No *Scandal*—and That's a Good Thing." *The Atlantic*, January 16, 2014. https://www.theatlantic.com/entertainment/archive /2014/01/-i-being-mary-jane-i-is-no-em-scandal-em-and-thats-a-good-thing /283118/.

Ouellette, Laurie and Julie Wilson. "Women's Work: Affective Labour and Convergence Culture." *Cultural Studies* 25, no.4–5, (2011): 548–565.

Pantene. "Pantene Gold Series: The Scientists behind It." YouTube video, 1:04, March 22, 2017. https://www.youtube.com/watch?v=pPVo_LQozLU.

Patten, Dominic. "OWN Breaks Up With 'Love Is _' Amidst EP Salim Akil Domestic Violence Claims." *Deadline*, December 19, 2018. https://deadline.com/2018/12 /love-is-canceled-salim-akil-lawsuit-controversy-own-1202523087/.

Peck, Janice. *The Age of Oprah: Cultural Icon for the Neoliberal Era*. Boulder: Paradigm Publishers, 2008.

Perry, Tyler, dir. *Daddy's Little Girls*. 2007; Santa Monica, CA: Lionsgate Films, 2007. DVD.

———, dir. *I Can Do Bad All By Myself*. 2009; Santa Monica, CA: Lionsgate Films, 2009. DVD.

———, dir. *Madea's Family Reunion*. 2006; Santa Monica, CA: Lionsgate Films, 2006. DVD.

Petrzela, Natalia M. and Christine B. Whelan. "Self-Help Gurus Like Tony Robbins Have Often Stood in the Way of Social Change." *Washington Post*, April 13, 2018.

Pierson, Emma, Camelie Simoiu, Jan Overgoor, Sam Corbett-Davies, Daniel Jenson, Amy Shoemaker, Vignesh Ramachandran, Phoebe Barghouty, Cheryl Phillips, Ravi Shroff, and Sharad Goel. "A Large-Scale Analysis of Racial Disparities in Police Stops across the United States." *Nature Human Behaviour* 4 (2020): 736–745. Accessed June 23, 2021. https://doi.org/10.1038/s41562-020-0858-1.

Prokop, Trudy. "Black Capitalism Works in Philadelphia." *Women's Wear Daily*, February 25, 1969, 36.

Public Broadcasting Service (PBS). "Tom Burrell on Revolutionizing Advertising." PBS, WTTW Archive, June 28, 2018. Video, 9:11. https://www.pbs.org/video/tom -burrell-revolutionizing-advertising-6u42gm/.

Puff, Simone. "Writing (about) the Black Female Body: An Exploration of Skin Color Politics in Advertising within *Ebony* and *Essence*." In *Black Women and Popular Culture: The Conversation Continues*, edited by Adria Y. Goldman, Vanatta S. Ford, Alexa A. Harris, and Natasha R. Howard, 225–246. Lanham, MD: Lexington Books, 2014.

Quinn, Dave. "Serena Williams Had Emergency C-Section and Health Complications After Daughter's Birth." *People.com*, January 10, 2018. https://people.com /parents/serena-williams-c-section-health-complications-daughter-alexis-cover/.

Rae, Issa (@IssaRae). Text and video. Twitter, September 7, 2016. https://twitter.com /IssaRae/status/773586256039075840.

———. "Issa Rae Recaps Season 1 Finale." *Entertainment Weekly*, November 28, 2016. http://ew.com/article/2016/11/28/insecure-blog-issa-rae-recaps-season-1-finale/.

Rae, Issa, Jen Regan, and Christopher Oscar Peña, writers. *Insecure*. Season 2, episode 8, "Hella Perspective." Directed by Melina Matsoukas, featuring Issa Rae and Jay Ellis. Aired September 10, 2017 on HBO.

Rae, Issa and Larry Wilmore, writers. *Insecure*. Season 1, episode 1, "Insecure as Fuck." Directed by Melina Matsoukas, featuring Issa Rae. Aired October 9, 2016 on HBO.

Ramsey, Franchesca and Nefetari Spencer, writers, *Black Girls Rock! Awards* show. Directed by Sandra Restrepo, featuring Niecy Nash. Aired September 8, 2019 on BET.

Reagan Foundation. "President Reagan's Radio Address to the Nation on Welfare Reform—8/1/87." Broadcast August 1, 1987, Washington, DC. YouTube video, 5:33, August 20, 2010. https://www.youtube.com/watch?v=MjnTQ8b6byY.

Rooks, Noliwe. *Ladies' Pages: African American Women's Magazines and the Culture That Made Them*. New Brunswick, NJ: Rutgers University Press, 2004.

Rose, Nikolas. *Governing the Soul: The Shaping of the Private Self*. London: Routledge, 1990.

Rubenstein, Janine. "Serena Williams Recalls Being 'Devastated' by Emergency C-Section and Postpartum Problems." *People*, April 26, 2018. https://people.com /parents/serena-williams-emergency-c-section-postpartum-problems/.

Rustin, Bayard. "In His Heart, Nixon Knows He's Wrong." *Philadelphia Tribune*, August 31, 1968.

———. "RUSTIN SAYS: Nixon-Agnew, Wallace Biggest Threat of Post-Reconstruction." *Afro-American*, August 31, 1968.

Sacks, Tina K. "Performing Black Womanhood: A Qualitative Study of Stereotypes and the Healthcare Encounter." *Critical Public Health* 28, no. 1 (2018): 59–69.

SeeHer. "Our Mission." SeeHer, Association of National Advertisers. Accessed October 24, 2021. https://www.seeher.com/about/.

Simonds, Wendy. "All Consuming Selves: Self-Help Literature and Women's Identities." In *Constructing the Self in a Mediated World*, edited by Debra Grodin and Thomas R. Lindlof, 15–29. Thousand Oaks, CA: SAGE Publications, 1996.

Smith-Shomade, Beretta E. *Pimpin' Ain't Easy: Selling Black Entertainment Television*. New York: Routledge, 2008.

———. *Shaded Lives: African-American Women and Television*. New Brunswick, NJ: Rutgers University Press, 2002.

Spires, Derrick R. *The Practice of Citizenship: Black Politics and Print Culture in the Early United States*. Philadelphia: University of Pennsylvania Press, 2019.

Sponsor: The Magazine of Broadcast Advertising 20, no. 15, July 25, 1966.

Springer, Kimberly. "Third Wave Black Feminism?" *Signs* 27, no. 4, (2002): 1059–1082.

Stiles, Thelma Jackson. "Essence Women." *Essence,* May 1975.

Story, Tim, dir. *Think Like a Man.* 2012; Los Angeles: Screen Gems, 2012. DVD.

Su, Bill. "The Evolution of Consumer Behavior in the Digital Ae." *Analytics for Humans,* November 16, 2017. https://medium.com/analytics-for-humans/the -evolution-of-consumer-behavior-in-the-digital-age-917a93c15888.

Sumner, Jane. "Essence Woman: Eddie Johnson." *Essence,* September 1975.

Swaminathan, Vanitha, Alina Sorescu, Jan-Benedict, E.M. Steenkamp, Thomas Clayton, Gibson O'Guinn, and Bernd Schmitt. "Branding in a Hyperconnected World: Refocusing Theories and Rethinking Boundaries." *Journal of Marketing* 84, no. 2 (2020): 24–46.

Taylor, Sandra R. "Write On!" *Essence,* May 1973.

Taylor, Susan. "A Beautiful New You!" *Essence,* July 1971.

———. "Beauty Lookout." *Essence,* January 1977.

———. "Critical Issues Affecting Black Women." C-SPAN video, 1:19:32, July 8, 1994. https://www.c-span.org/video/?58537-1/critical-issues-affecting-black-women.

———. "Haiti Chéri." *Essence,* March 1973.

———. "Shape 'N' Up." *Essence,* March 1972.

Taylor, Susan L. "An Intimate Talk with Oprah." *Essence,* August 1987.

———. "In the Beginning." In *Essence: 25 Years Celebrating Black Women,* edited by Patricia Mignon Hinds, 23–55. New York: Harry N. Abrams.

———. "In the Spirit: Our Achievements." *Essence,* October 1989.

———. *In the Spirit: The Inspirational Writings of Susan L. Taylor.* New York: HarperCollins, 1993.

———. Interview by James Briggs Murray. Video recording. Moving Image and Recorded Sound Collection, Schomburg Center for Research in Black Culture, May 5, 1987.

Thedarkroome. "Bill Cosby Pound Cake Speech." YouTube video, 3:40 at 1:52, July 9, 2015. https://www.youtube.com/watch?v=CG5r5ByCbMI&t=112s.

Thomas, Dexter. "Why Everyone's Saying 'Black Girls Are Magic'." *Los Angeles Times,* September. 9, 2015. https://www.latimes.com/nation/nationnow/la-na-nn -everyones-saying-black-girls-are-magic-20150909-htmlstory.html.

Thompson, Gianina. "The Woman behind CoverGirl's 'I Am What I Make Up' Marketing Campaign." *The Undefeated,* March 20, 2018. https://theundefeated .com/features/ukonwa-ojo-covergirl-ayesha-curry-issa-rae-i-am-what-i-make-up -marketing-campaign/.

Thornton, Cedric. "Michelle Ebanks Steps Down as CEO of Essence." *Black Enterprise,* March 11, 2020. https://www.blackenterprise.com/michelle-ebanks-steps -down-as-ceo-of-essence/.

Trescott, Jacqueline. "The Battle for 'Essence'." *Washington Post,* April 26, 1977.

Turrow, Joseph. *Breaking Up America: Advertisers and the New Media World.* Chicago: University of Chicago Press, 1997.

Udin, Sala. "Serve the People." *New Pittsburgh Courier,* January 25, 1975.

Van Deburg, William L. *New Day in Babylon: The Black Power Movement and American Culture, 1965–1975.* Chicago: University of Chicago Press, 1992.

Vanzant, Iyanla and Bebe Moore Campbell. "The Powers That Free." *Essence,* October 1989.

Waithe, Lena, writer. *Twenties*. Season 1, episode 1, "Pilot." Directed by Justin Tipping, featuring Jonica T. Gibbs. Aired March 4, 2020 on BET.

Walker, Alice. *In Search of Our Mothers' Gardens: Womanist Prose*. San Diego: Harcourt Brace Jovanovich, 1983.

Walker, Susannah. *Style & Status: Selling Beauty to African American Women, 1920–1975*. Lexington, KY: The University Press of Kentucky, 2007.

Wanzo, Rebecca. "Beyond a 'Just' Syntax: Black Actresses, Hollywood and Complex Personhood." *Women and Performance: A Journal of Feminist Theory* 16, no. 1 (2006): 135–152.

Warner, Kristen. "[Home] Girls: Insecure and HBO's Risky Racial Politics." *Los Angeles Review of Books*, October 21, 2016. https://lareviewofbooks.org/article /home-girls-insecure-and-hbos-risky-racial-politics/.

Washington, Harriet A. *Medical Apartheid: The Dark History of Medical Experimentation on Black Americans from Colonial Times to the Present*. New York: Harlem Moon, 2006.

Weathers, Diane. "At Home with Iyanla Vanzant." *Essence*, July 1996.

Weems Jr., Robert E. *Desegregating the Dollar: African American Consumerism in the Twentieth Century*. New York: New York University Press, 1998.

Weems Jr., Robert E. and Lewis A. Randolph. *Business in Black and White: American Presidents and Black Entrepreneurs in the Twentieth Century*. New York: New York University Press, 2009.

Weinberger, Stephen. "*The Birth of a Nation* and the Making of the NAACP." *Journal of American Studies* 45, no. 1 (2011): 77–93.

West, Michael O. "Whose Black Power?: The Business of Black Power and Black Power's Business." In *The Business of Black Power: Community Development, Capitalism, and Corporate Responsibility in Postwar America*, edited by Lauren Warren Hill and Julia Rabig, 274–303. Rochester, NY: University of Rochester Press, 2012.

Westkaemper, Emily. *Selling Women's History: Packing Feminism in Twentieth-Century American Popular Culture*. New Brunswick, NJ: Rutgers University Press, 2017.

White, Joyce. "Susan Taylor on Beauty." *Essence*, January 1978.

Williams, Serena. "What My Life-Threatening Experience Taught Me about Giving Birth." *CNN*, February 20, 2018. https://www.cnn.com/2018/02/20/opinions /protect-mother-pregnancy-williams-opinion/index.html.

Wolfe, Patrick. "Race and Citizenship." *OAH Magazine of History*, October 2004.

Women's Institute for Freedom of the Press. "Boxed In: Women on Screen and Behind the Scenes in Prime-Time TV." *Media Report to Women* 30, no. 4, (2002): 6.

Wynter, Sylvia. "Unsettling the Colonial of Being/Power/Truth/Freedom: Towards the Human, After Man, Its Overrepresentation—An Argument." *CR: The New Centennial Review* 3, no. 3 (2003): 257–337.

Yale University. "Marriage, Family on the Decline for Highly Educated Black Women." *Yale News*. August 8, 2009. https://news.yale.edu/2009/08/08/marriage -family-decline-highly-educated-black-women.

Youn, Soo. "Black Women Are Being Targeted in Misinformation Campaigns, A Report Shows." *The Lily*, September 20, 2020. https://www.thelily.com/black-women -are-being-targeted-in-misinformation-campaigns-a-report-shows-heres-what-to -know/.

Younge, Sheila F. "Essence Woman: Vy Higginsen." *Essence*, December 1972.

Index

About the Author

TIMEKA N. TOUNSEL is an assistant professor of African American studies and media studies at Pennsylvania State University. Her work has been published in academic and scholarly venues including the *Journal of Communication*, *Souls*, and *Elle.com*.